ONE DIRTY TREE

Publishers Tom Kaczynski and Jordan Shiveley

Uncivilized Books
P.O. Box 6534
Minneapolis, MN 55406
USA
uncivilizedbooks.com

ISBN: 978-1-941250-27-3

First Edition, October 2018

10 9 8 7 6 5 4 3 2 1

Printed in China

"Give me a child until he is 7 and I will show you the man."

— Aristotle

ONE DIRTY TREE

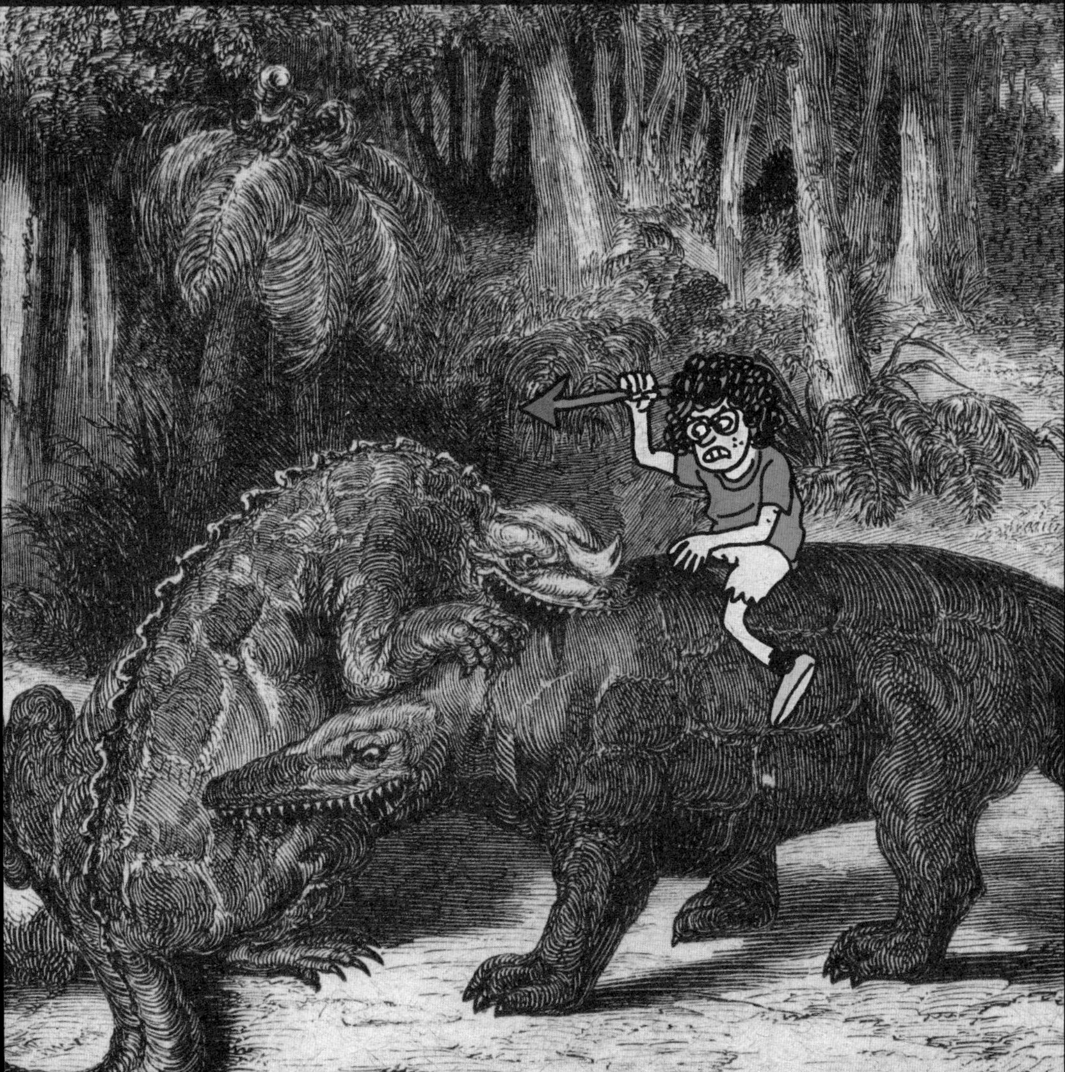

a novella by

Noah Van Sciver

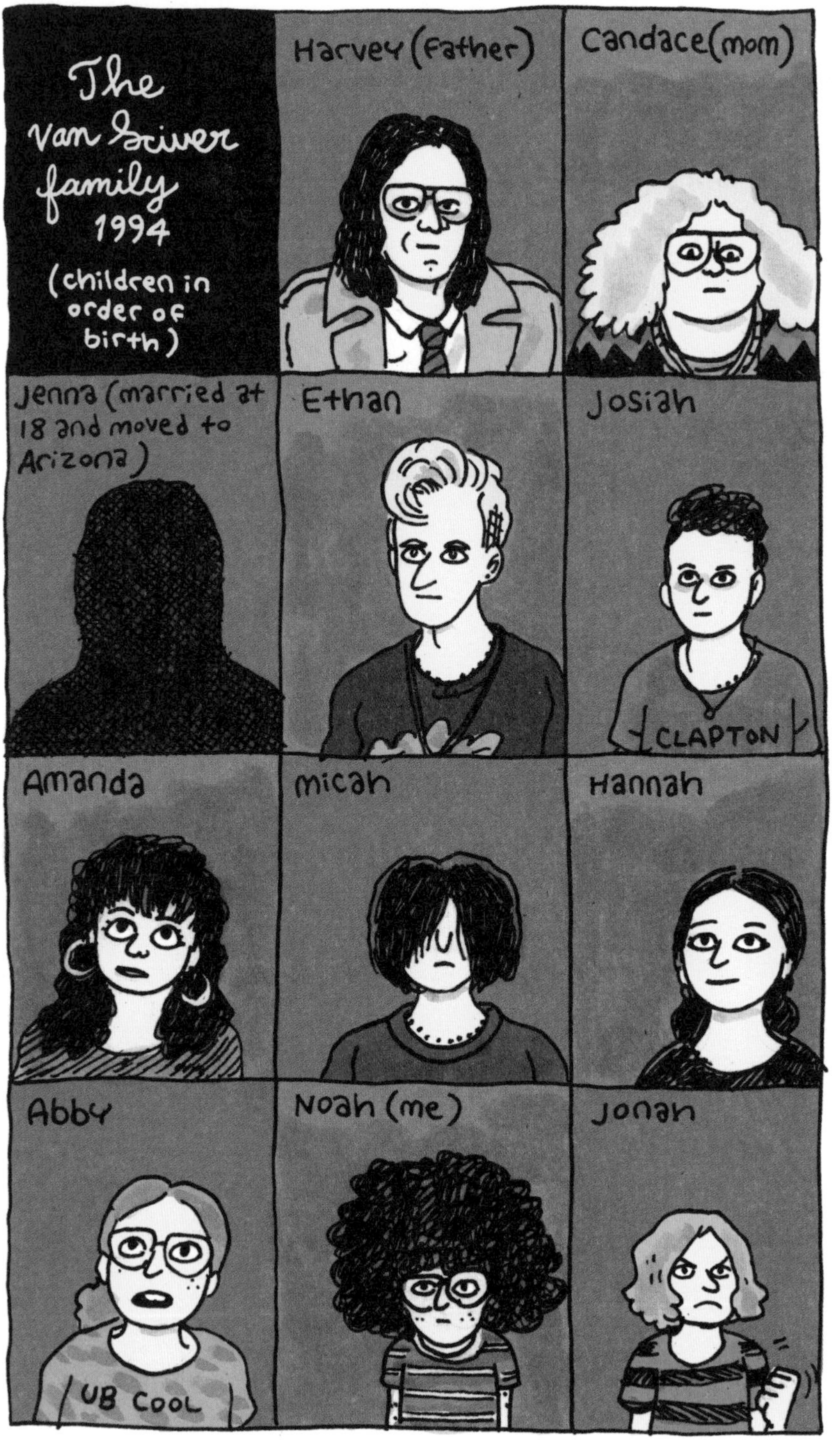
The van Sciver family 1994
(children in order of birth)
Harvey (father)
Candace (mom)
Jenna (married at 18 and moved to Arizona)
Ethan
Josiah
CLAPTON
Amanda
Micah
Hannah
Abby
UB COOL
Noah (me)
Jonah

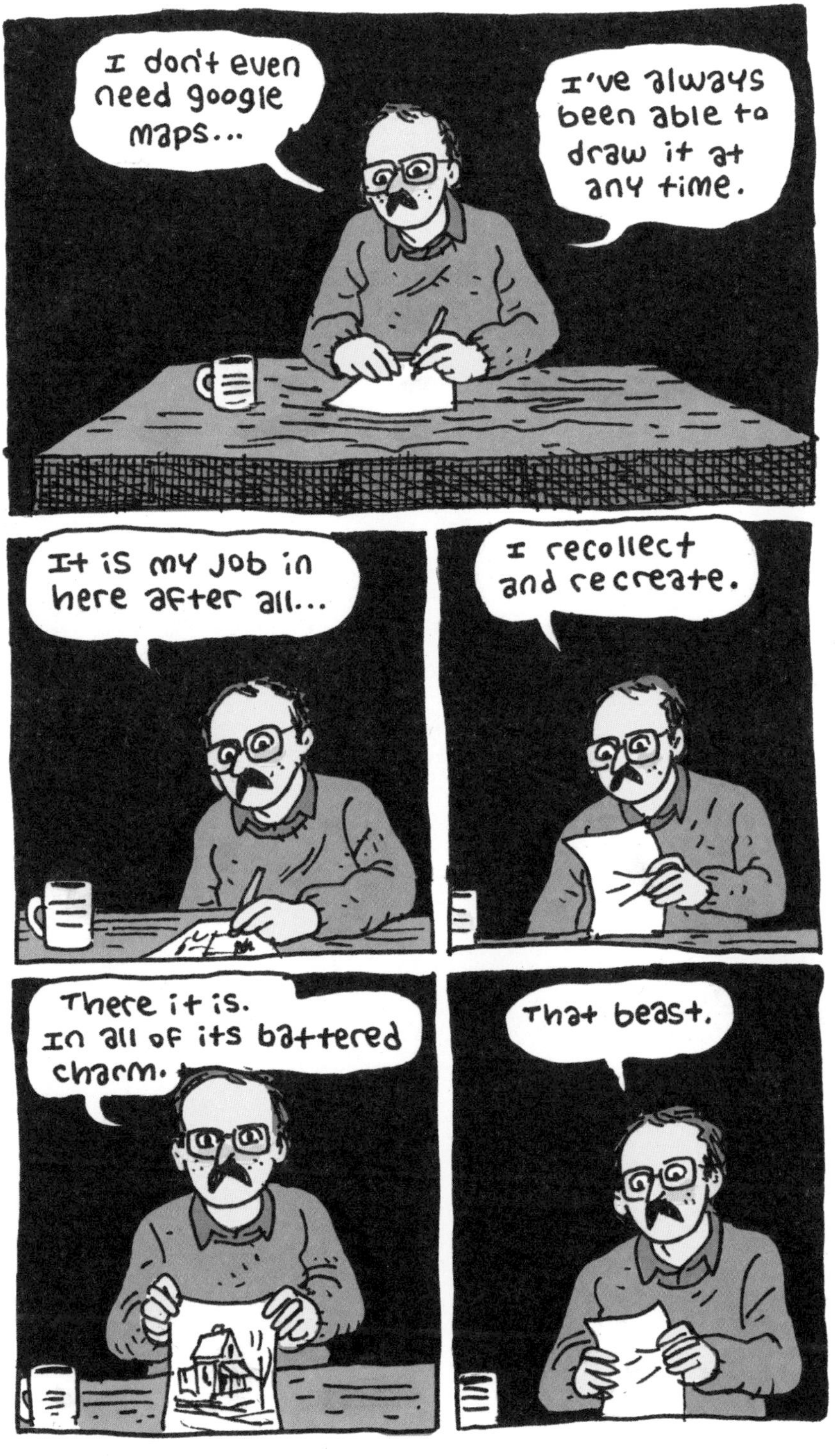
I don't even need google maps...
I've always been able to draw it at any time.
It is my job in here after all...
I recollect and recreate.
There it is. In all of its battered charm.
That beast.

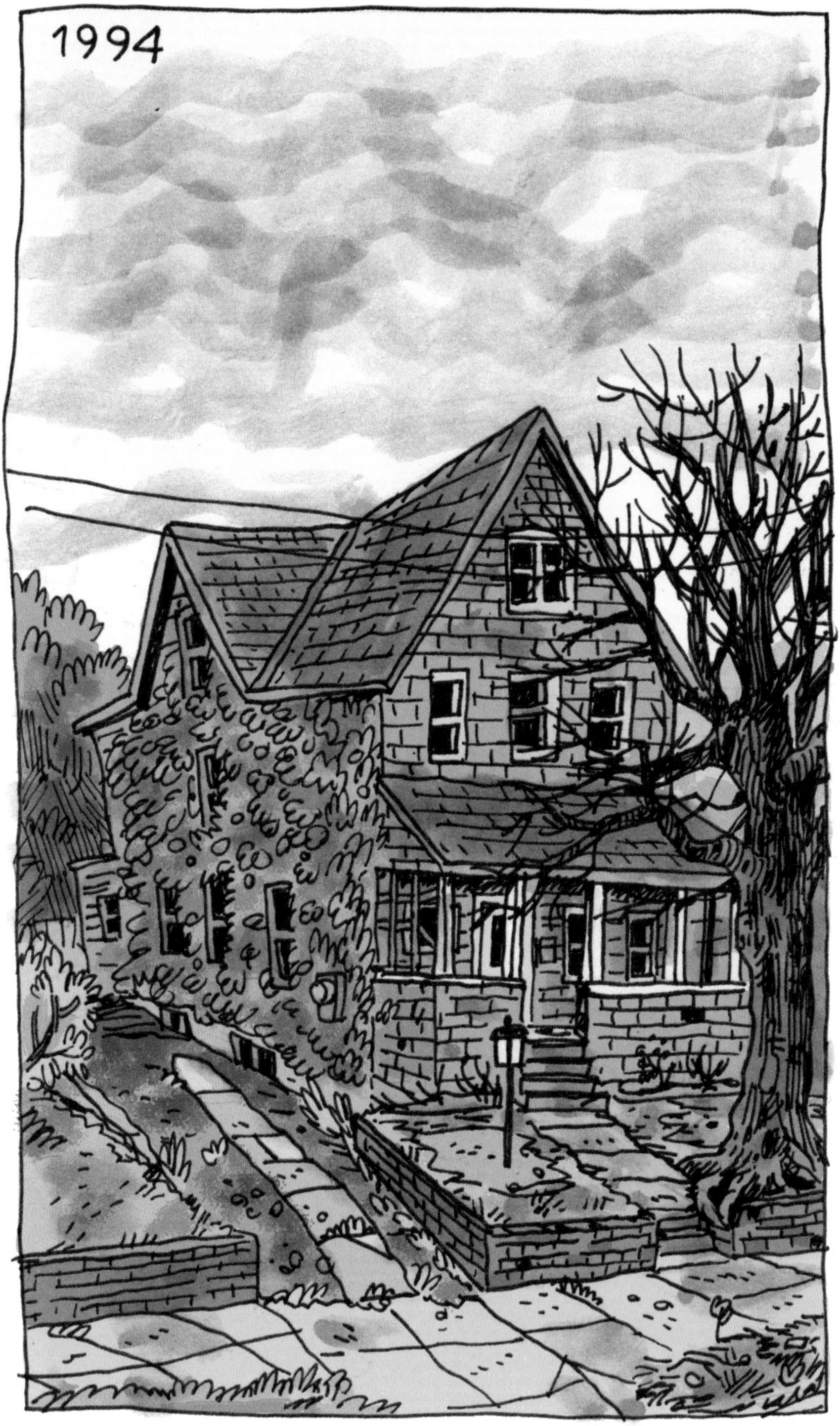
1994

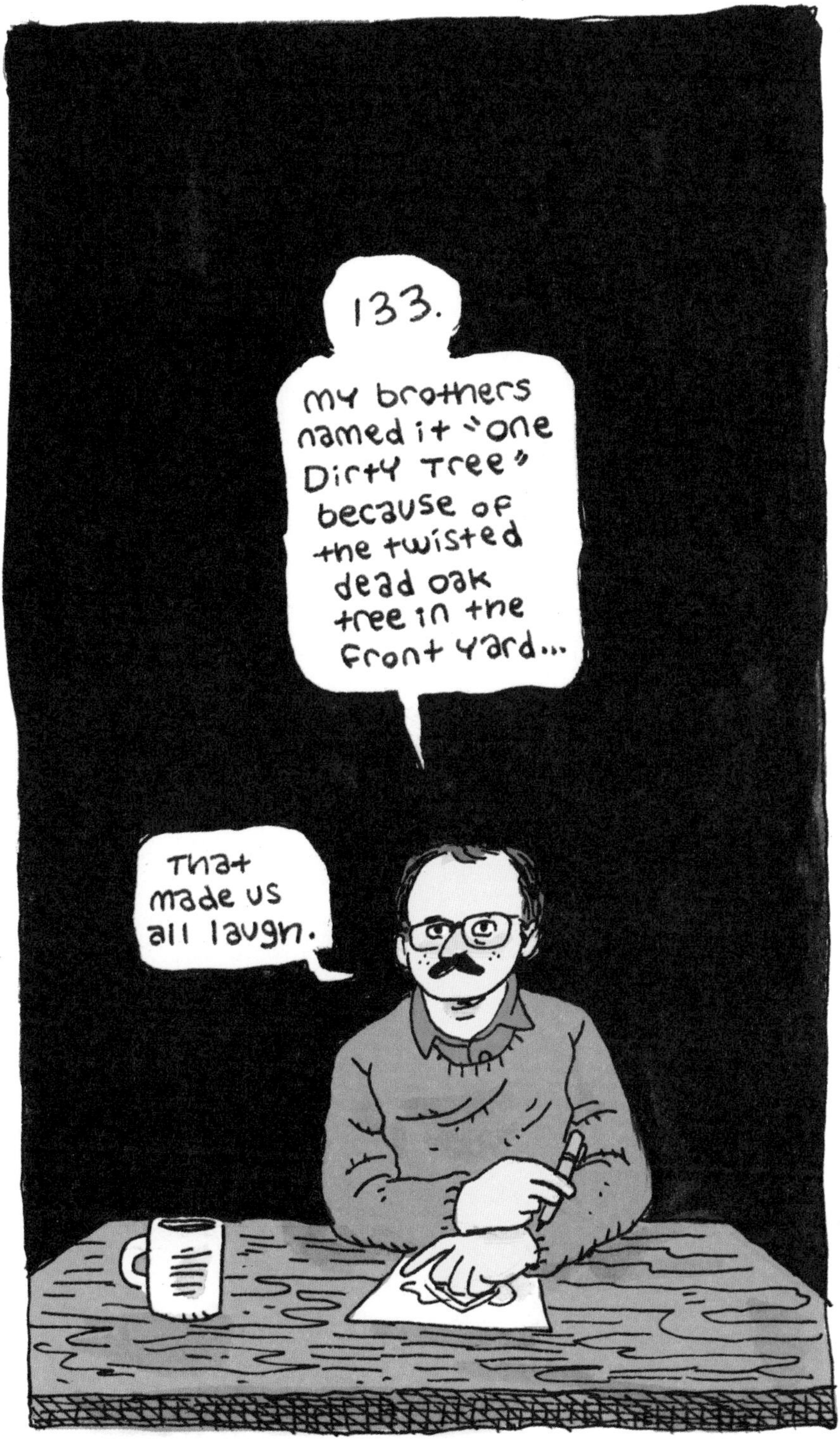
133.
my brothers named it "one Dirty Tree" because of the twisted dead oak tree in the front yard...
That made us all laugh.

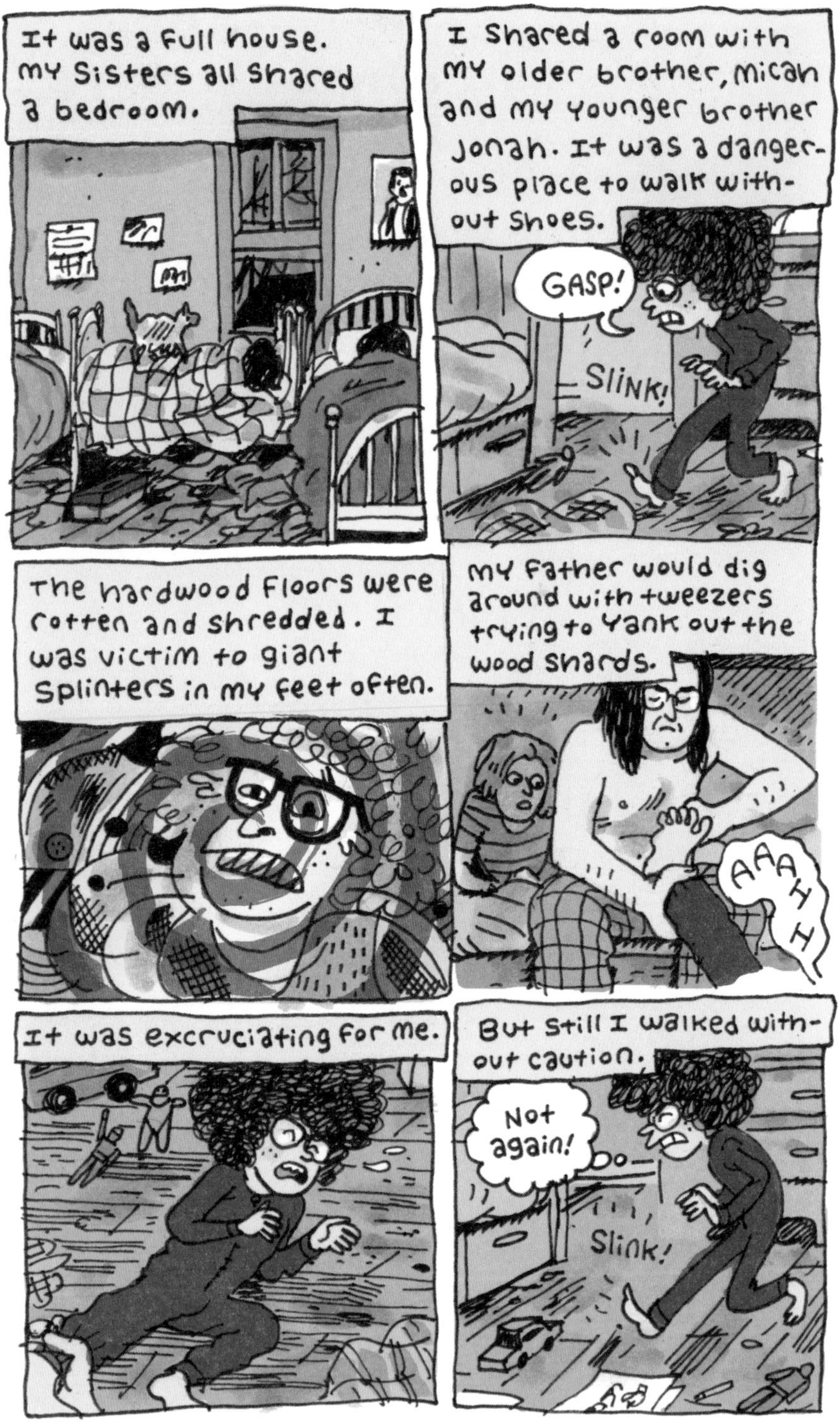
It was a full house. my sisters all shared a bedroom.
I shared a room with my older brother, Micah and my younger brother Jonah. It was a danger-ous place to walk with-out shoes.
GASP!
SLINK!
The hardwood floors were rotten and shredded. I was victim to giant splinters in my feet often.
My father would dig around with tweezers trying to yank out the wood shards.
AAAHHH
It was excruciating for me.
But still I walked with-out caution.
Not again!
Slink!

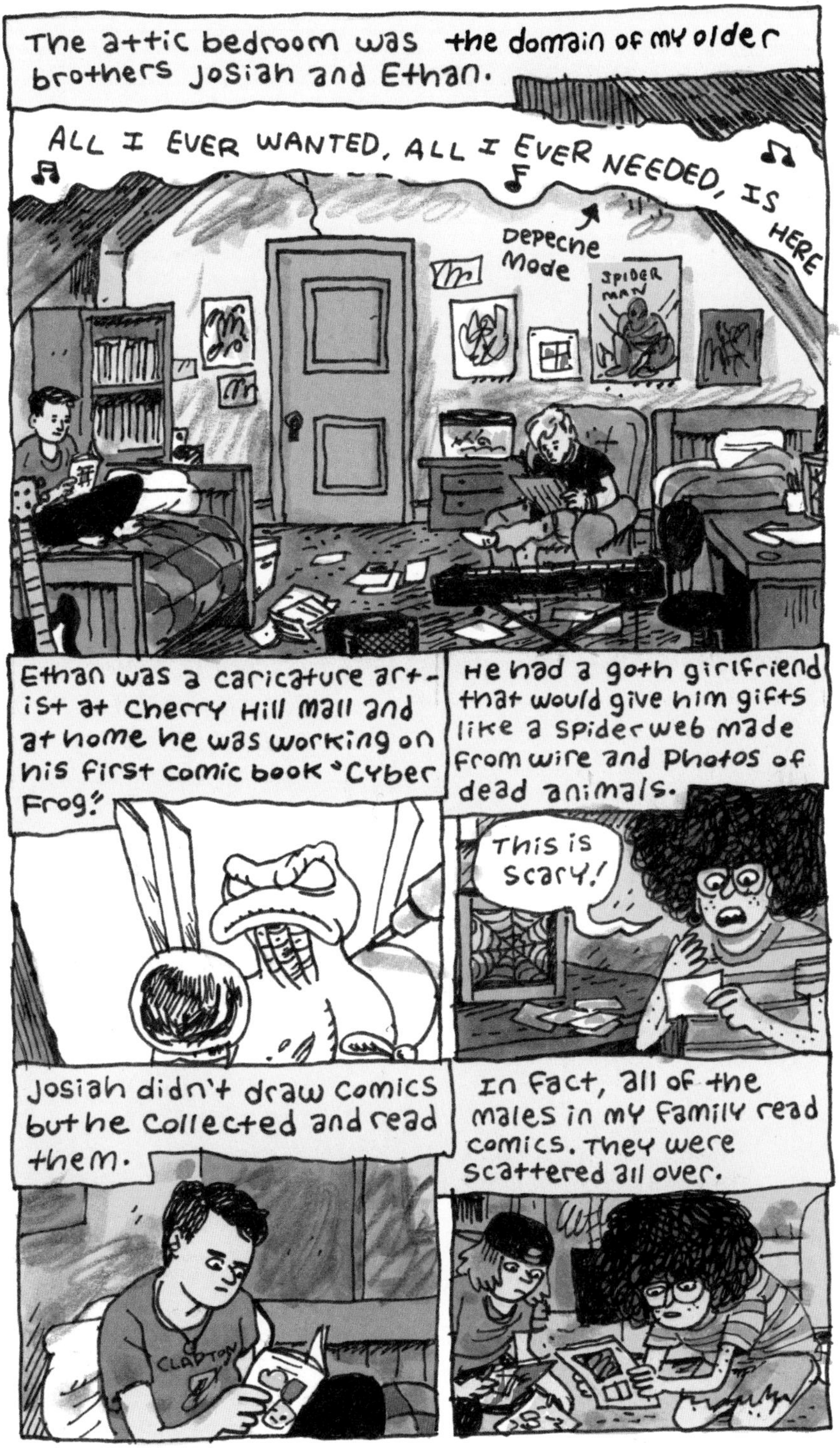
The attic bedroom was the domain of my older brothers Josiah and Ethan.
ALL I EVER WANTED, ALL I EVER NEEDED, IS HERE
Depeche Mode
SPIDER MAN
Ethan was a caricature artist at Cherry Hill Mall and at home he was working on his first comic book "Cyber Frog."
He had a goth girlfriend that would give him gifts like a spiderweb made from wire and photos of dead animals.
This is scary!
Josiah didn't draw comics but he collected and read them.
CLAPTON
In fact, all of the males in my family read comics. They were scattered all over.

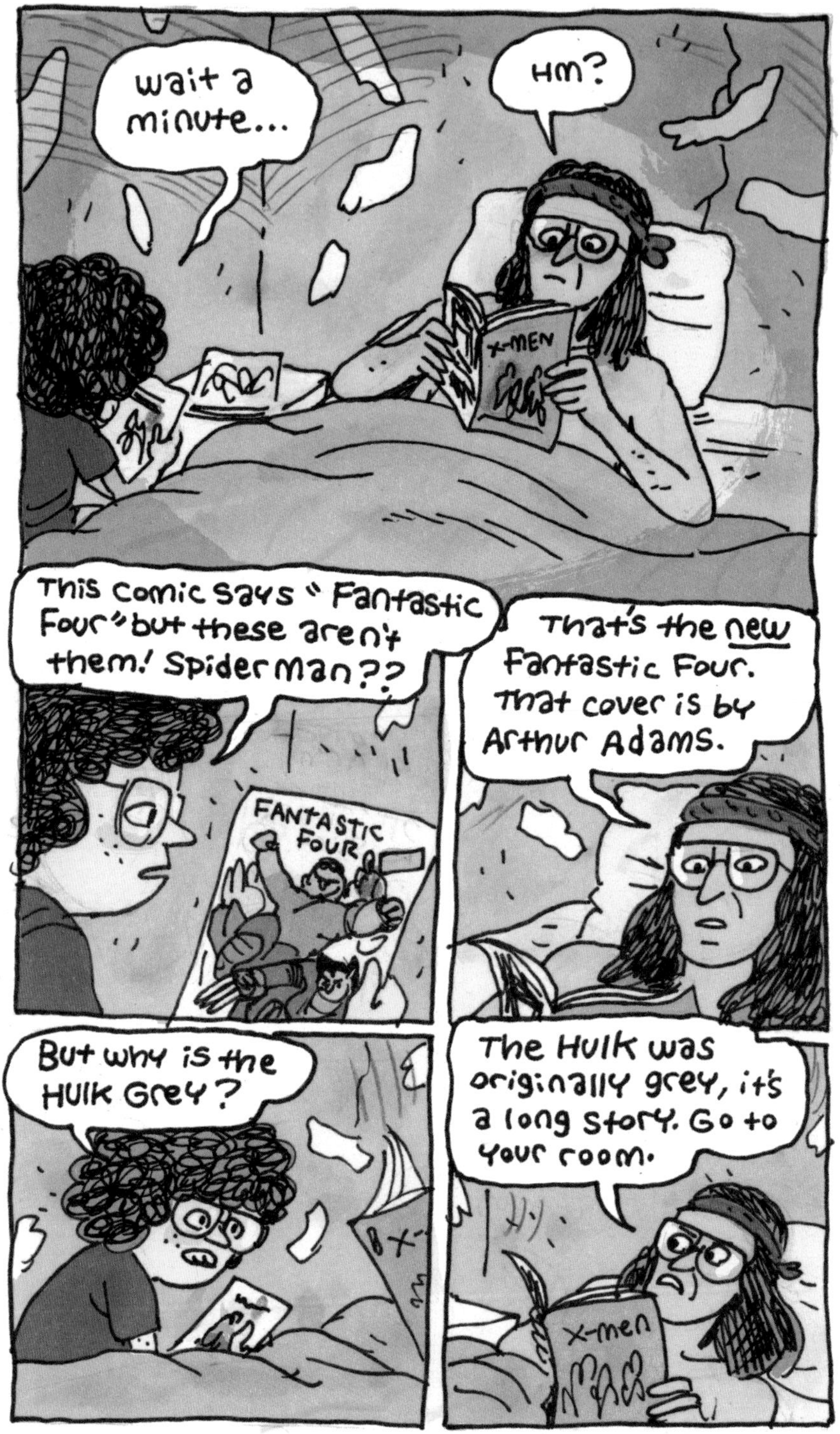
wait a minute...
HM?
X-MEN
This comic says "Fantastic Four" but these aren't them! Spider Man??
FANTASTIC FOUR
That's the new Fantastic Four. That cover is by Arthur Adams.
But why is the HUlk Grey?
The Hulk was originally grey, it's a long story. Go to your room.
X-men

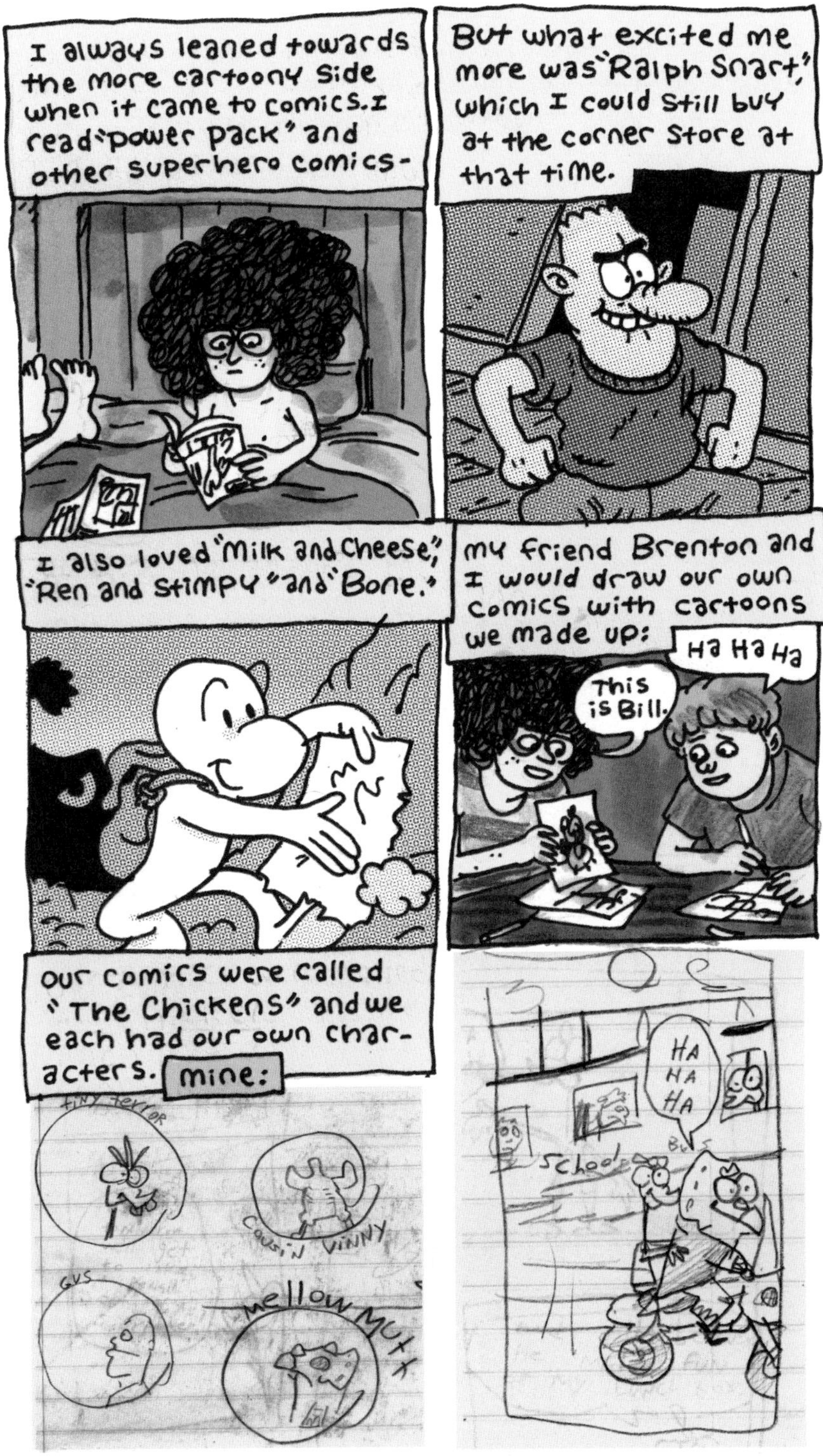
I always leaned towards the more cartoony side when it came to comics. I read "Power Pack" and other superhero comics-
But what excited me more was "Ralph Snart," which I could still buy at the corner store at that time.
I also loved "Milk and Cheese," "Ren and Stimpy" and "Bone."
my friend Brenton and I would draw our own comics with cartoons we made up:
HA HA HA
This is Bill.
our comics were called "The Chickens" and we each had our own characters.
mine:
tiny terror
Cousin VINNY
GUS
mellow MUTT
HA HA HA
School

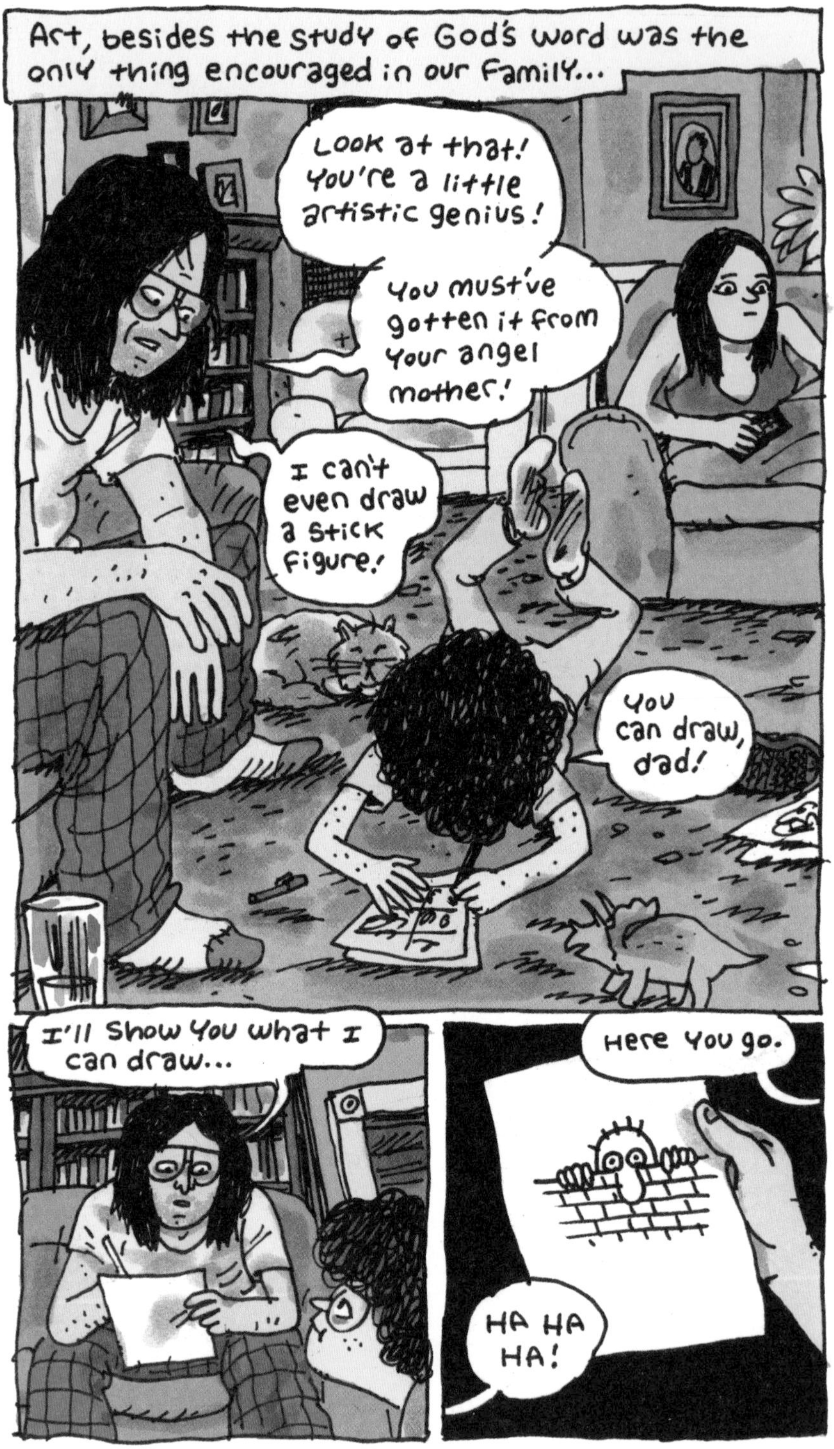

Art, besides the study of God's word was the only thing encouraged in our family...
Look at that! You're a little artistic genius!
You must've gotten it from your angel mother!
I can't even draw a stick figure!
You can draw, dad!
I'll show you what I can draw...
Here you go.
HA HA HA!

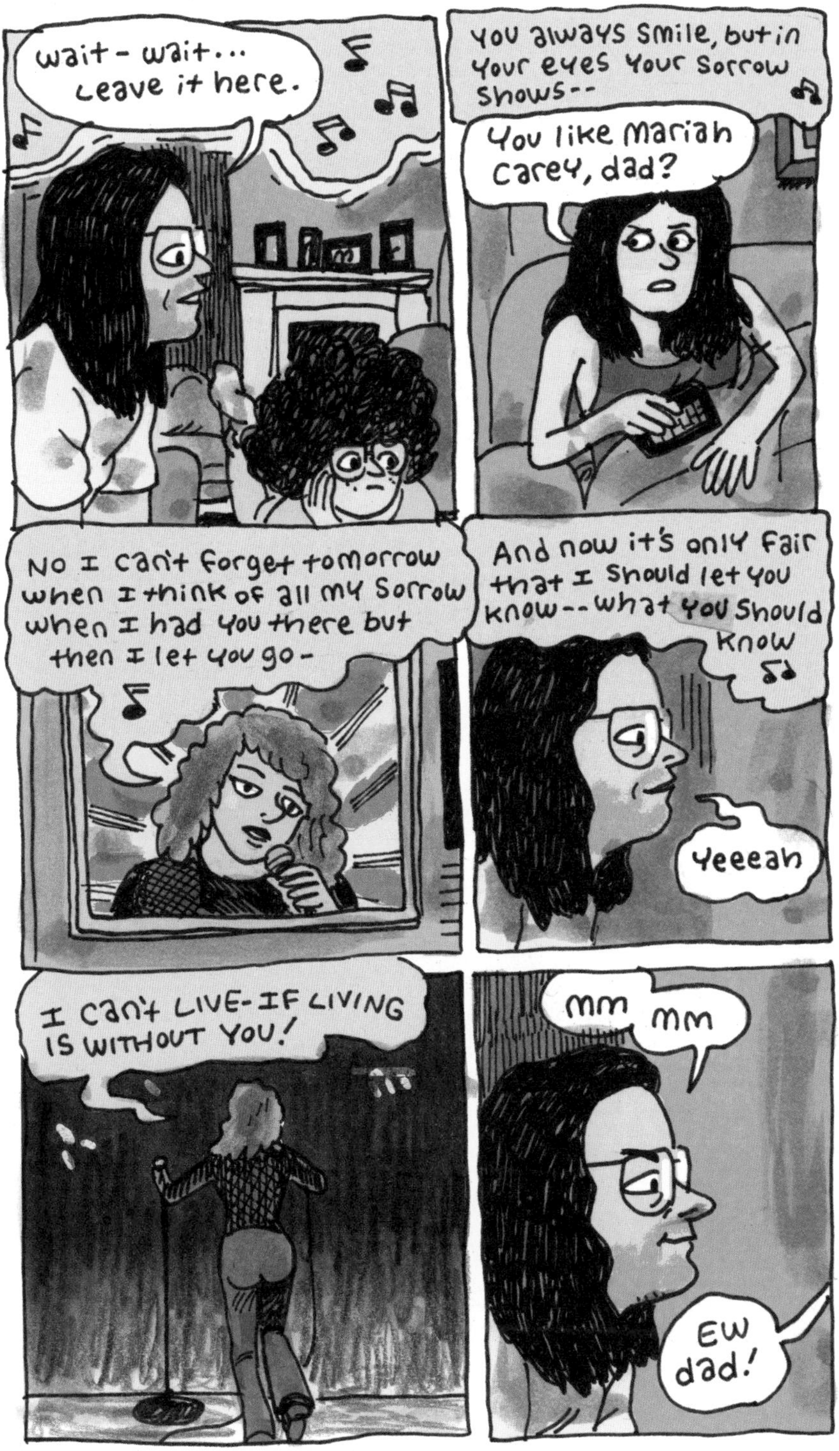
wait- wait...
leave it here.
You always smile, but in your eyes your sorrow shows--
You like Mariah Carey, dad?
No I can't forget tomorrow when I think of all my sorrow when I had you there but then I let you go-
And now it's only fair that I should let you know--what you should know
Yeeeah
I CAN'T LIVE- IF LIVING IS WITHOUT YOU!
mm mm
EW dad!

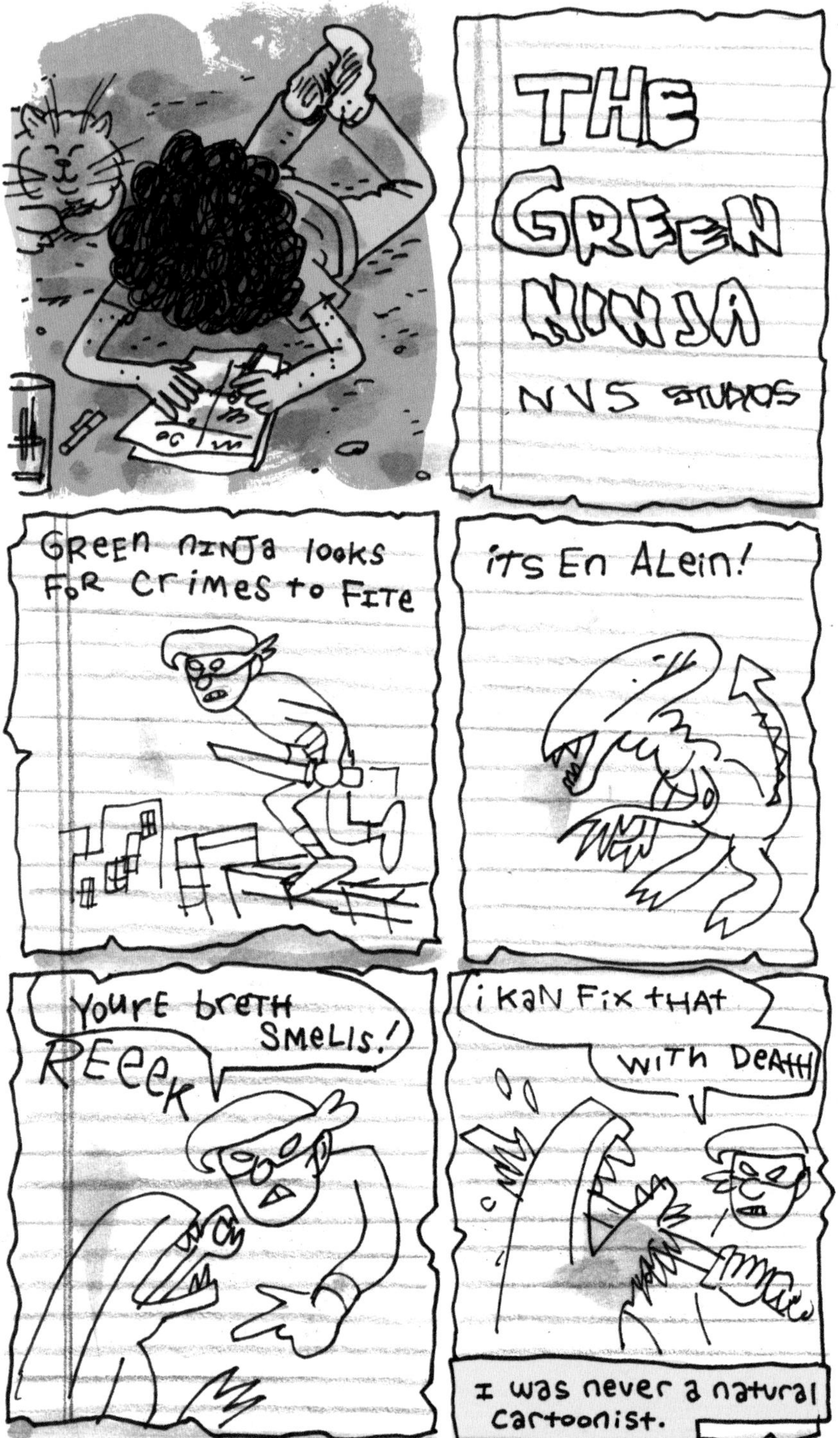
THE GREEN NINJA
NVS STUDIOS
Green ninja looks for crimes to fite
its En Alein!
Youre breth smells!
REeek
i kaN Fix tHAt with DeAtH
I was never a natural cartoonist.

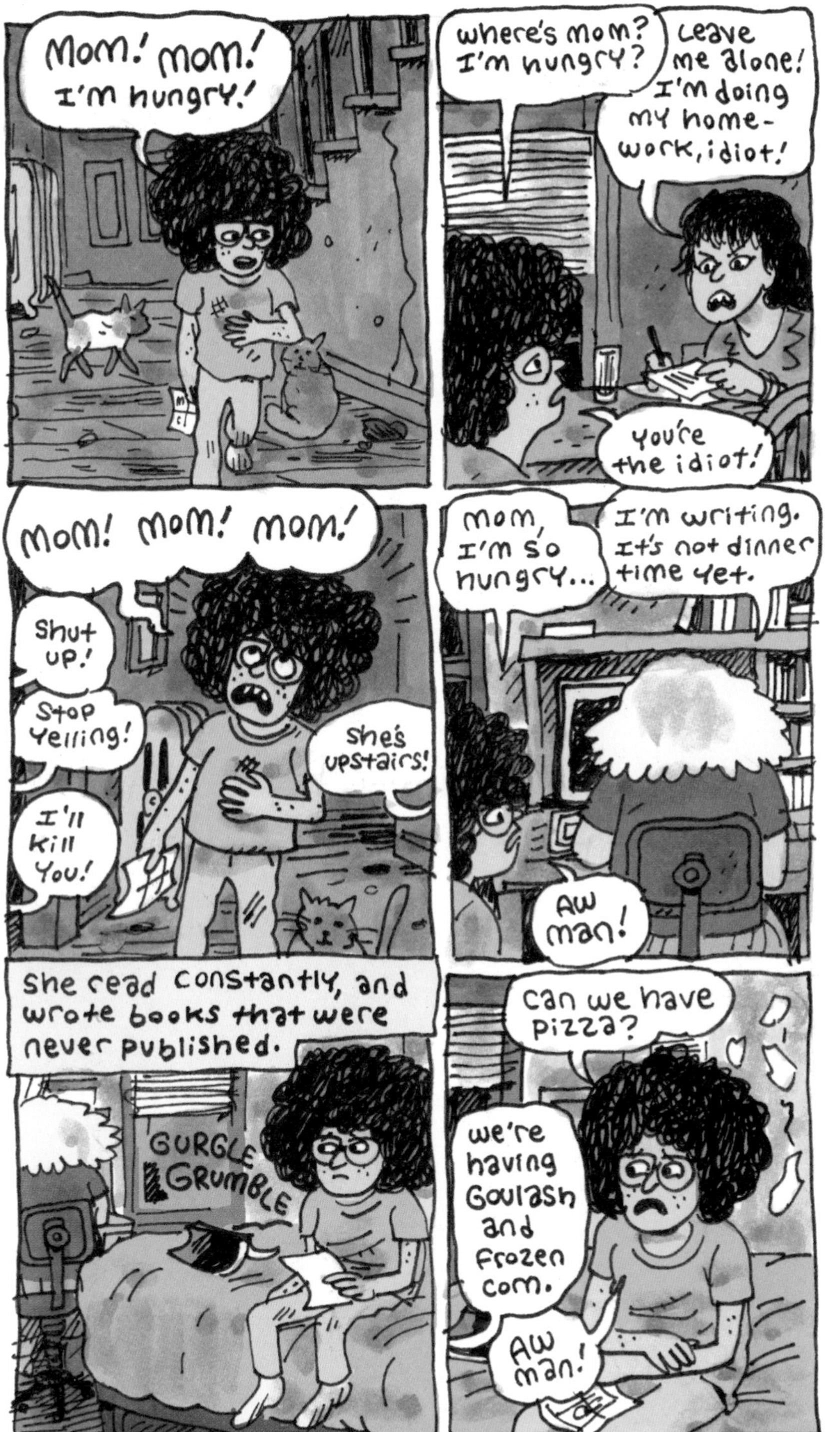
Mom! mom! I'm hungry!
where's mom? I'm hungry?
Leave me alone! I'm doing my home-work, idiot!
You're the idiot!
Mom! mom! mom!
Shut up!
Stop yelling!
I'll kill You!
She's upstairs!
mom, I'm so hungry...
I'm writing. It's not dinner time yet.
Aw man!
She read constantly, and wrote books that were never published.
GURGLE GRUMBLE
Can we have pizza?
we're having Goulash and frozen corn.
Aw man!

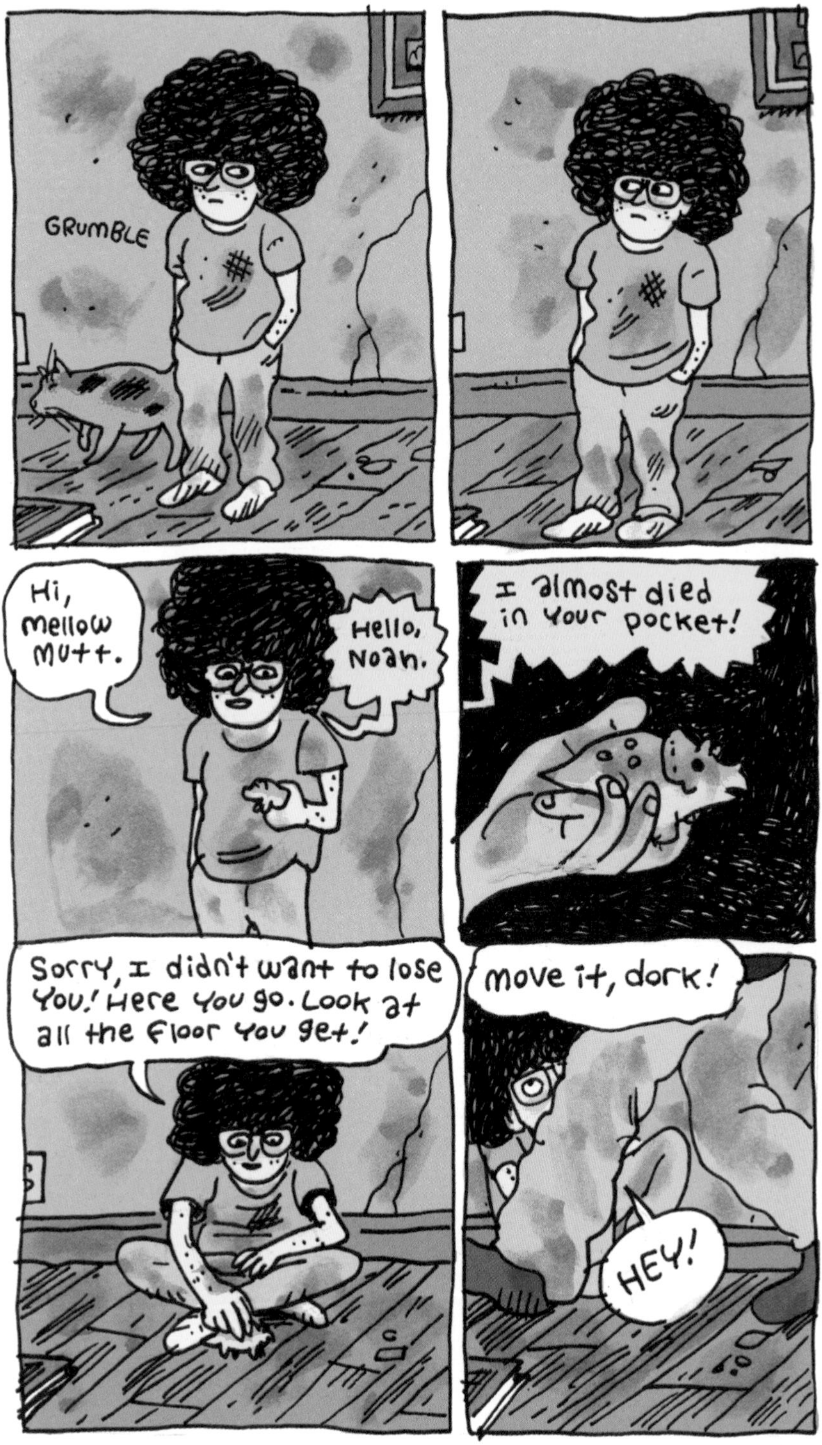
GRUMBLE
Hi, mellow Mutt.
Hello, Noah.
I almost died in your pocket!
Sorry, I didn't want to lose you! Here you go. Look at all the floor you get!
Move it, dork!
HEY!

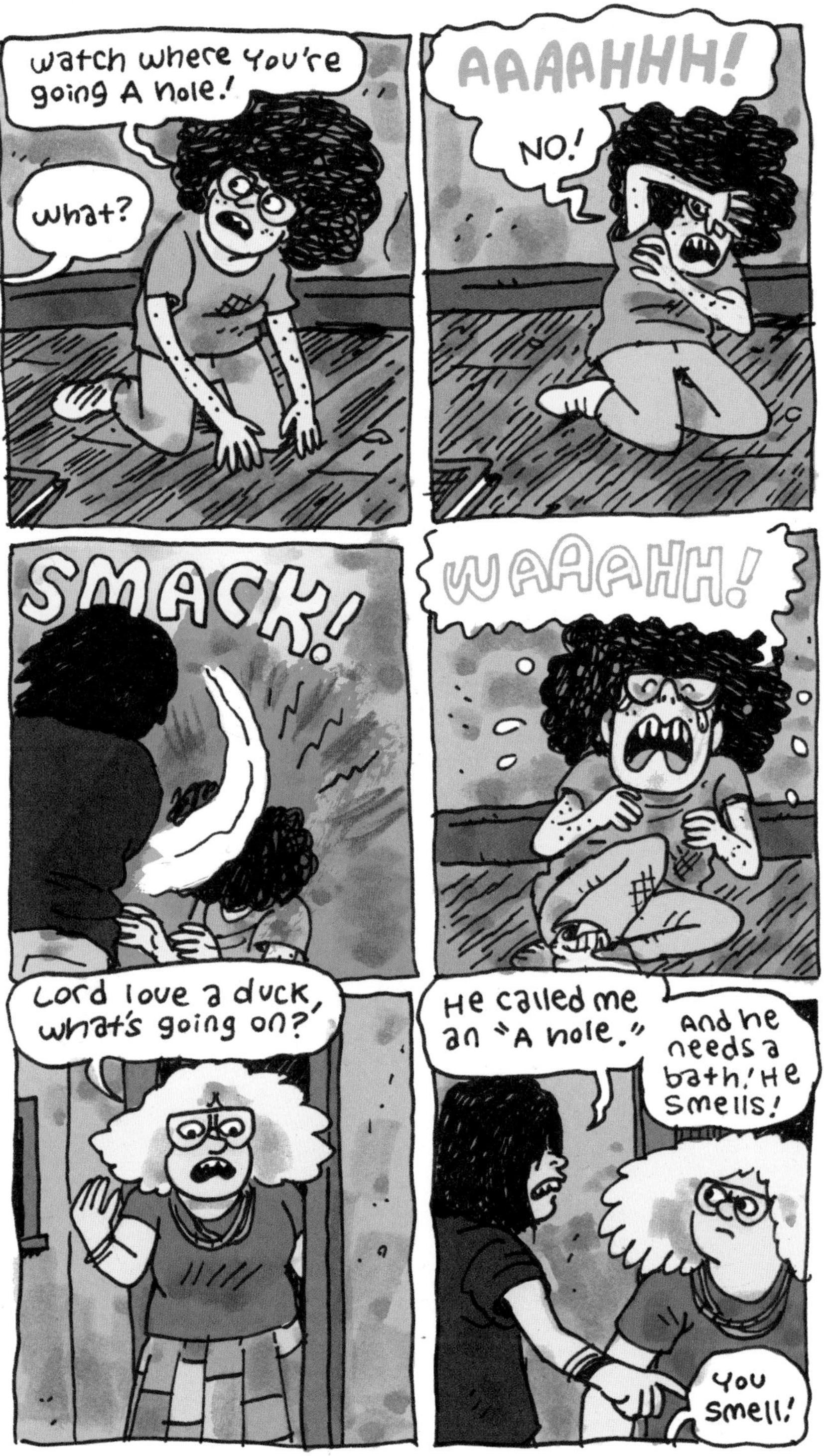

watch where you're going A hole!
what?
AAAAHHH!
NO!
SMACK!
WAAAHH!
Lord love a duck, what's going on?
He called me an "A hole."
And he needs a bath! He smells!
You smell!

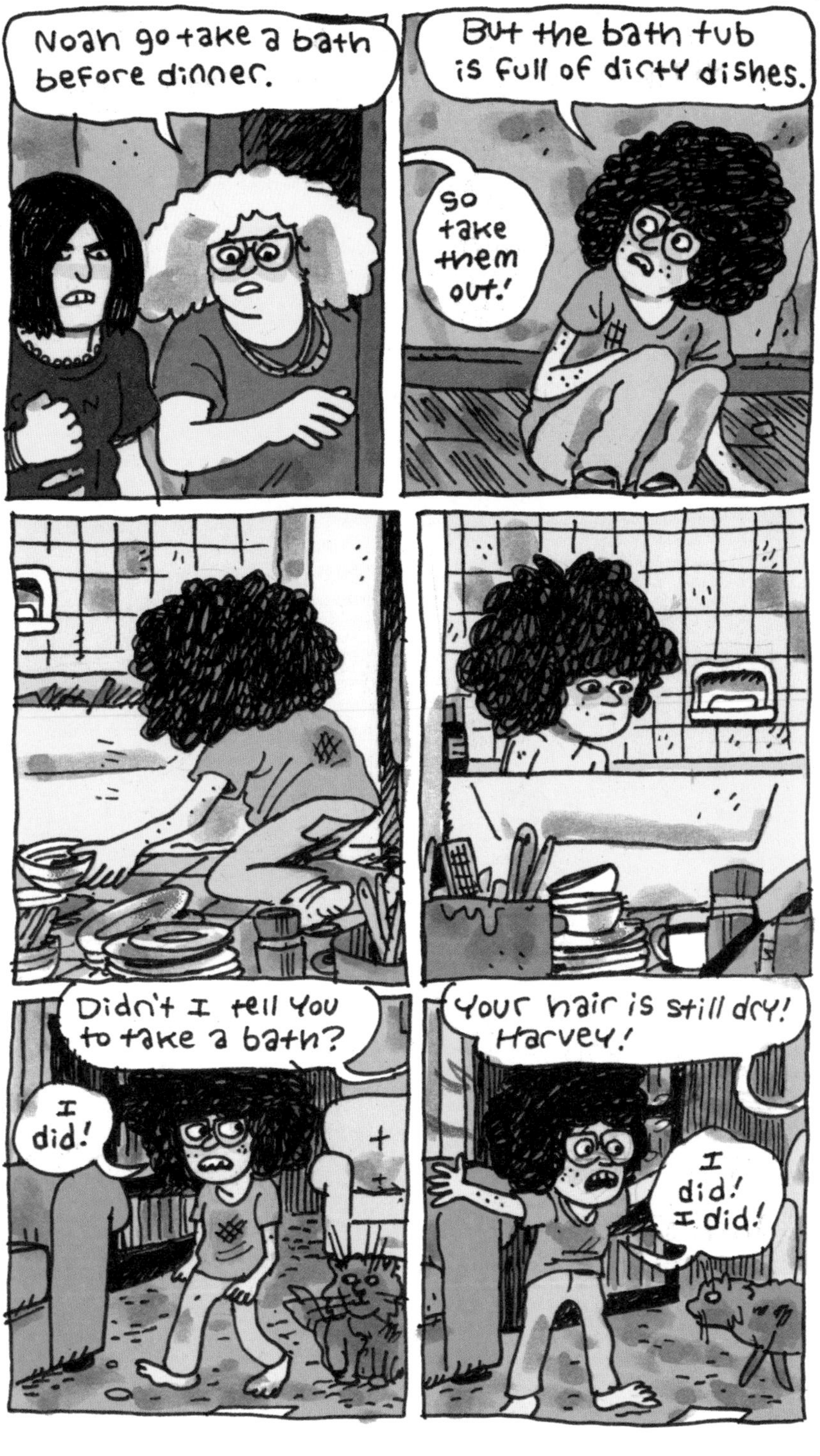
Noah go take a bath before dinner.
But the bath tub is full of dirty dishes.
So take them out!
Didn't I tell you to take a bath?
I did!
Your hair is still dry! Harvey!
I did! I did!

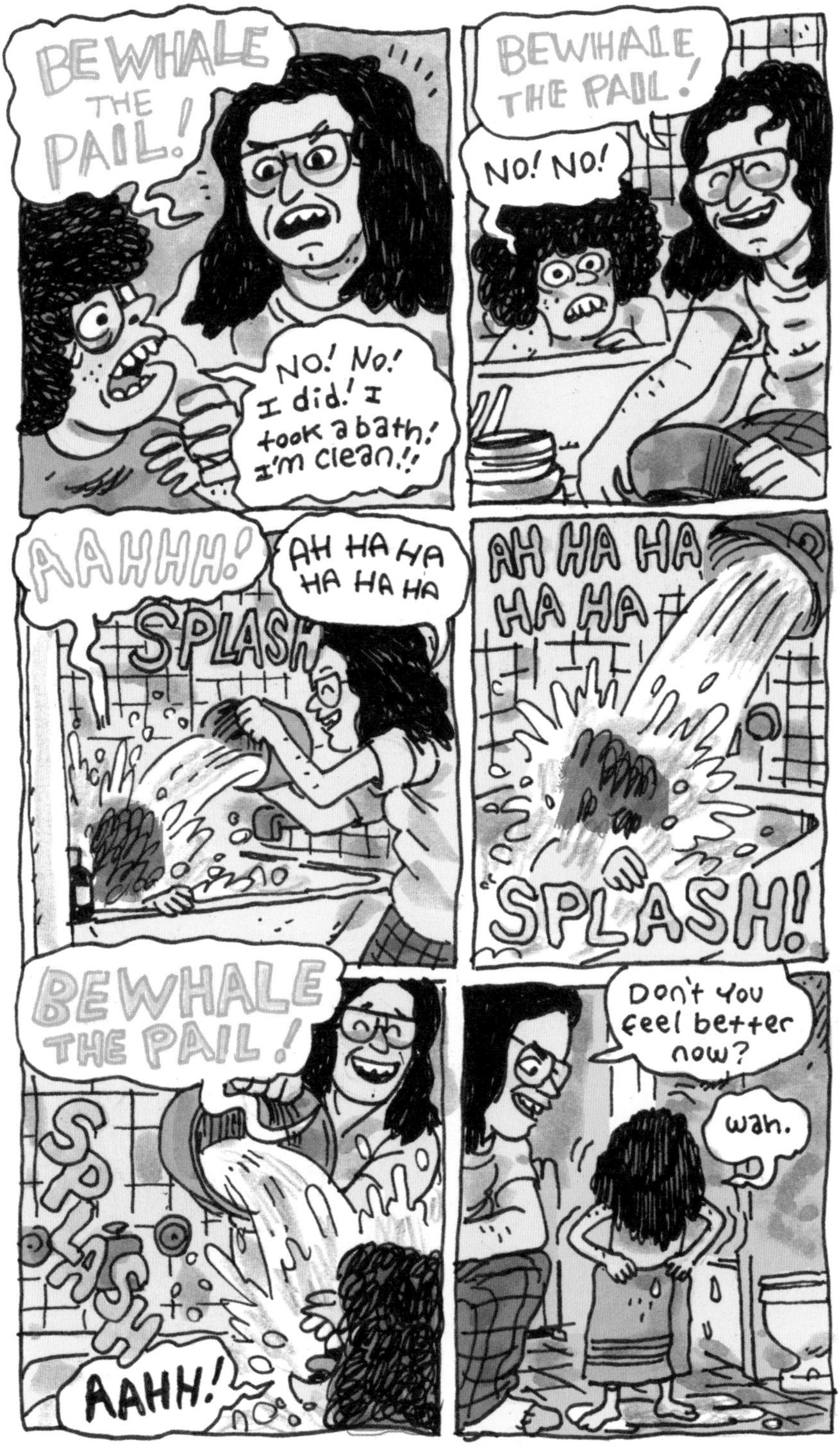
BEWHALE THE PAIL!
No! No! I did! I took a bath! I'm clean!!
BEWHALE, THE PAIL!
NO! NO!
AAHHH!
AH HA HA HA HA HA
SPLASH
AH HA HA HA HA
SPLASH!
BEWHALE THE PAIL!
SPLASH
AAHH!
Don't you feel better now?
wah.

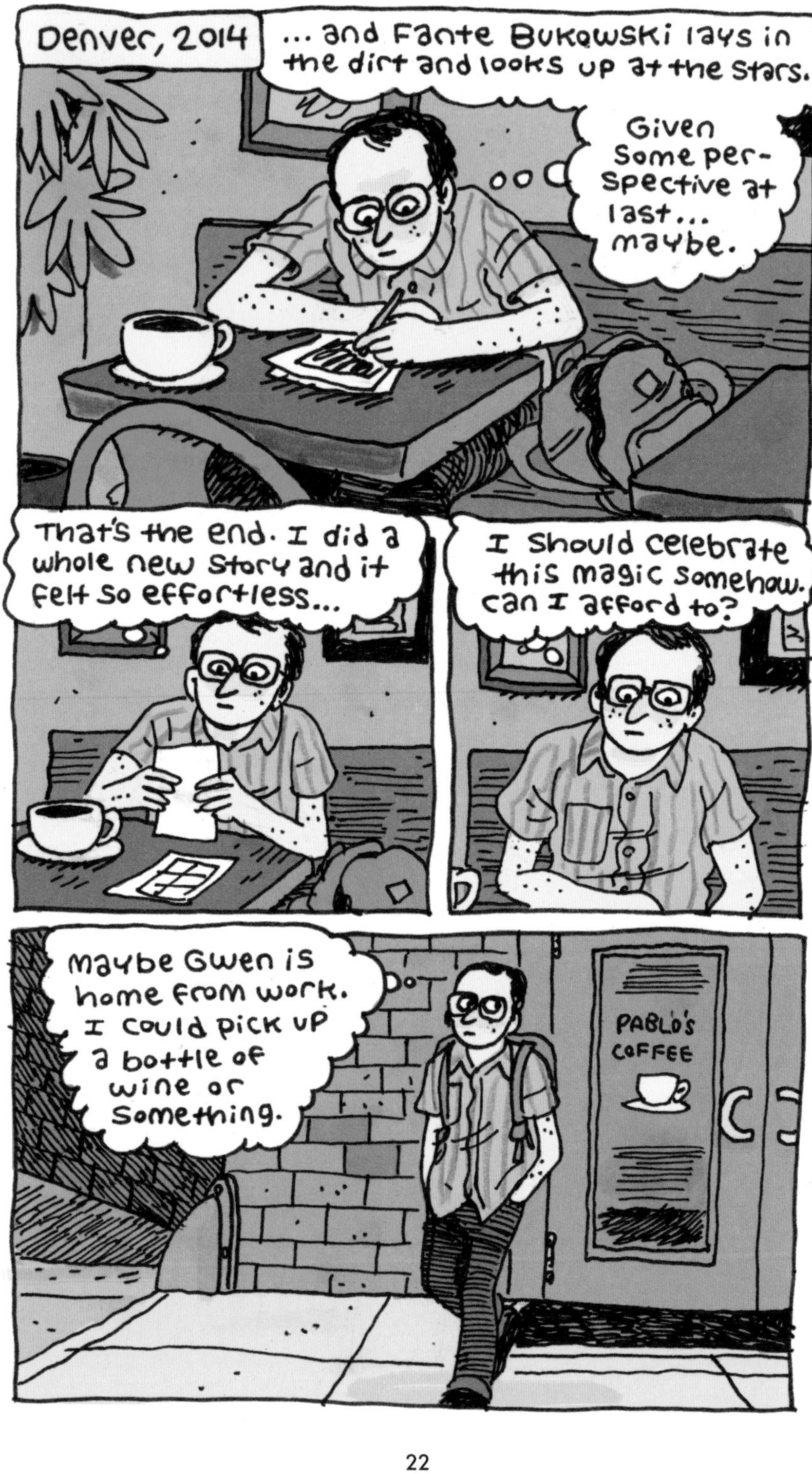

Denver, 2014
... and Fante Bukowski lays in the dirt and looks up at the stars.
Given some perspective at last... maybe.
That's the end. I did a whole new story and it felt so effortless...
I should celebrate this magic somehow. Can I afford to?
Maybe Gwen is home from work. I could pick up a bottle of wine or something.
PABLO'S COFFEE

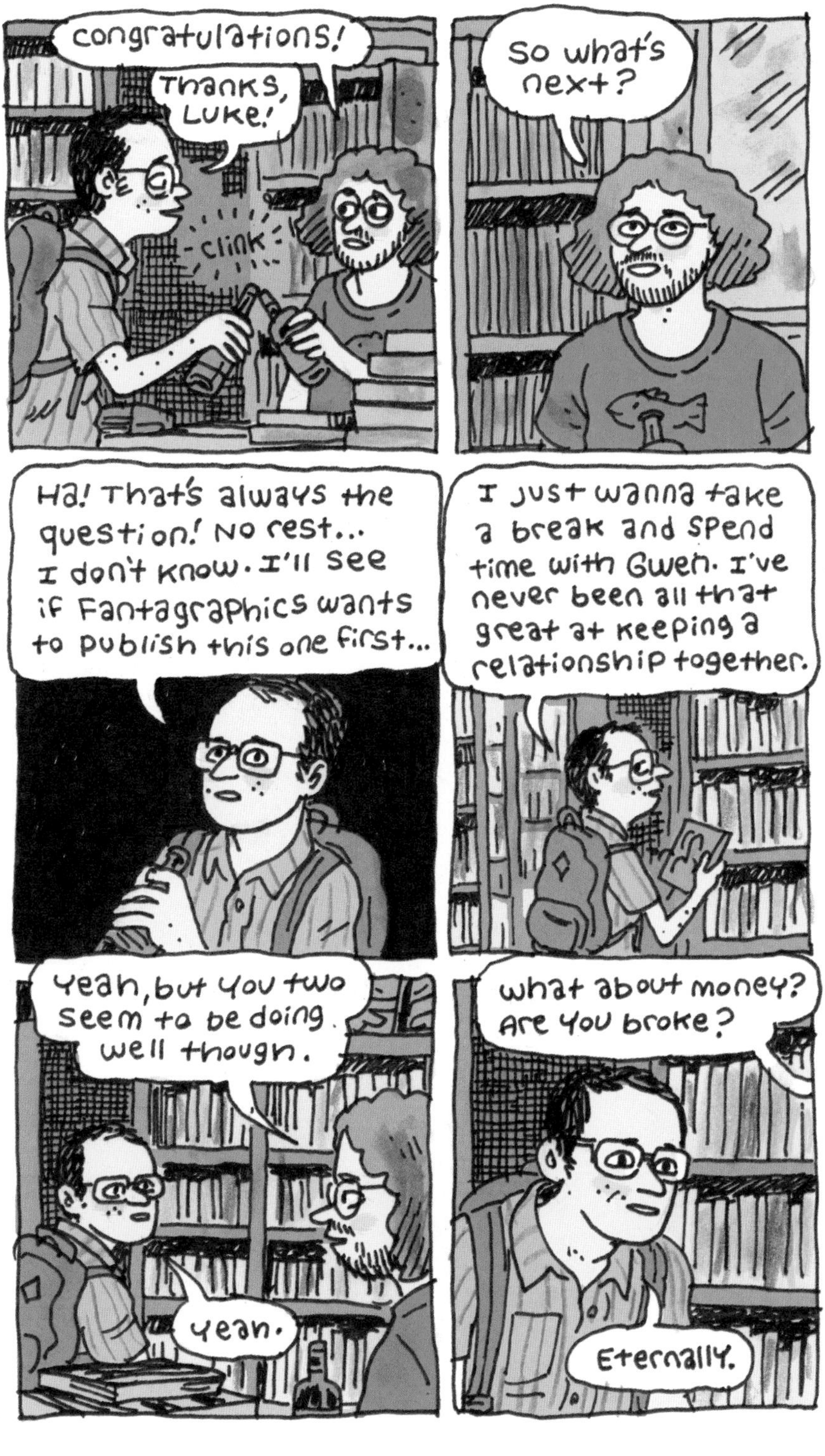
congratulations!
Thanks, Luke!
clink
So what's next?
Ha! That's always the question! No rest... I don't know. I'll see if Fantagraphics wants to publish this one first...
I just wanna take a break and spend time with Gwen. I've never been all that great at keeping a relationship together.
Yeah, but you two seem to be doing well though.
Yeah.
What about money? Are you broke?
Eternally.

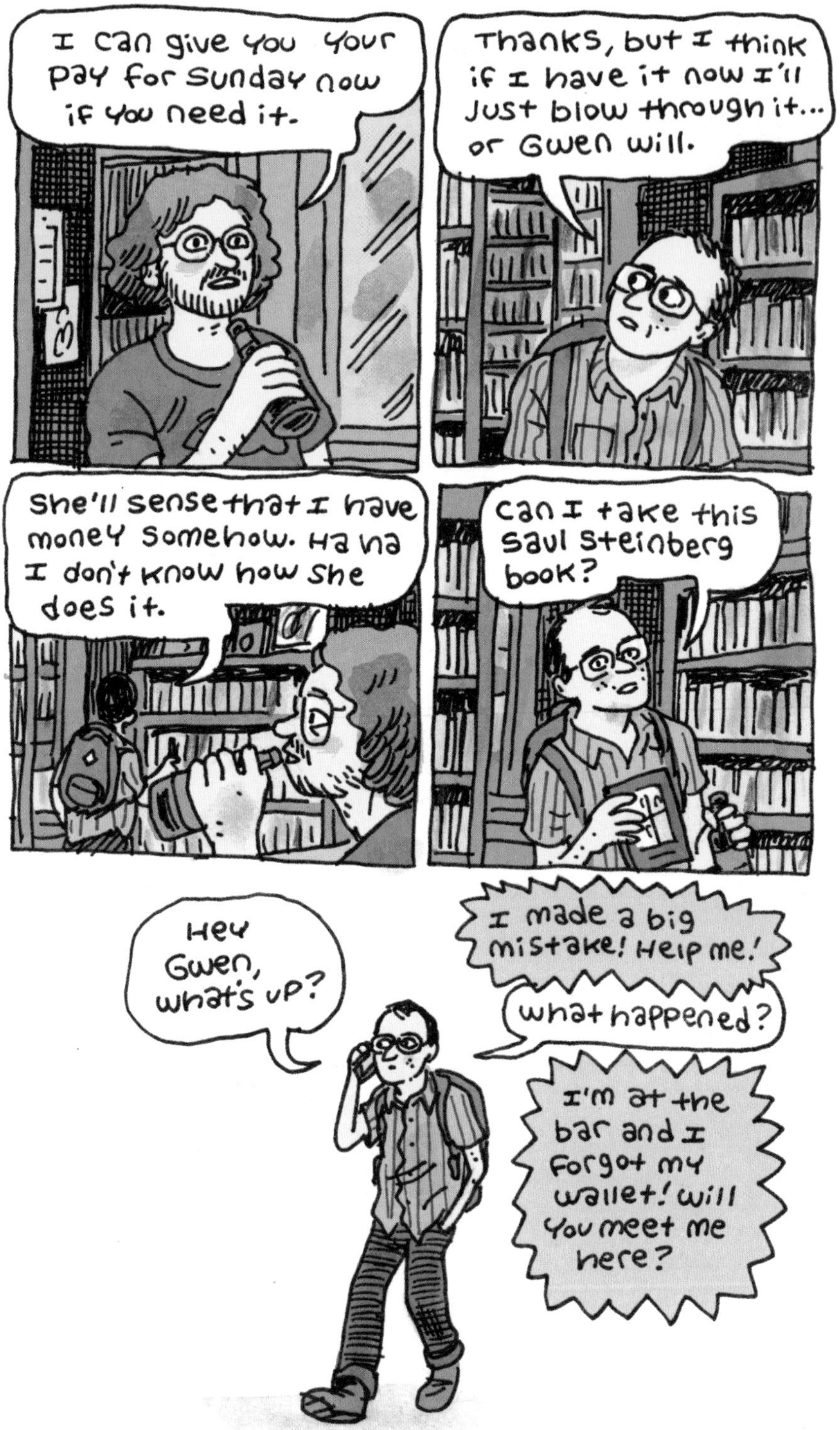
I can give you your pay for Sunday now if you need it.
Thanks, but I think if I have it now I'll just blow through it... or Gwen will.
She'll sense that I have money somehow. Ha ha I don't know how she does it.
Can I take this Saul Steinberg book?
Hey Gwen, what's up?
I made a big mistake! Help me!
What happened?
I'm at the bar and I forgot my wallet! Will you meet me here?

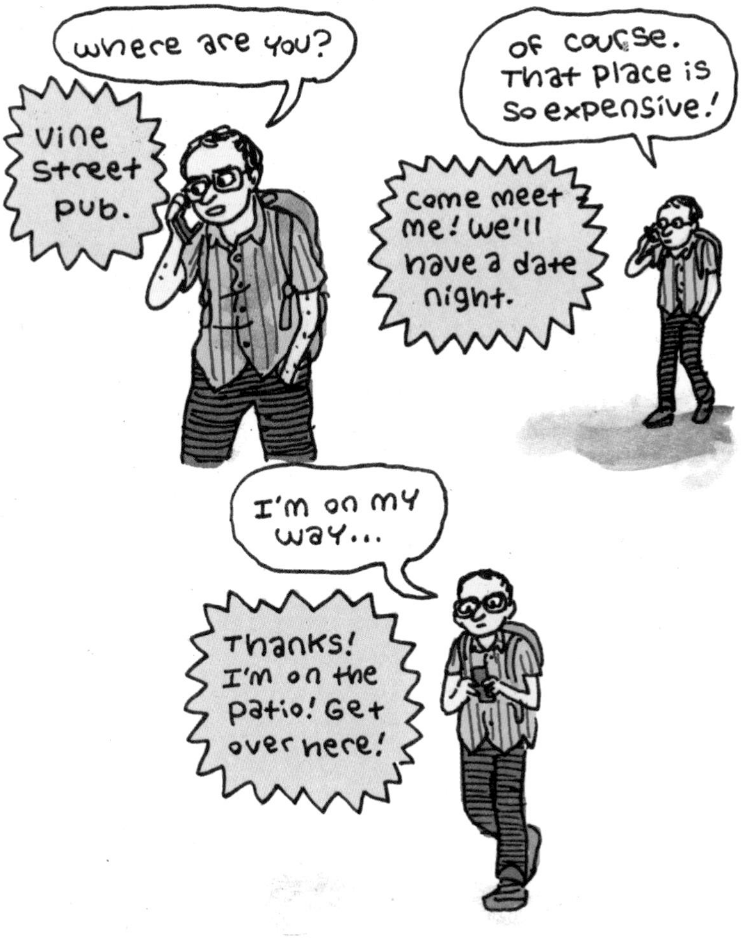
where are you?
vine street pub.
of course. That place is so expensive!
come meet me! we'll have a date night.
I'm on my way...
Thanks! I'm on the patio! Get over here!

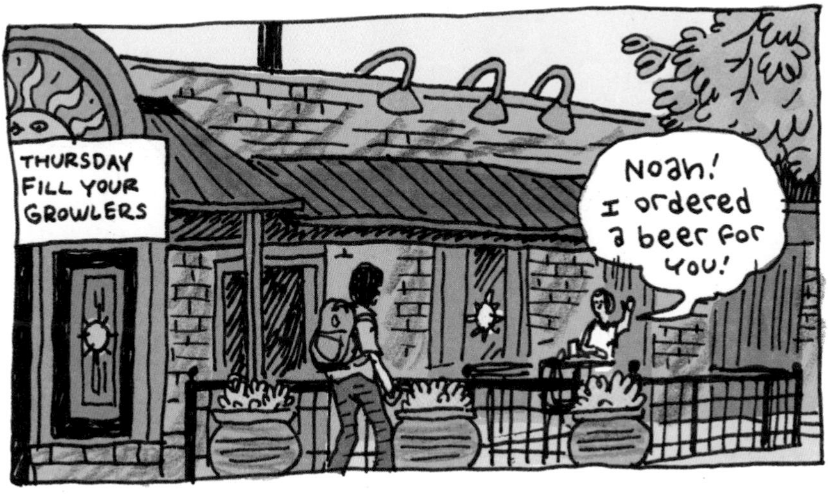
THURSDAY FILL YOUR GROWLERS
Noah! I ordered a beer for you!

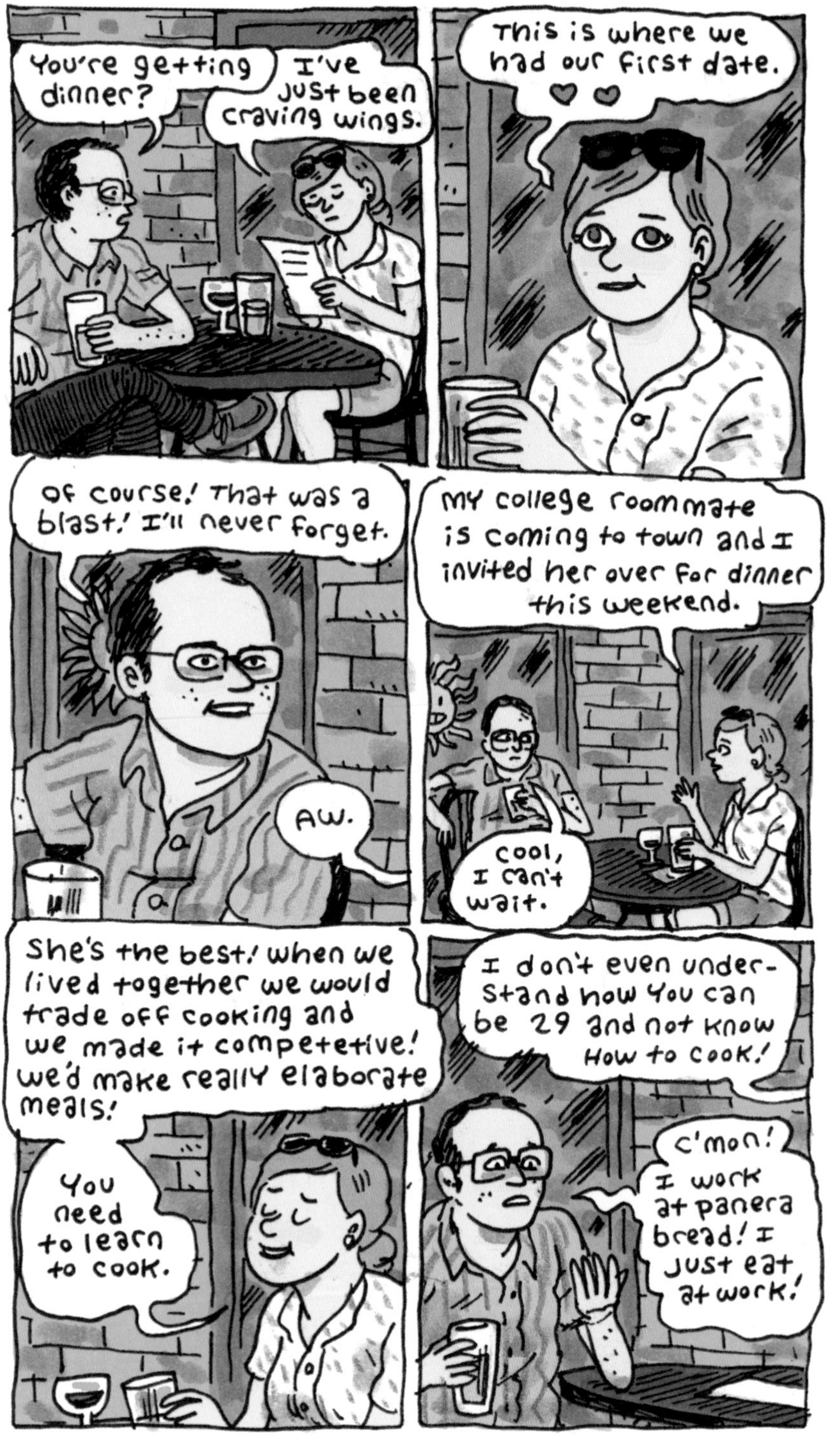
You're getting dinner?
I've just been craving wings.
This is where we had our first date.
Of course! That was a blast! I'll never forget.
Aw.
My college roommate is coming to town and I invited her over for dinner this weekend.
Cool, I can't wait.
She's the best! When we lived together we would trade off cooking and we made it competetive! We'd make really elaborate meals!
You need to learn to cook.
I don't even under-stand how you can be 29 and not know how to cook!
C'mon!
I work at Panera Bread! I just eat at work!

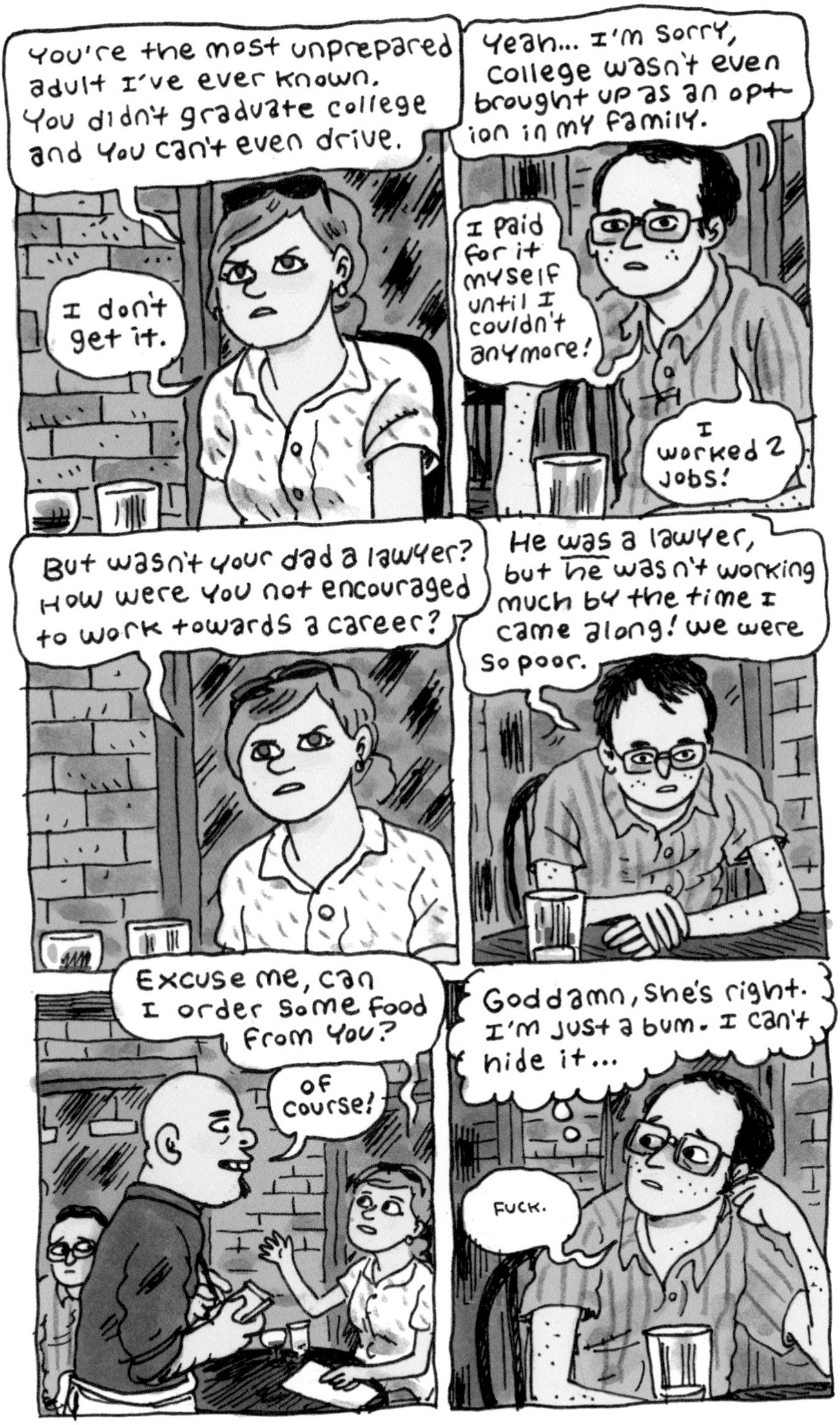
You're the most unprepared adult I've ever known. You didn't graduate college and you can't even drive.
I don't get it.
Yeah... I'm sorry, college wasn't even brought up as an option in my family.
I paid for it myself until I couldn't anymore!
I worked 2 jobs!
But wasn't your dad a lawyer? How were you not encouraged to work towards a career?
He was a lawyer, but he wasn't working much by the time I came along! We were so poor.
Excuse me, can I order some food from you?
Of course!
Goddamn, she's right. I'm just a bum. I can't hide it...
FUCK.

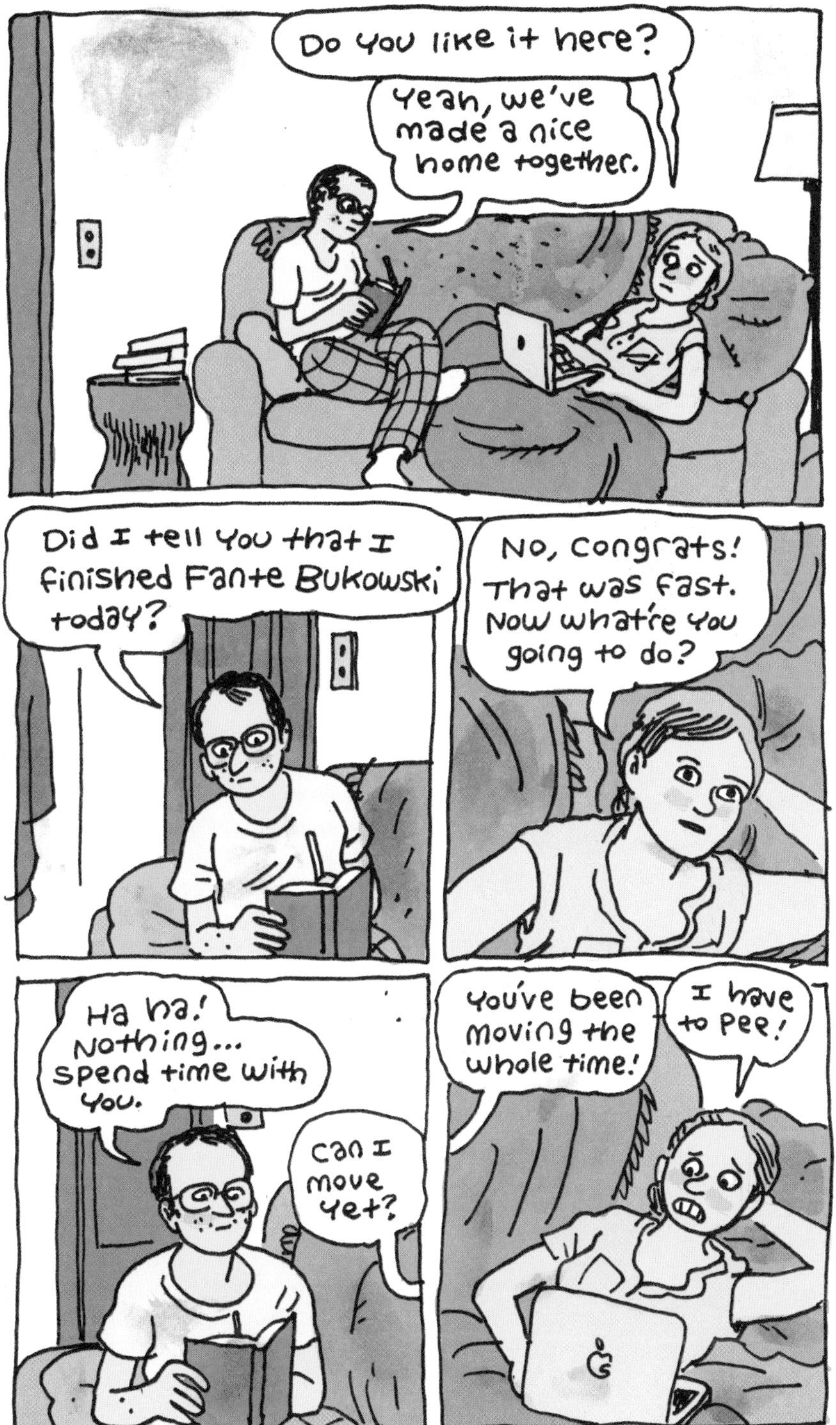
Do you like it here?
Yeah, we've made a nice home together.
Did I tell you that I finished Fante Bukowski today?
No, congrats! That was fast. Now what're you going to do?
Ha ha! Nothing... spend time with you.
Can I move yet?
You've been moving the whole time!
I have to pee!

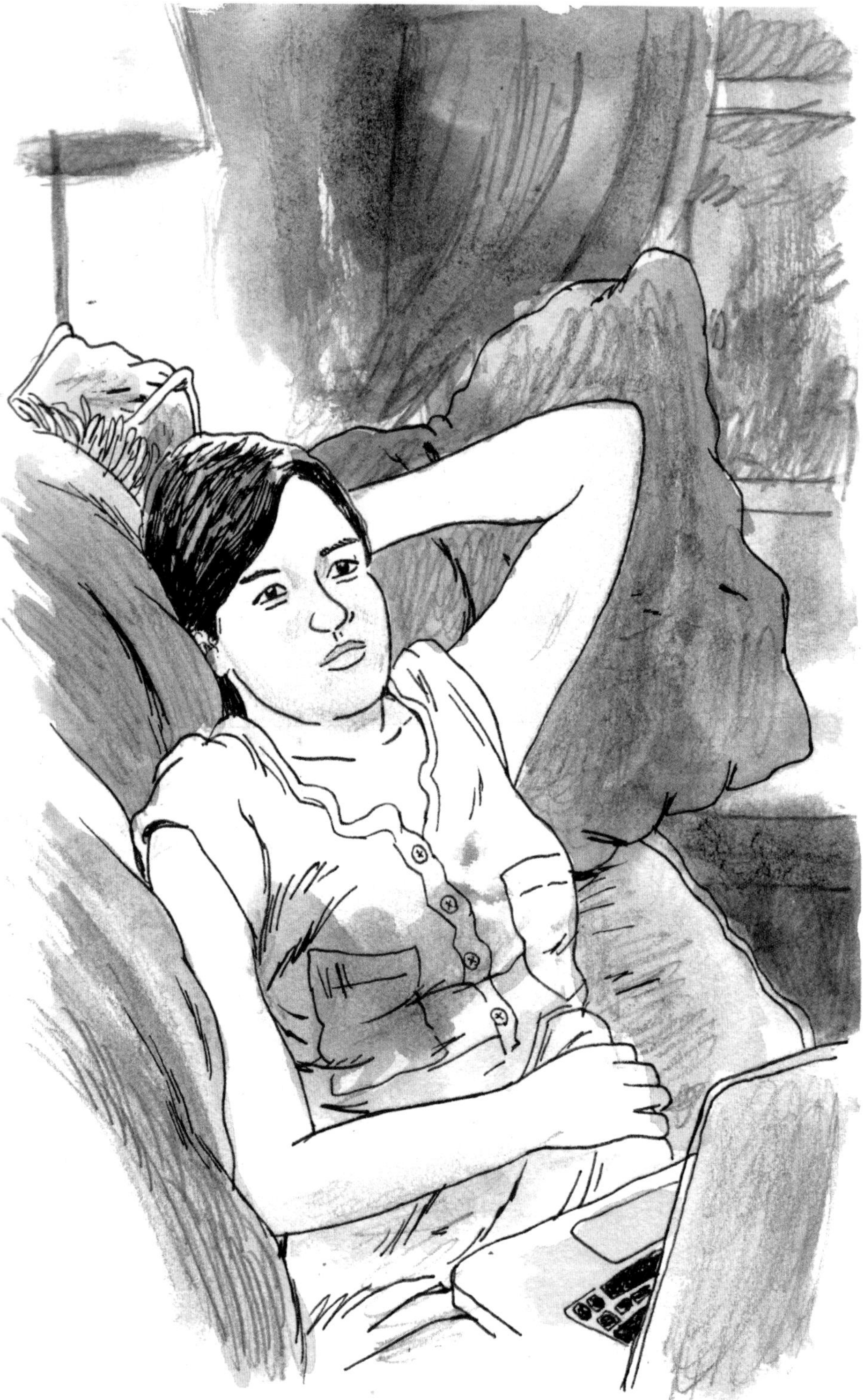

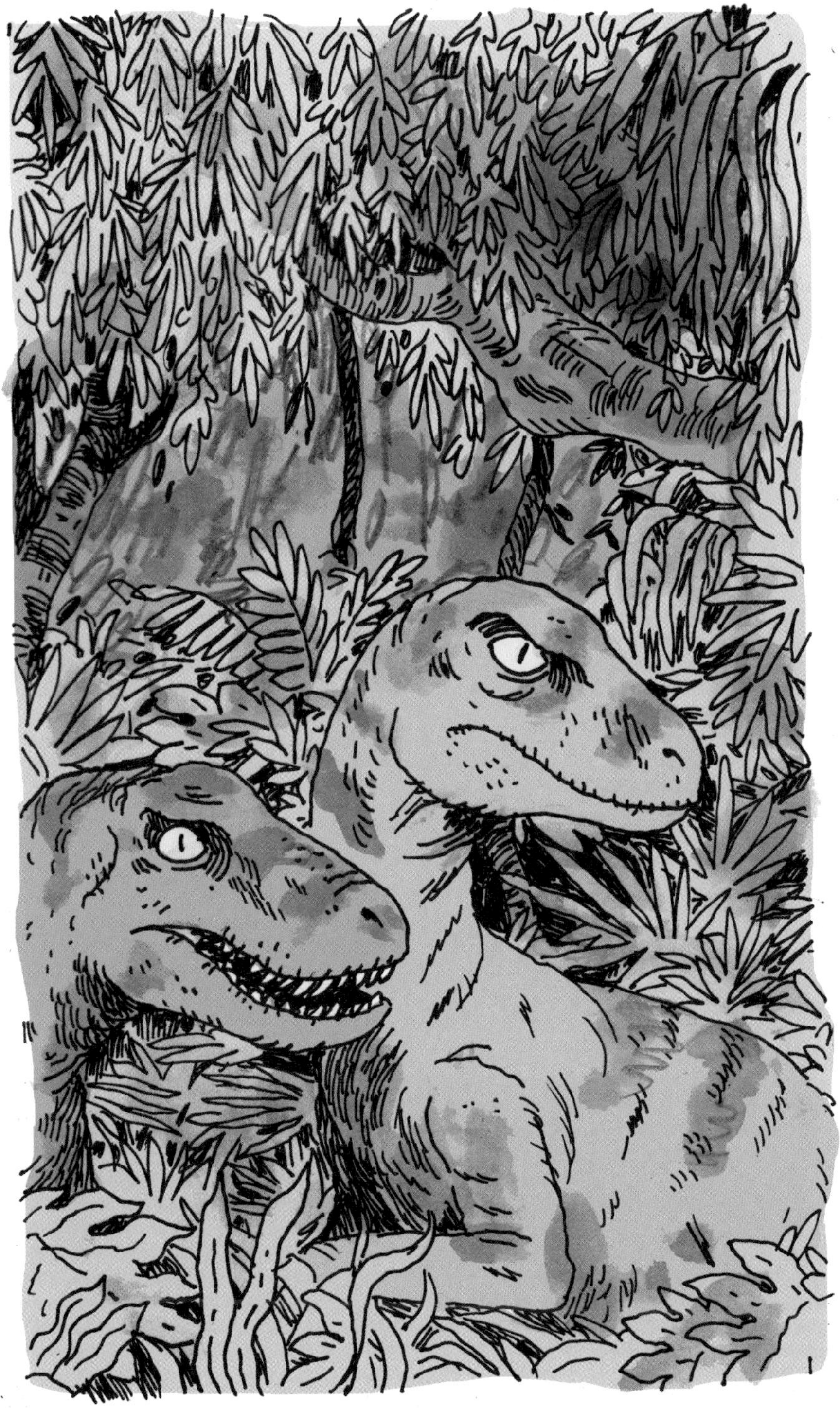

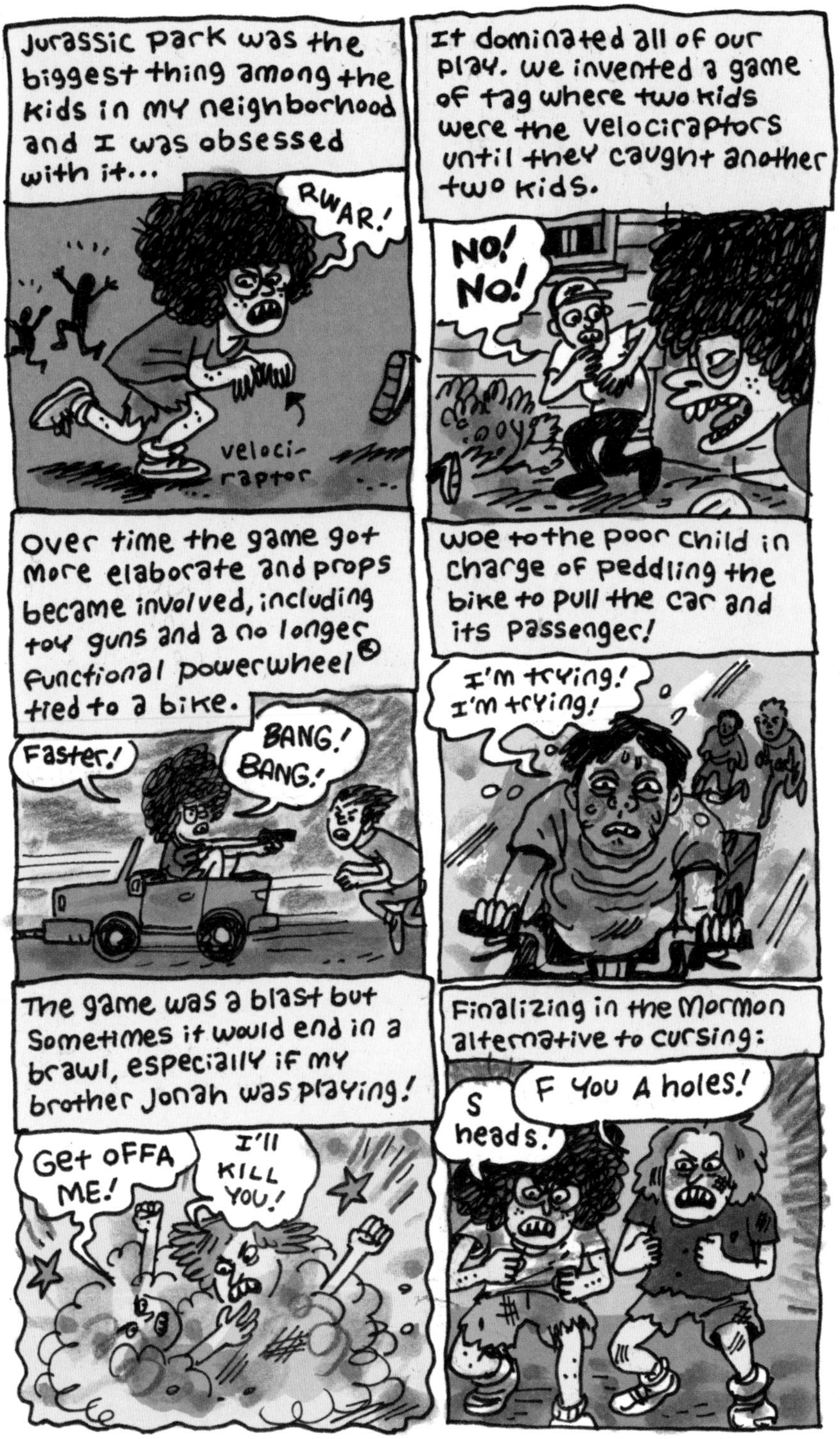
Jurassic Park was the biggest thing among the kids in my neighborhood and I was obsessed with it...
RWAR!
veloci-raptor
It dominated all of our play. We invented a game of tag where two kids were the velociraptors until they caught another two kids.
NO! NO!
Over time the game got more elaborate and props became involved, including toy guns and a no longer functional powerwheel® tied to a bike.
Faster!
BANG! BANG!
Woe to the poor child in charge of peddling the bike to pull the car and its passenger!
I'm trying! I'm trying!
The game was a blast but sometimes it would end in a brawl, especially if my brother Jonah was playing!
Get OFFA ME!
I'll KILL YOU!
Finalizing in the Mormon alternative to cursing:
S heads.
F You A holes!

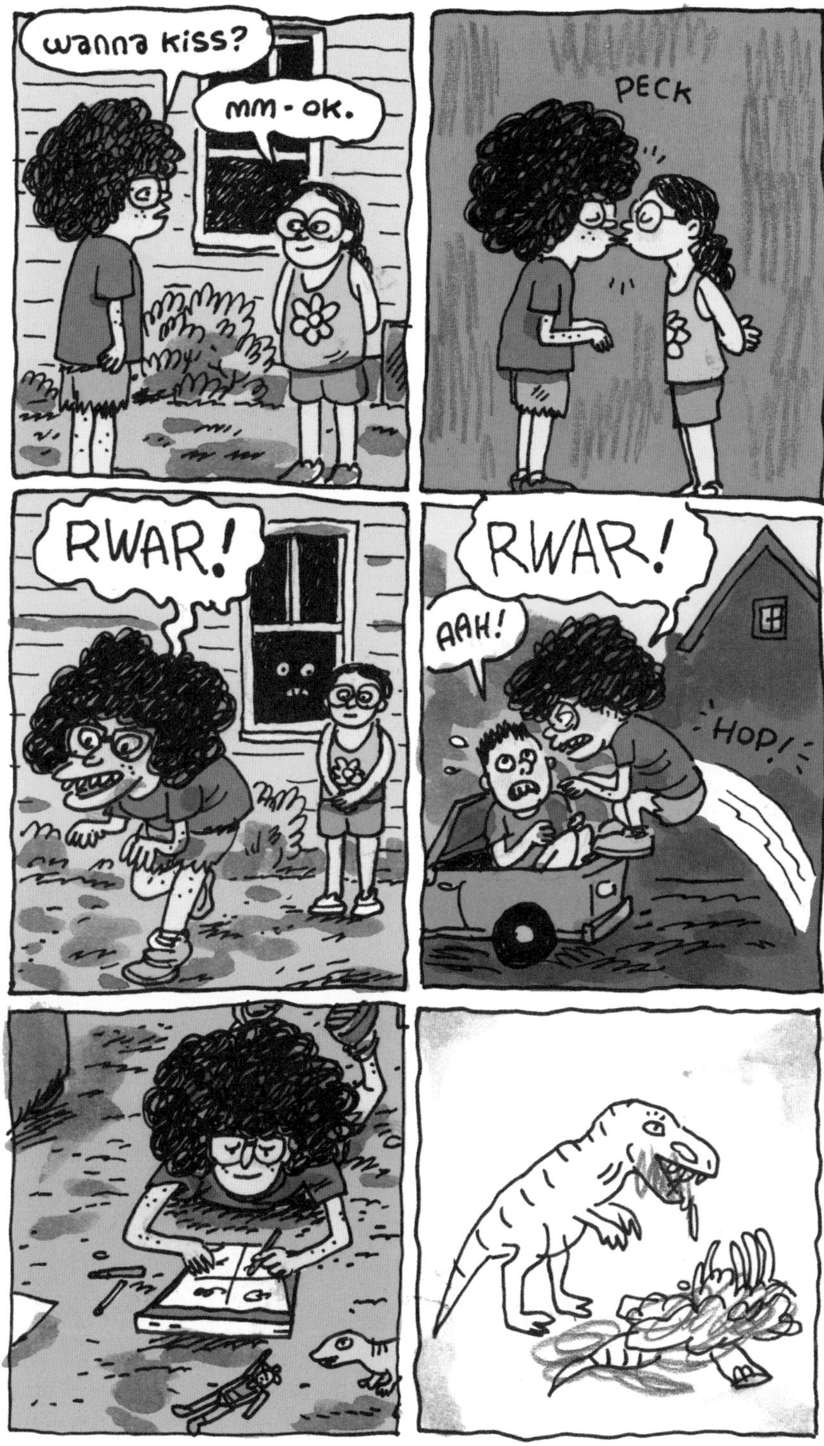
wanna kiss?
mm - ok.
PECK
RWAR!
RWAR!
AAH!
HOP!

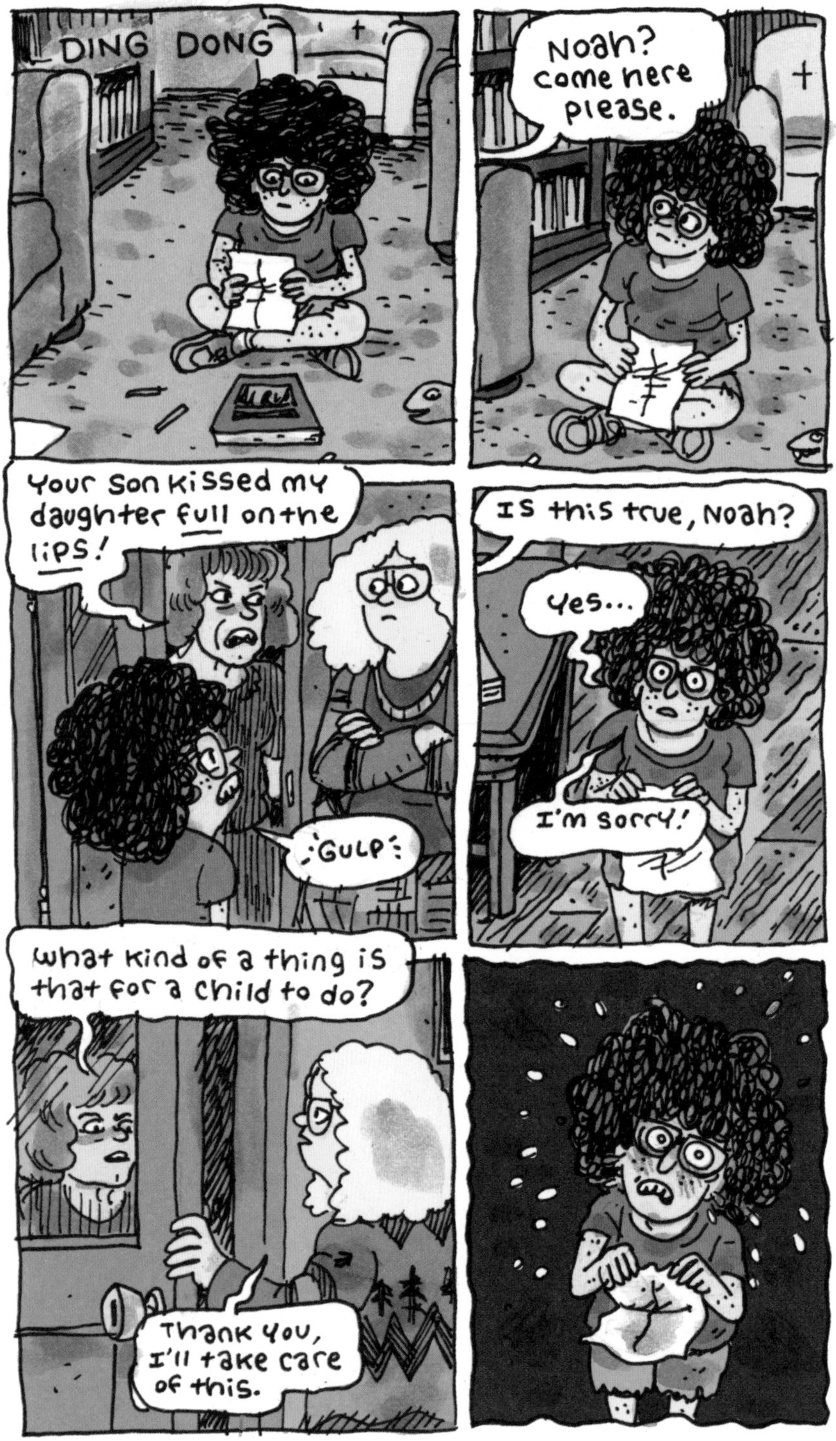
DING DONG
Noah? come here please.
Your son kissed my daughter full on the lips!
GULP
Is this true, Noah?
Yes...
I'm sorry!
What kind of a thing is that for a child to do?
Thank you, I'll take care of this.

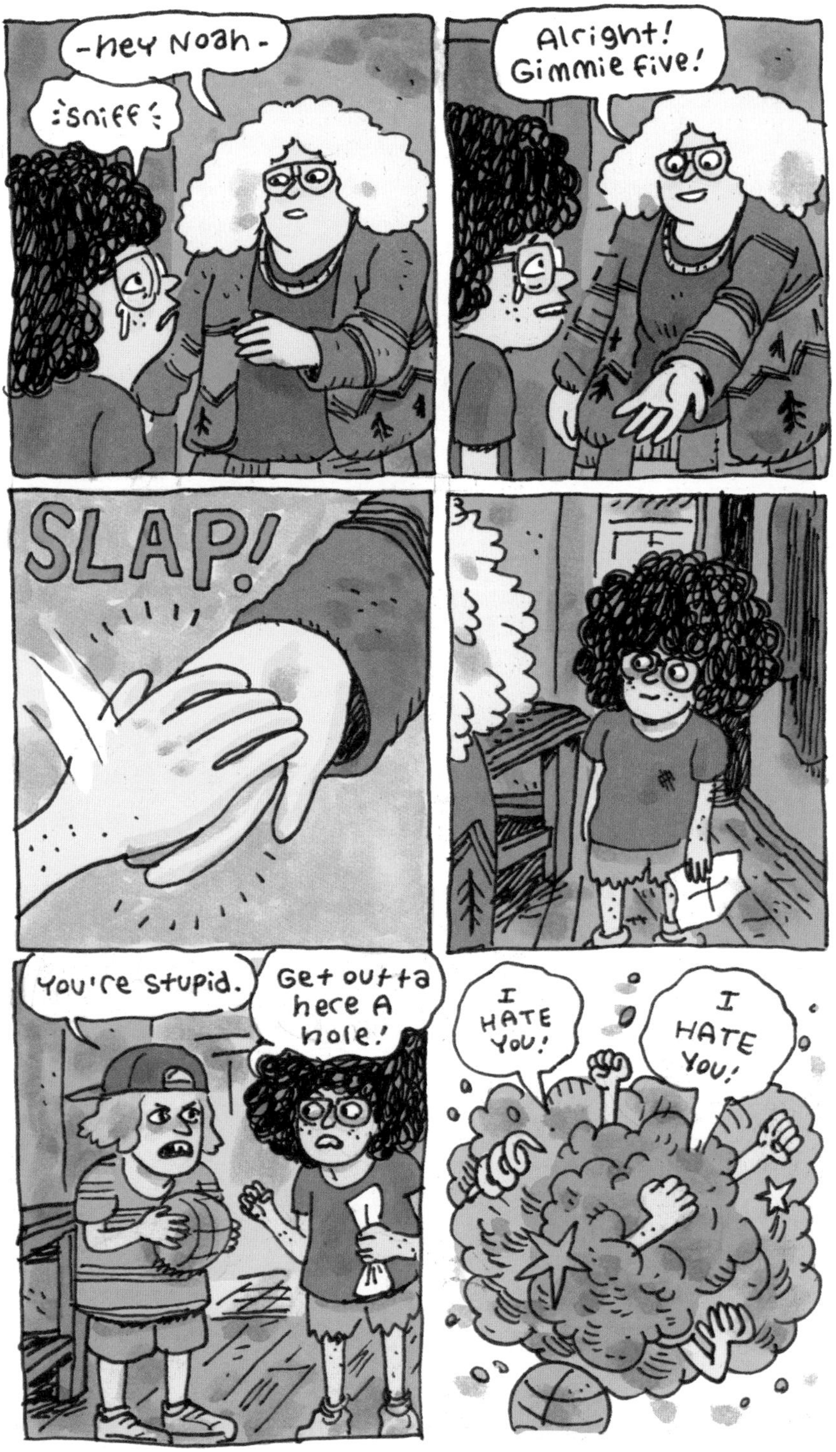

:sniff:
-hey Noah-
Alright! Gimmie five!
SLAP!
You're stupid.
Get outta here A hole!
I HATE YOU!
I HATE YOU!

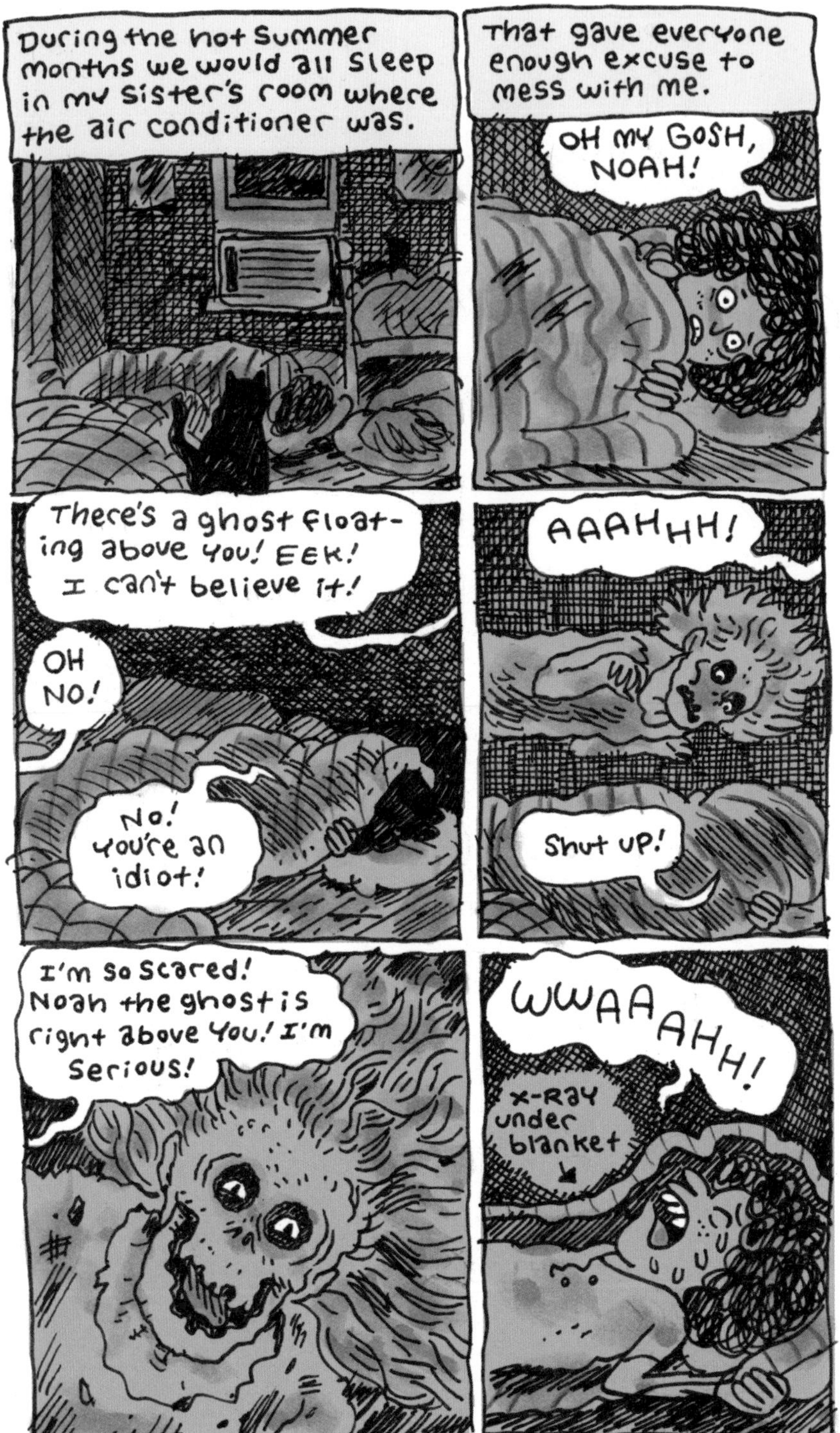
During the hot summer months we would all sleep in my sister's room where the air conditioner was.
That gave everyone enough excuse to mess with me.
OH MY GOSH, NOAH!
There's a ghost floating above you! EEK! I can't believe it!
OH NO!
No! You're an idiot!
AAAHHH!
Shut up!
I'm so scared! Noah the ghost is right above you! I'm serious!
WWAAAAHH!
X-RAY under blanket

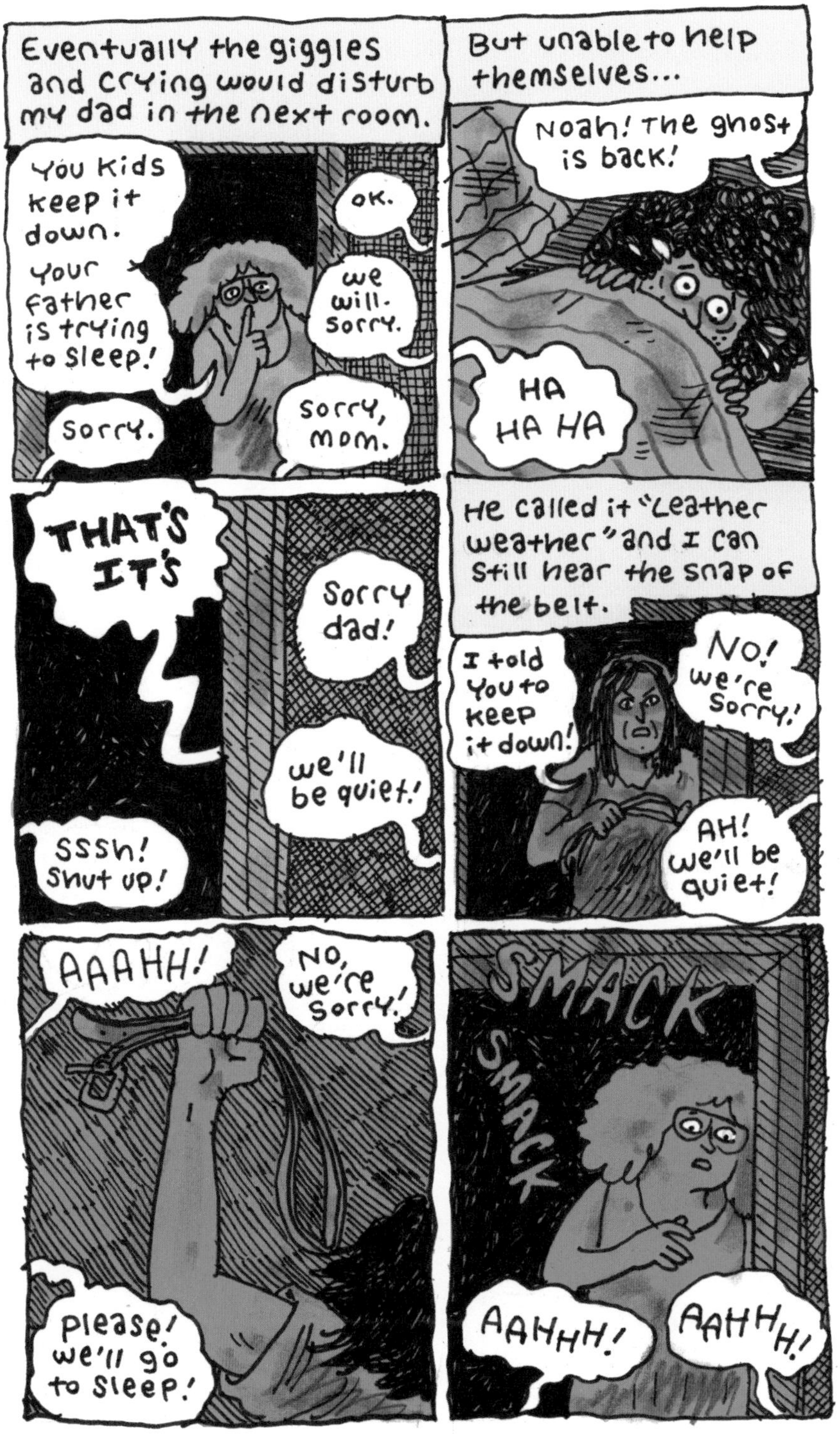
Eventually the giggles and crying would disturb my dad in the next room.
You kids keep it down.
Your father is trying to sleep!
ok.
we will. sorry.
Sorry.
sorry, mom.
But unable to help themselves...
Noah! The ghost is back!
HA HA HA
THAT'S IT'S
Sorry dad!
we'll be quiet!
sssh! shut up!
He called it "Leather weather" and I can still hear the snap of the belt.
I told you to keep it down!
No! we're sorry!
AH! we'll be quiet!
AAAHH!
No, we're sorry!
please! we'll go to sleep!
SMACK
SMACK
SMACK
AAHHH!
AAHHH!

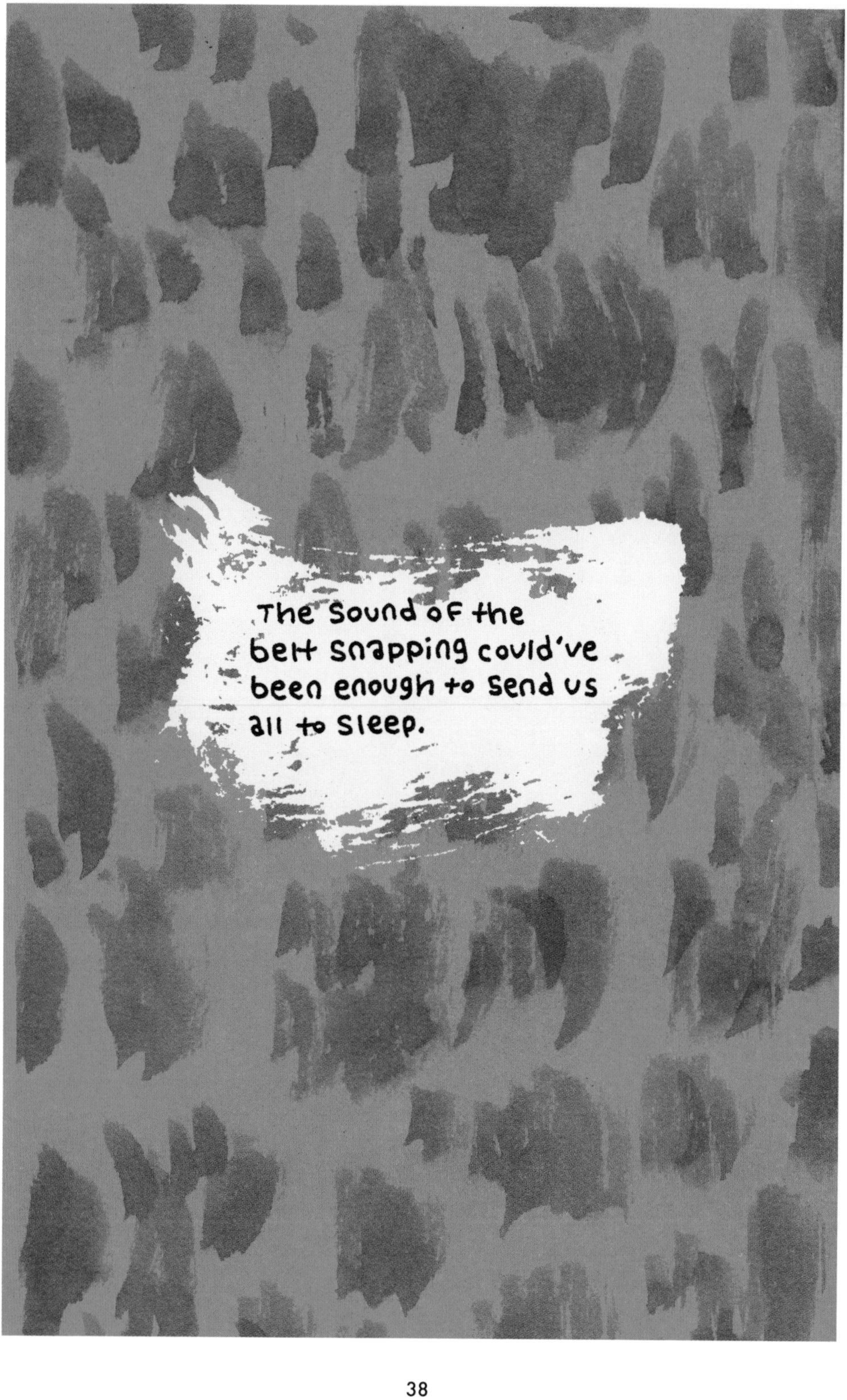
The sound of the belt snapping could've been enough to send us all to sleep.

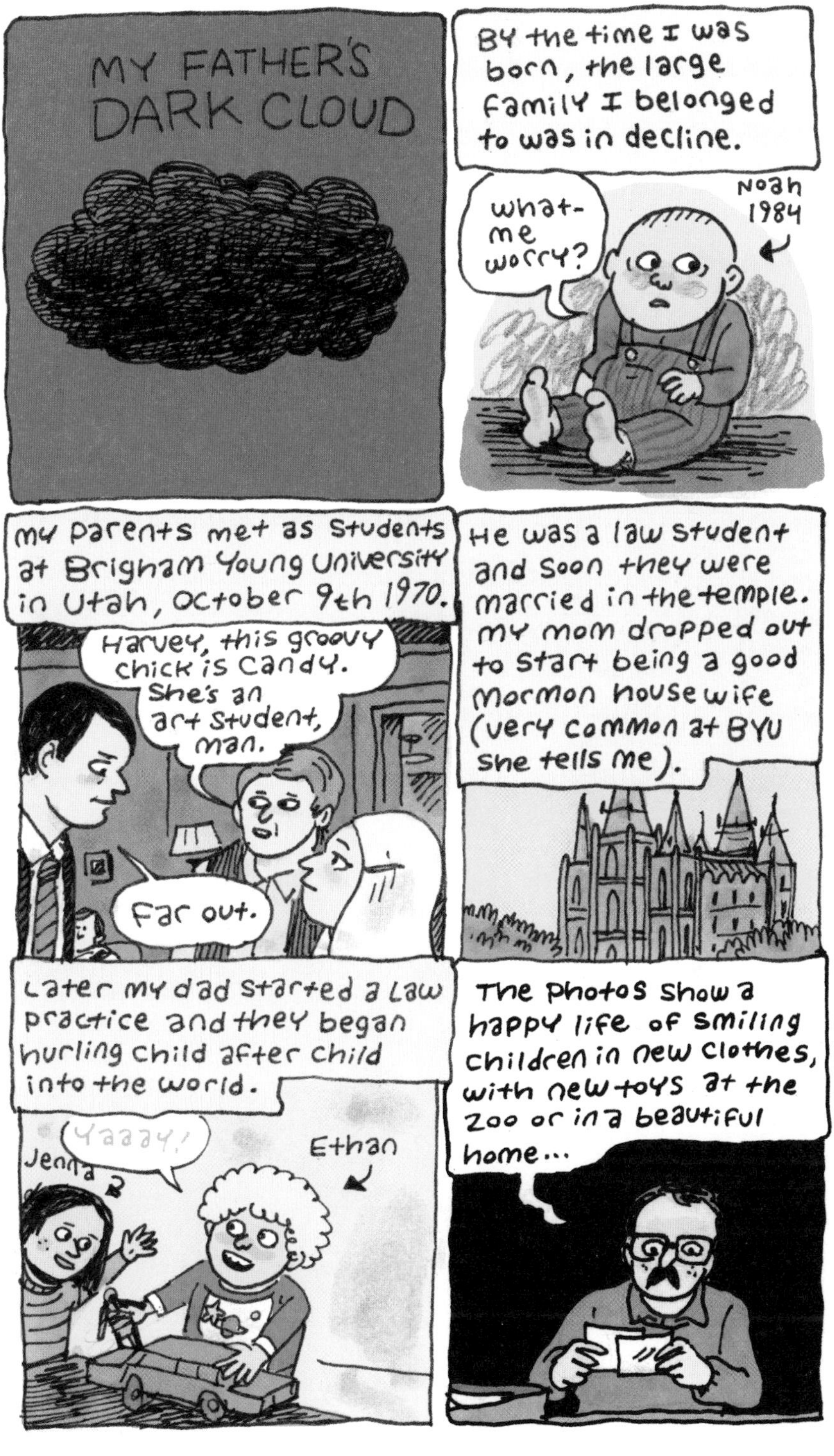
MY FATHER'S DARK CLOUD
BY the time I was born, the large family I belonged to was in decline.
what-me worry?
Noah 1984
my parents met as students at Brigham Young University in Utah, October 9th 1970.
Harvey, this groovy chick is Candy. She's an art student, man.
Far out.
He was a law student and soon they were married in the temple. my mom dropped out to start being a good mormon housewife (very common at BYU she tells me).
Later my dad started a law practice and they began hurling child after child into the world.
Yaaay!
Jenna
Ethan
The photos show a happy life of smiling children in new clothes, with new toys at the zoo or in a beautiful home...

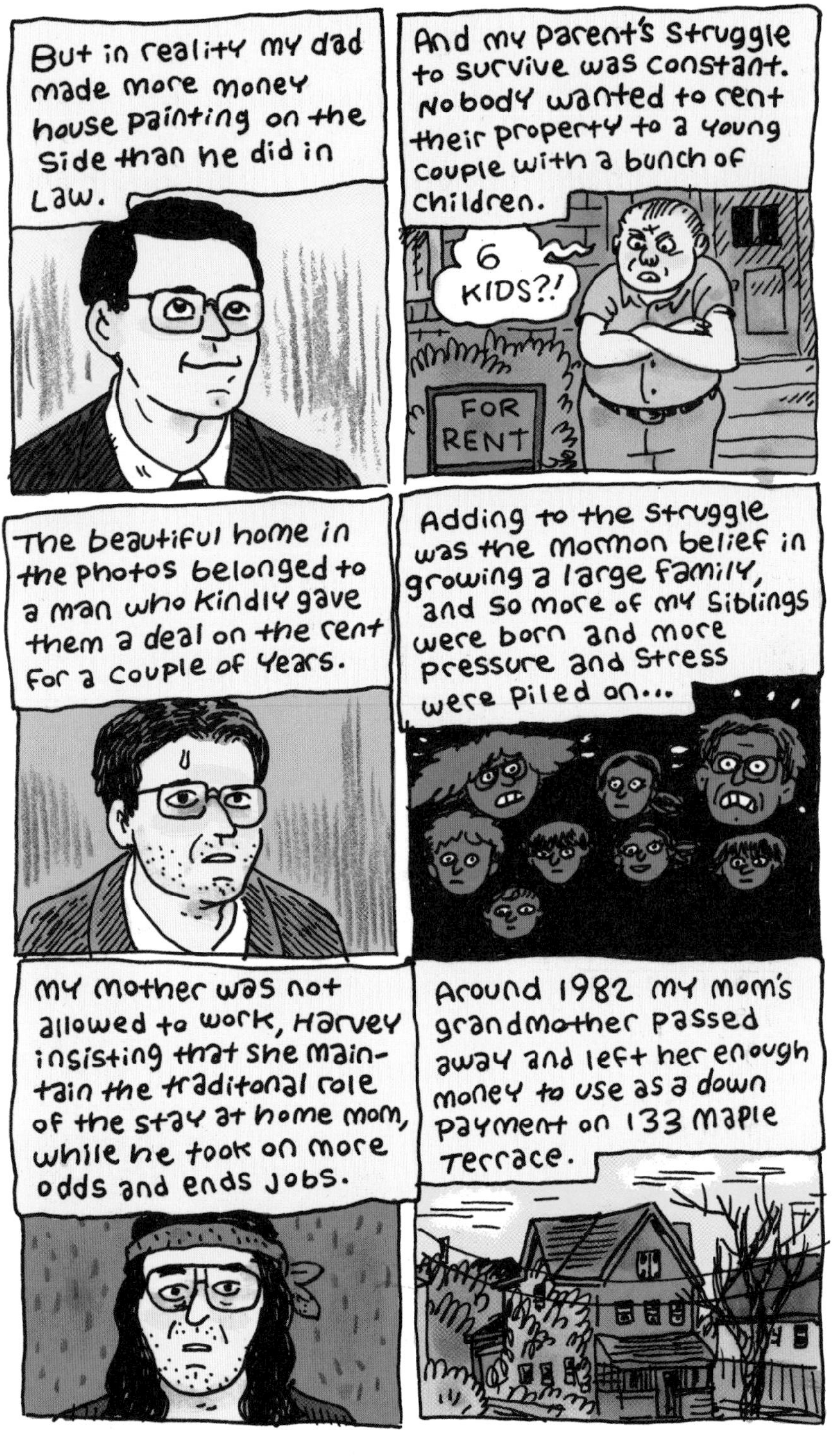
But in reality my dad made more money house painting on the side than he did in law.
And my parent's struggle to survive was constant. Nobody wanted to rent their property to a young couple with a bunch of children.
6 KIDS?!
FOR RENT
The beautiful home in the photos belonged to a man who kindly gave them a deal on the rent for a couple of years.
Adding to the struggle was the mormon belief in growing a large family, and so more of my siblings were born and more pressure and stress were piled on...
My mother was not allowed to work, Harvey insisting that she maintain the traditonal role of the stay at home mom, while he took on more odds and ends jobs.
Around 1982 my mom's grandmother passed away and left her enough money to use as a down payment on 133 Maple Terrace.

It was there, over the next few years, that my mother became pregnant with the last 3 children (myself included).

While my father's hustle to provide withered and we scraped by on barely anything.

A Stella d'oro cookie. → A cheap van Sciver breakfast.

Harvey's behavior became very strange, planning big projects that he never finished, including tearing out our kitchen, while our mother was away on a trip, and never rebuilding it.

During my childhood we had to do our dishes in the bath tub.

There's a s'getti ring around the tub!

He began staying home from work and spending his time in bed writing poetry (an epic Mormon poem titled "the Crossing") while listening to Neil Young.

He had been diagnosed as having bi-polar disorder and could lose his temper easily.

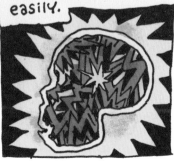

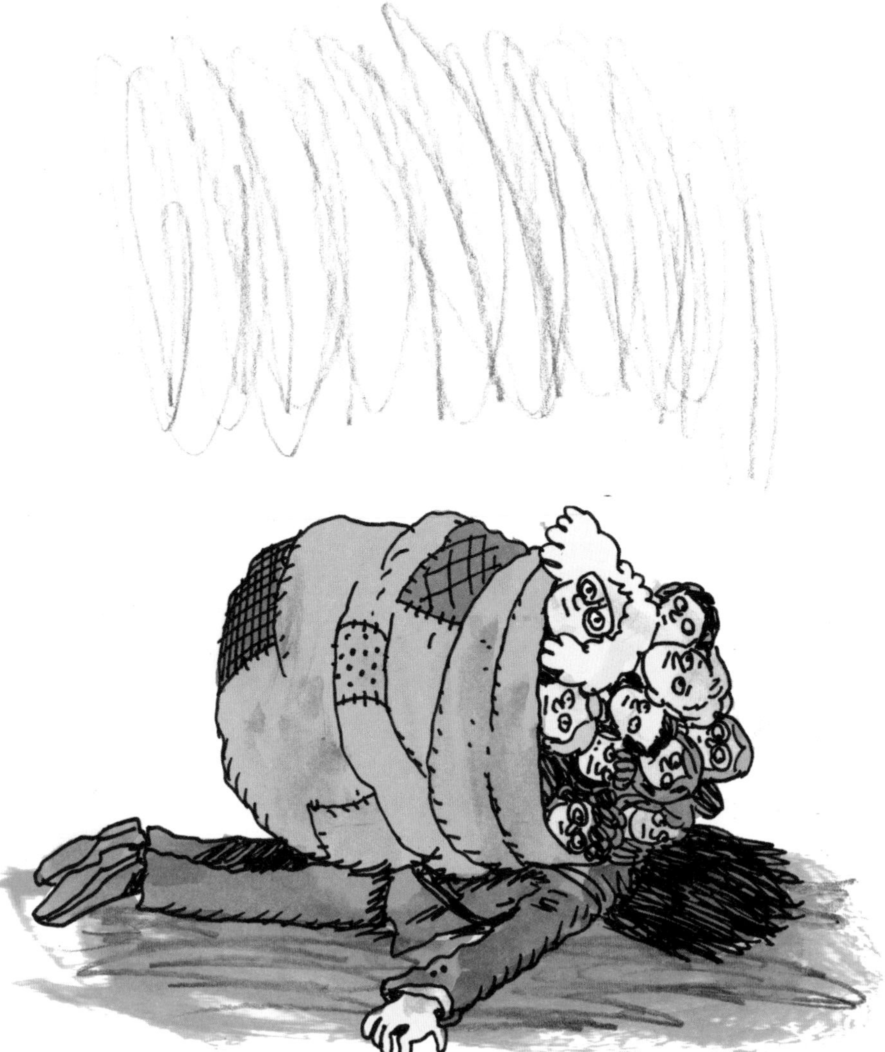

CRUSHED BY THE WEIGHT.

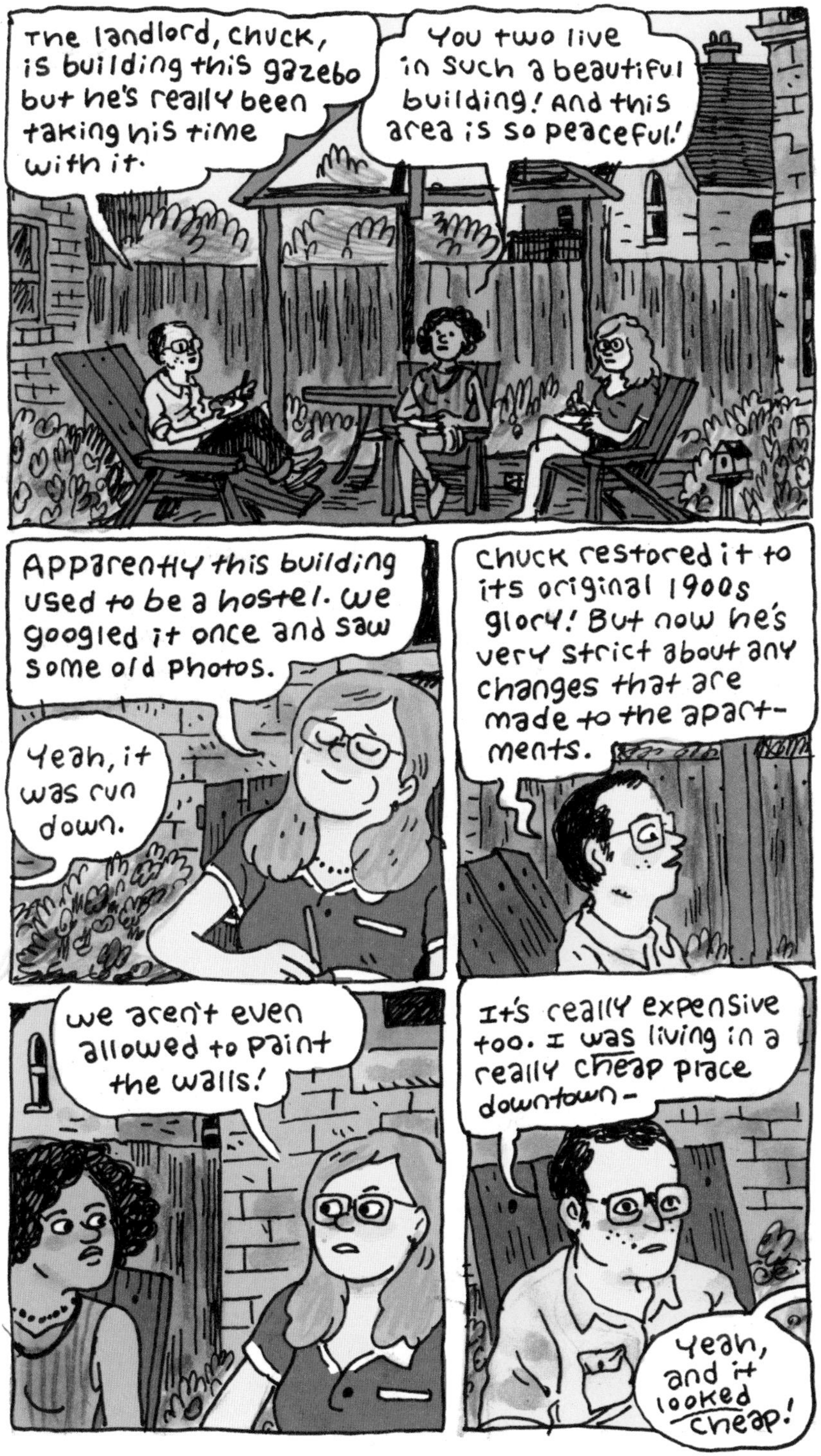
The landlord, Chuck, is building this gazebo but he's really been taking his time with it.
You two live in such a beautiful building! And this area is so peaceful!
Apparently this building used to be a hostel. We googled it once and saw some old photos.
Yeah, it was run down.
Chuck restored it to its original 1900s glory! But now he's very strict about any changes that are made to the apartments.
We aren't even allowed to paint the walls!
It's really expensive too. I was living in a really cheap place downtown-
Yeah, and it looked cheap!

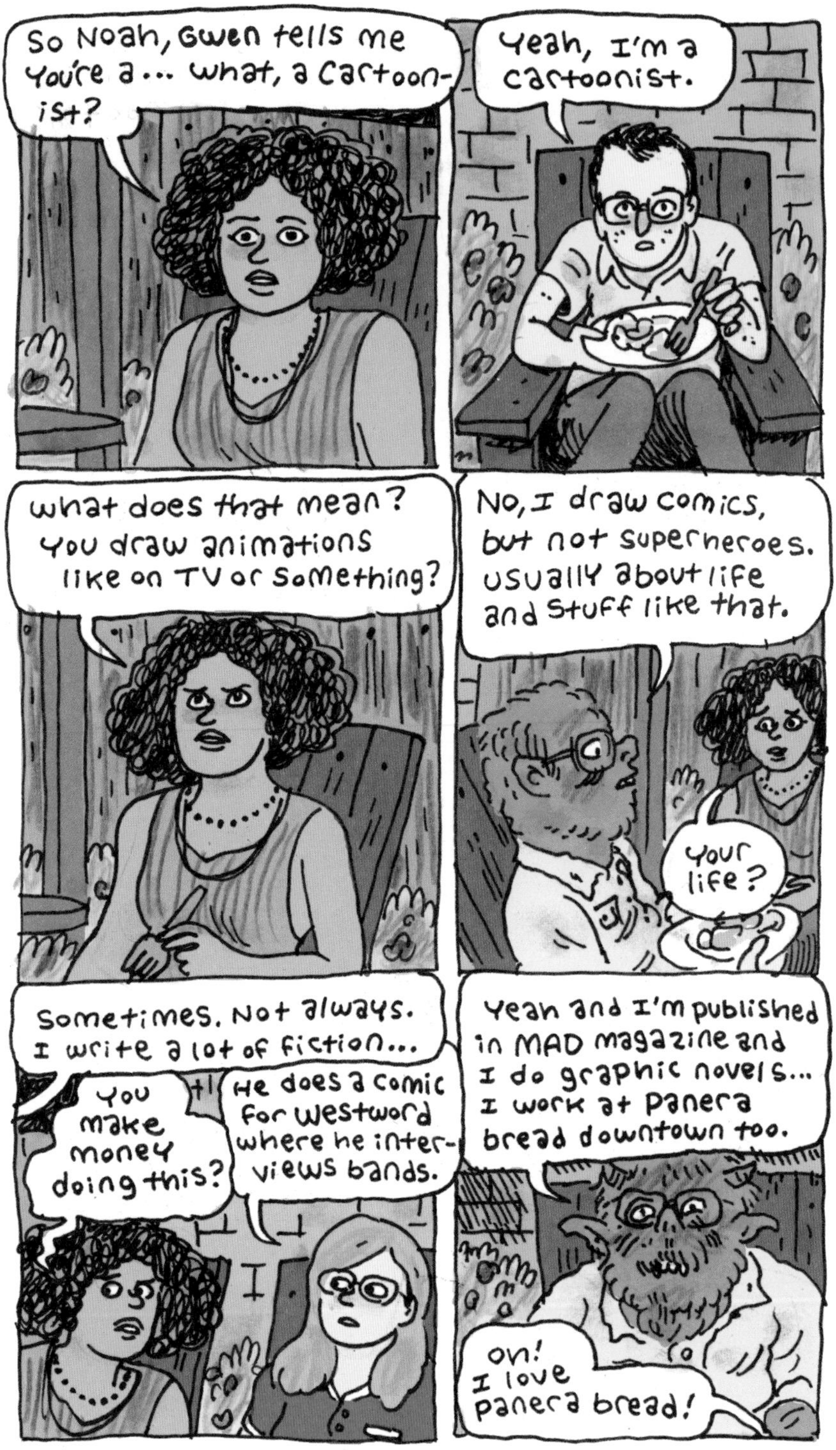
So Noah, Gwen tells me you're a... what, a cartoonist?
Yeah, I'm a cartoonist.
what does that mean? you draw animations like on TV or something?
No, I draw comics, but not superheroes. usually about life and stuff like that.
your life?
Sometimes. Not always. I write a lot of fiction...
You make money doing this?
He does a comic for westword where he interviews bands.
Yeah and I'm published in MAD magazine and I do graphic novels... I work at Panera bread downtown too.
oh! I love Panera bread!

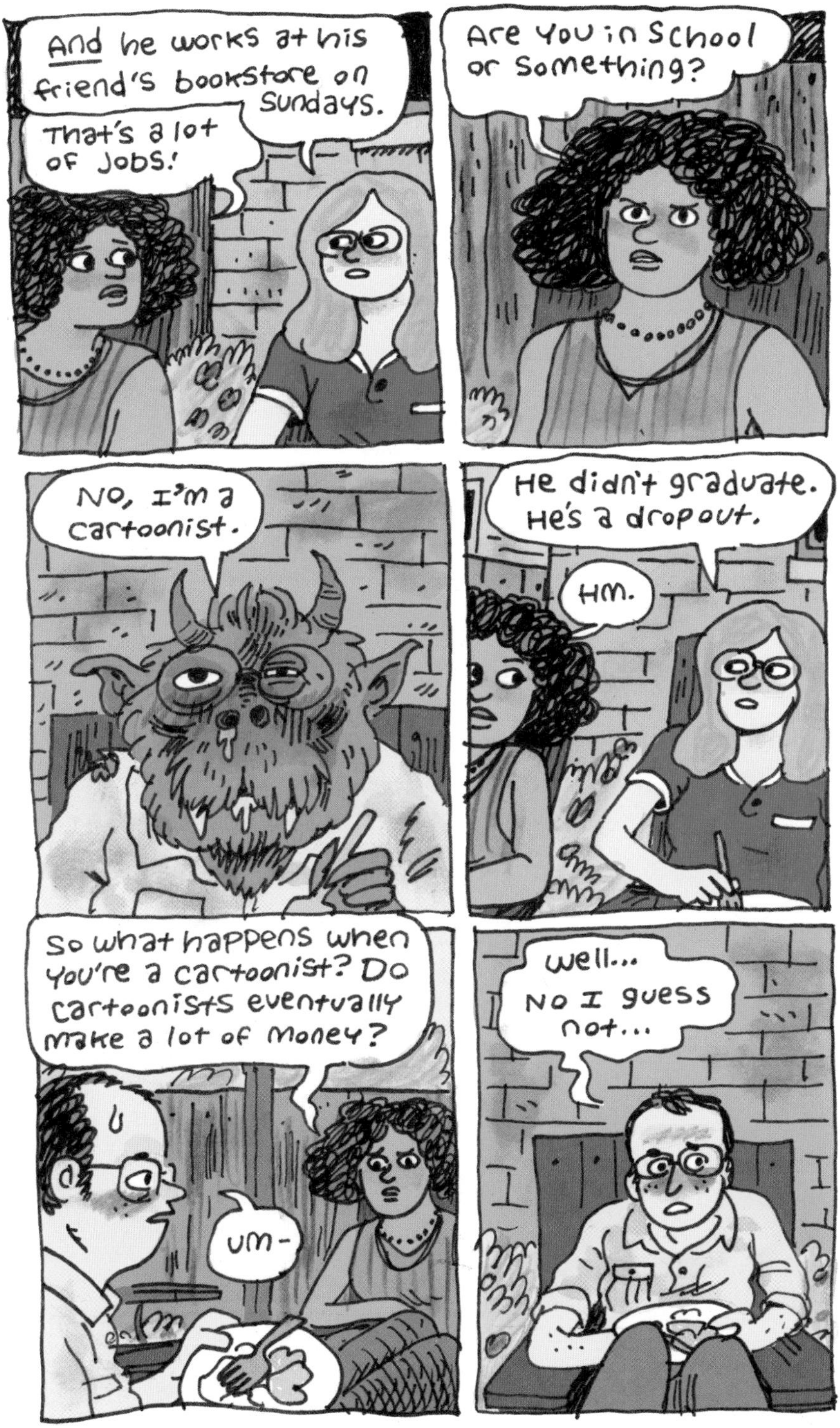
And he works at his friend's bookstore on Sundays.
That's a lot of jobs!
Are you in school or something?
No, I'm a cartoonist.
He didn't graduate. He's a dropout.
HM.
So what happens when you're a cartoonist? Do cartoonists eventually make a lot of money?
um-
well...
No I guess not...

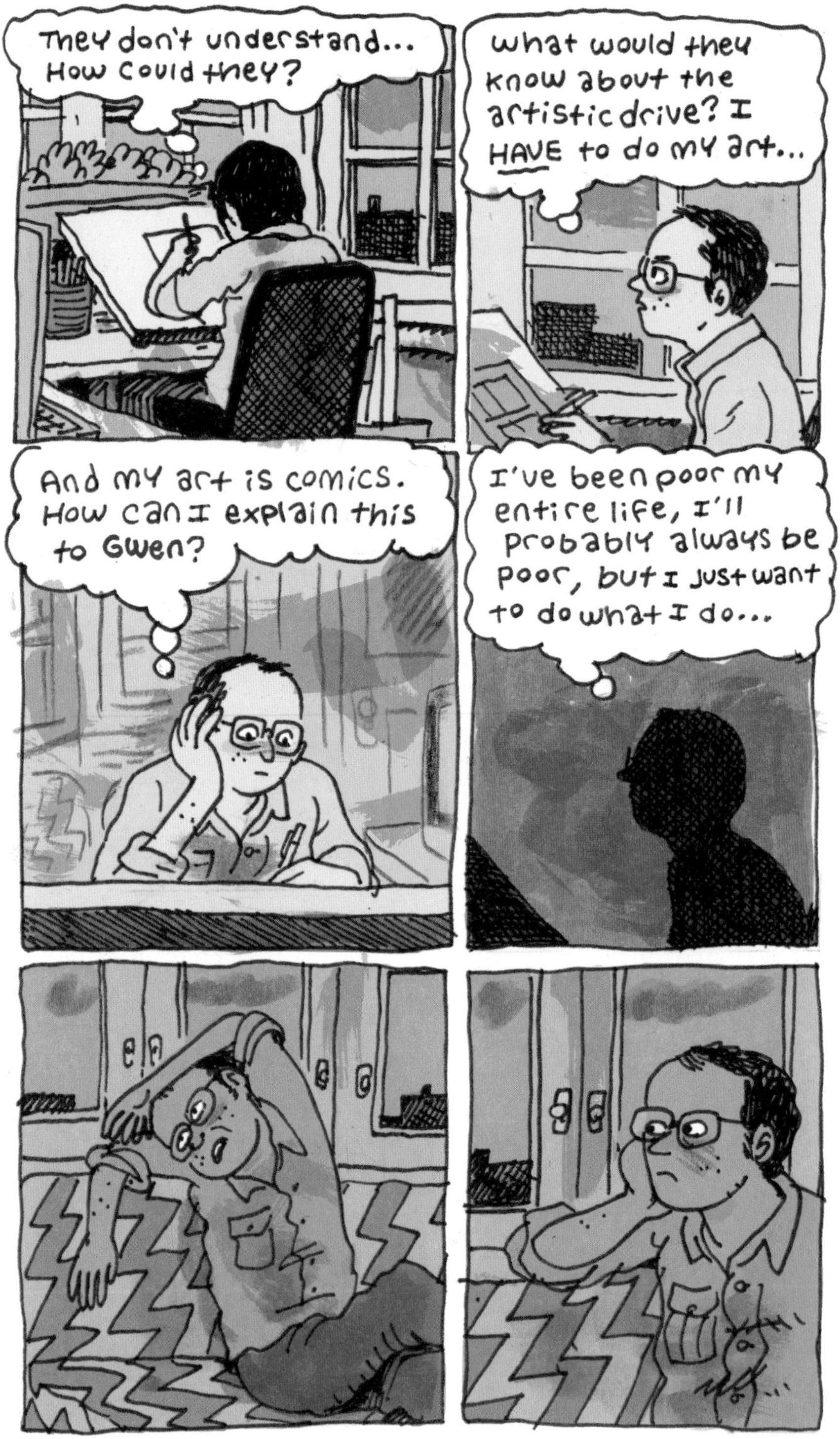
They don't understand... How could they?
What would they know about the artistic drive? I HAVE to do my art...
And my art is comics. How can I explain this to Gwen?
I've been poor my entire life, I'll probably always be poor, but I just want to do what I do...

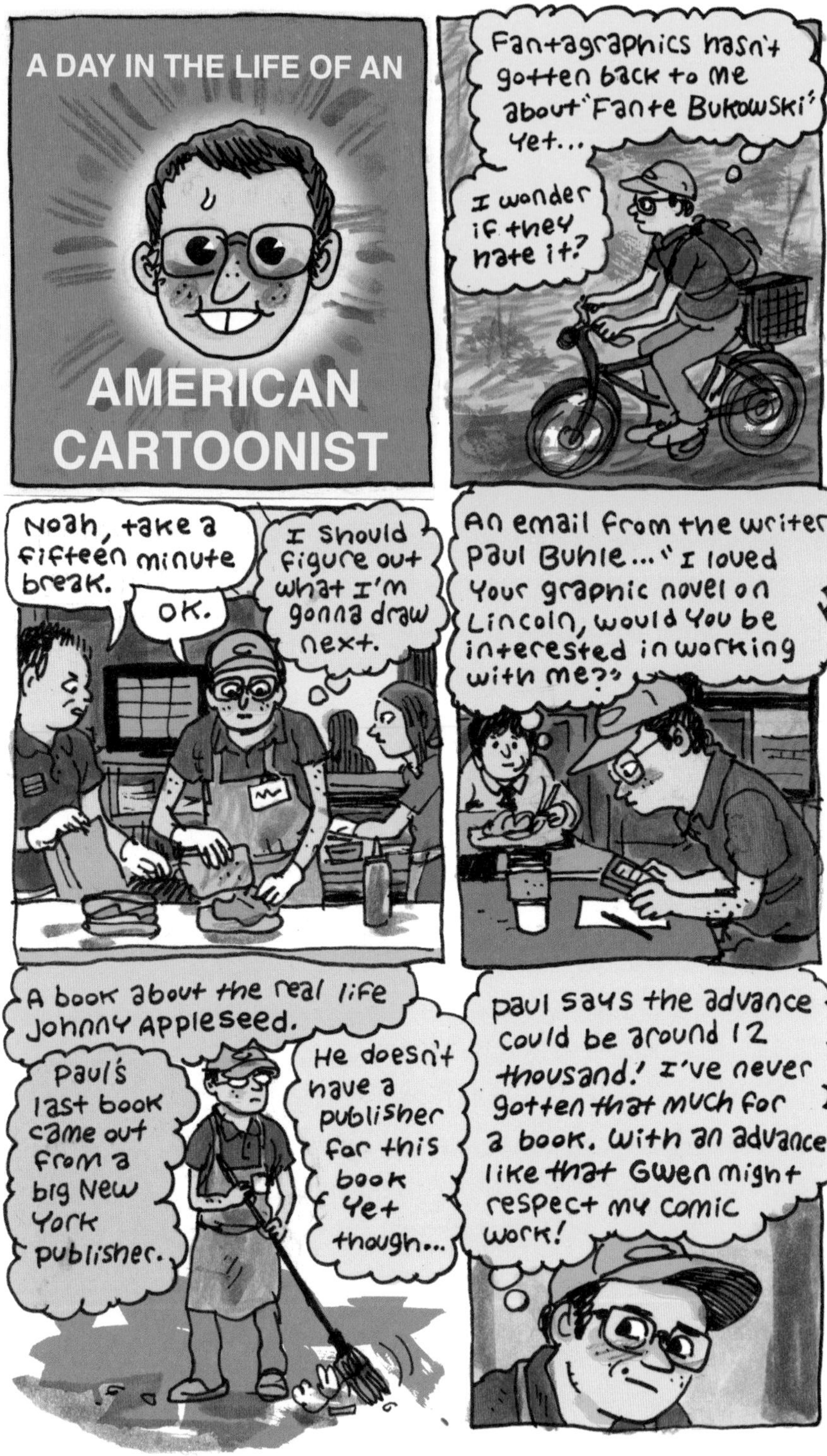
A DAY IN THE LIFE OF AN
AMERICAN CARTOONIST
Fantagraphics hasn't gotten back to me about "Fante Bukowski" yet...
I wonder if they hate it?
Noah, take a fifteen minute break.
OK.
I should figure out what I'm gonna draw next.
An email from the writer Paul Buhle... "I loved your graphic novel on Lincoln, would you be interested in working with me?"
A book about the real life Johnny Appleseed.
Paul's last book came out from a big New York publisher.
He doesn't have a publisher for this book yet though...
Paul says the advance could be around 12 thousand! I've never gotten that much for a book. With an advance like that Gwen might respect my comic work!

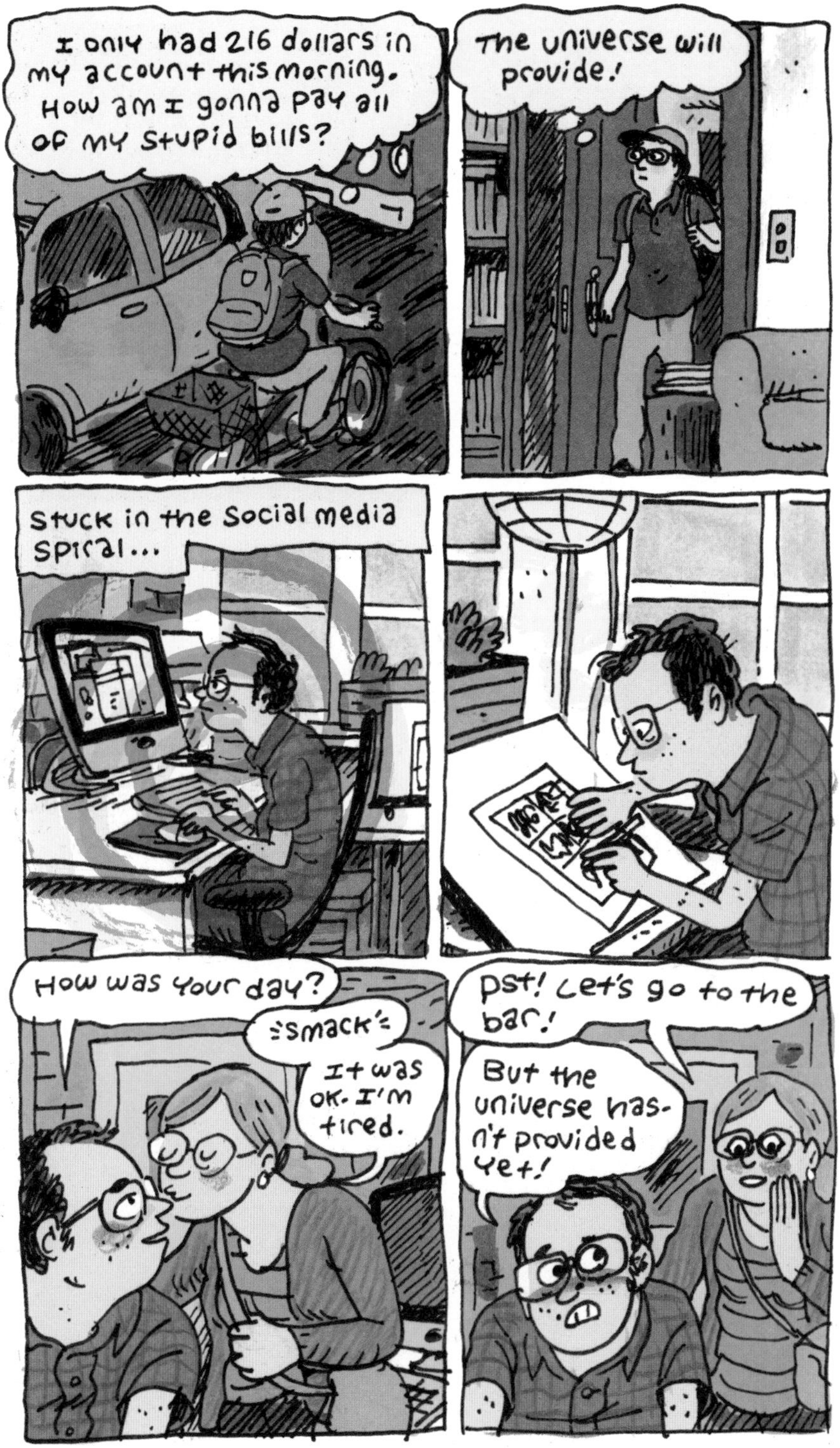
I only had 216 dollars in my account this morning. How am I gonna pay all of my stupid bills?
The universe will provide!
Stuck in the social media spiral...
How was your day?
smack
It was OK. I'm tired.
pst! Let's go to the bar!
But the universe has-n't provided yet!

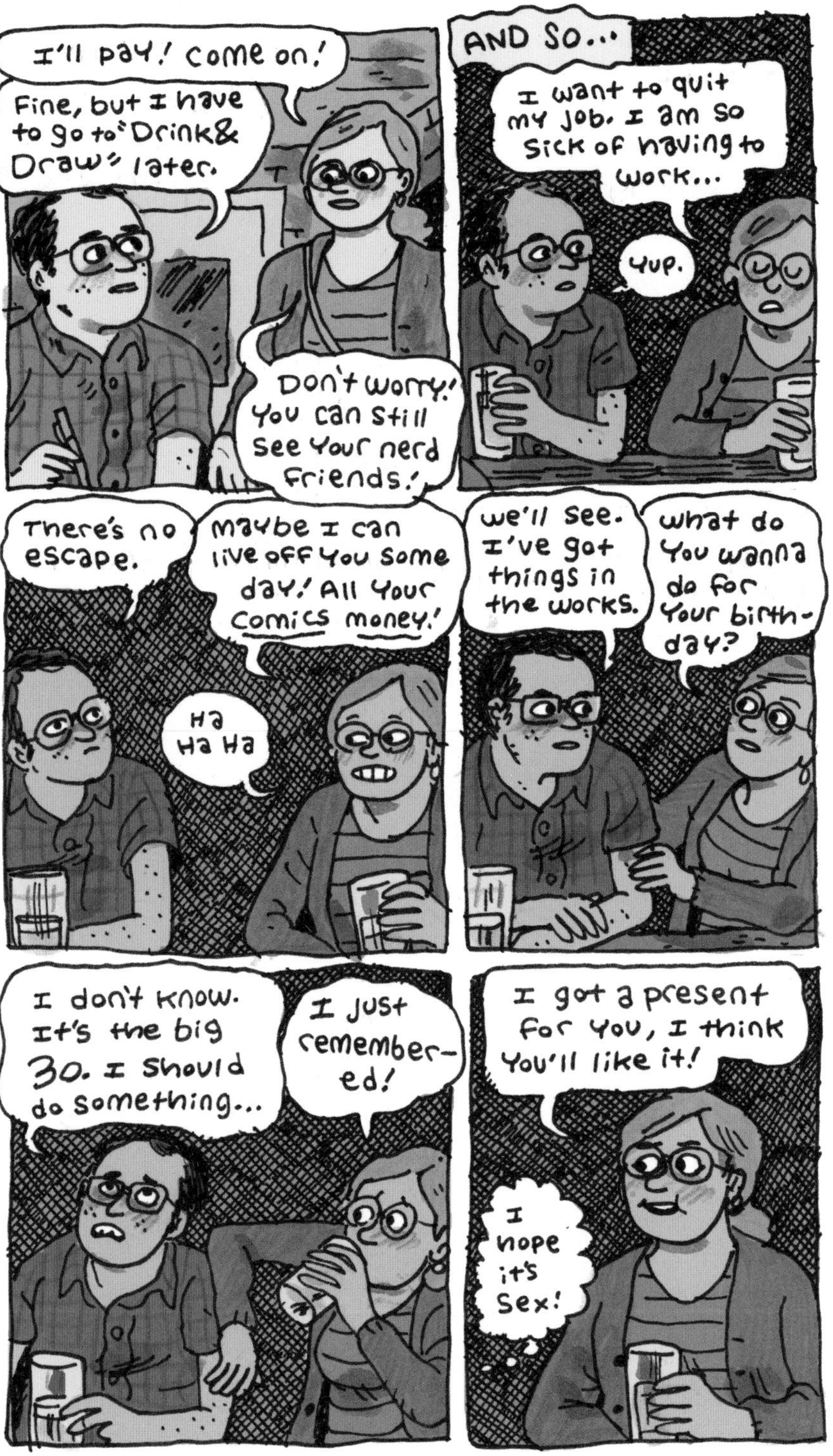
I'll pay! Come on!
Fine, but I have to go to "Drink & Draw" later.
Don't worry! You can still see your nerd friends!
AND SO...
I want to quit my job. I am so sick of having to work...
Yup.
There's no escape.
Maybe I can live off you some day! All your comics money!
Ha Ha Ha
We'll see. I've got things in the works.
What do you wanna do for your birthday?
I don't know. It's the big 30. I should do something...
I just remembered!
I got a present for you, I think you'll like it!
I hope it's sex!

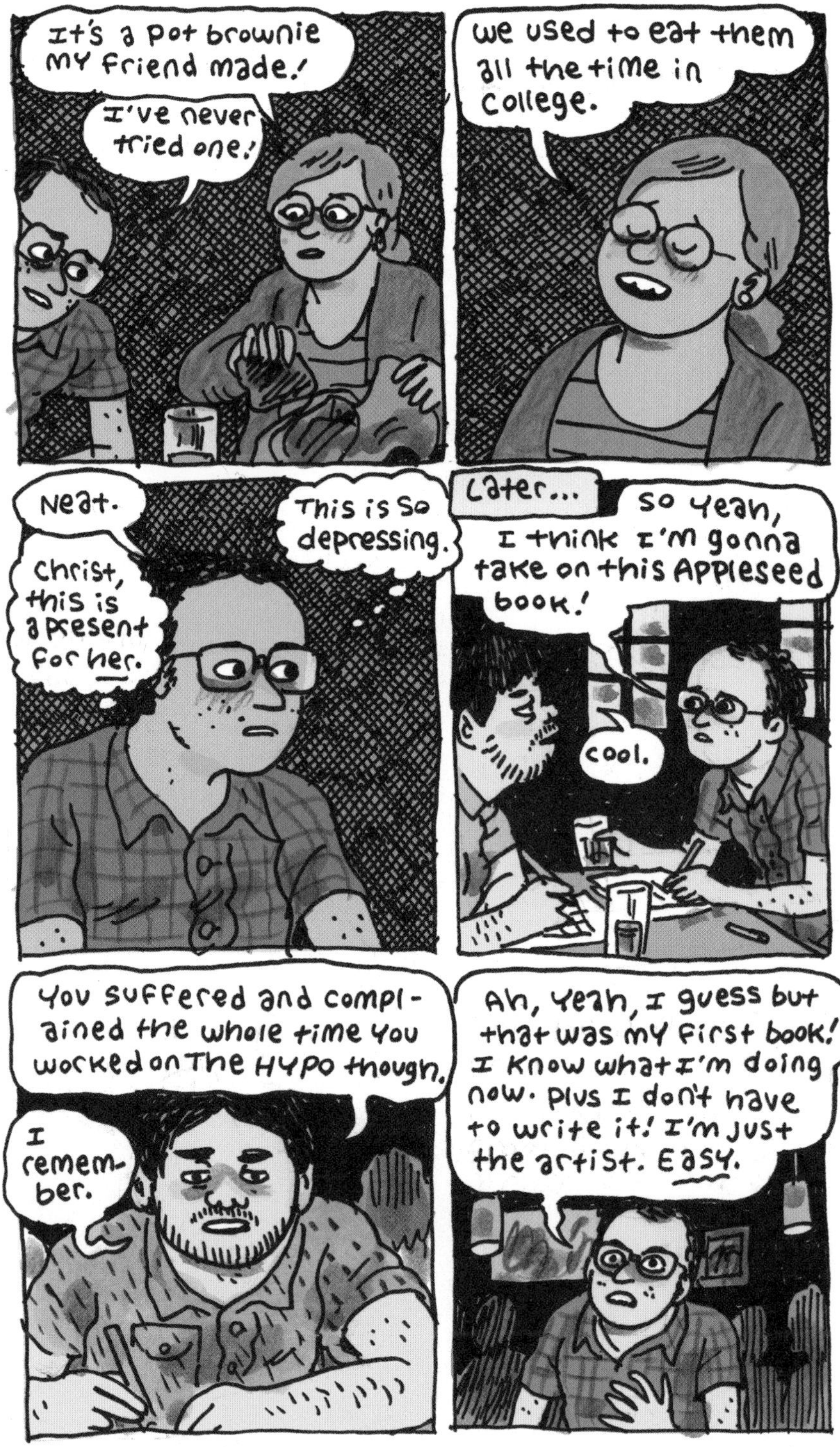
It's a pot brownie my friend made!
I've never tried one!
We used to eat them all the time in college.
Neat.
Christ, this is a present for her.
This is so depressing.
Later...
So yeah, I think I'm gonna take on this Appleseed book!
Cool.
You suffered and compl-ained the whole time you worked on The HYPO though.
I remem-ber.
Ah, yeah, I guess but that was my first book! I know what I'm doing now. Plus I don't have to write it! I'm just the artist. Easy.

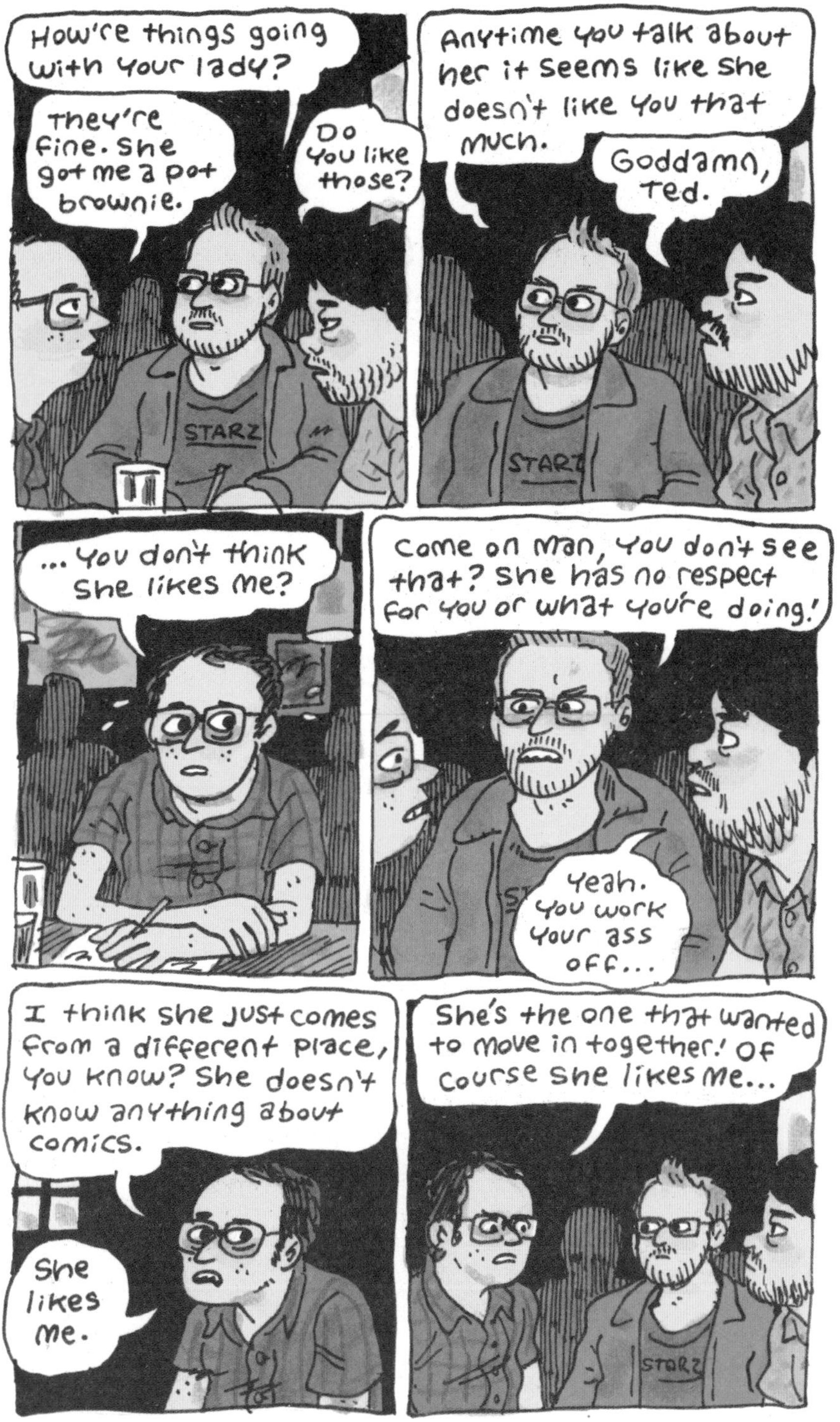
How're things going with your lady?
They're fine. She got me a pot brownie.
Do you like those?
Anytime you talk about her it seems like she doesn't like you that much.
Goddamn, Ted.
...You don't think she likes me?
Come on man, you don't see that? She has no respect for you or what you're doing!
Yeah. You work your ass off...
I think she just comes from a different place, you know? She doesn't know anything about comics.
She likes me.
She's the one that wanted to move in together! Of course she likes me...

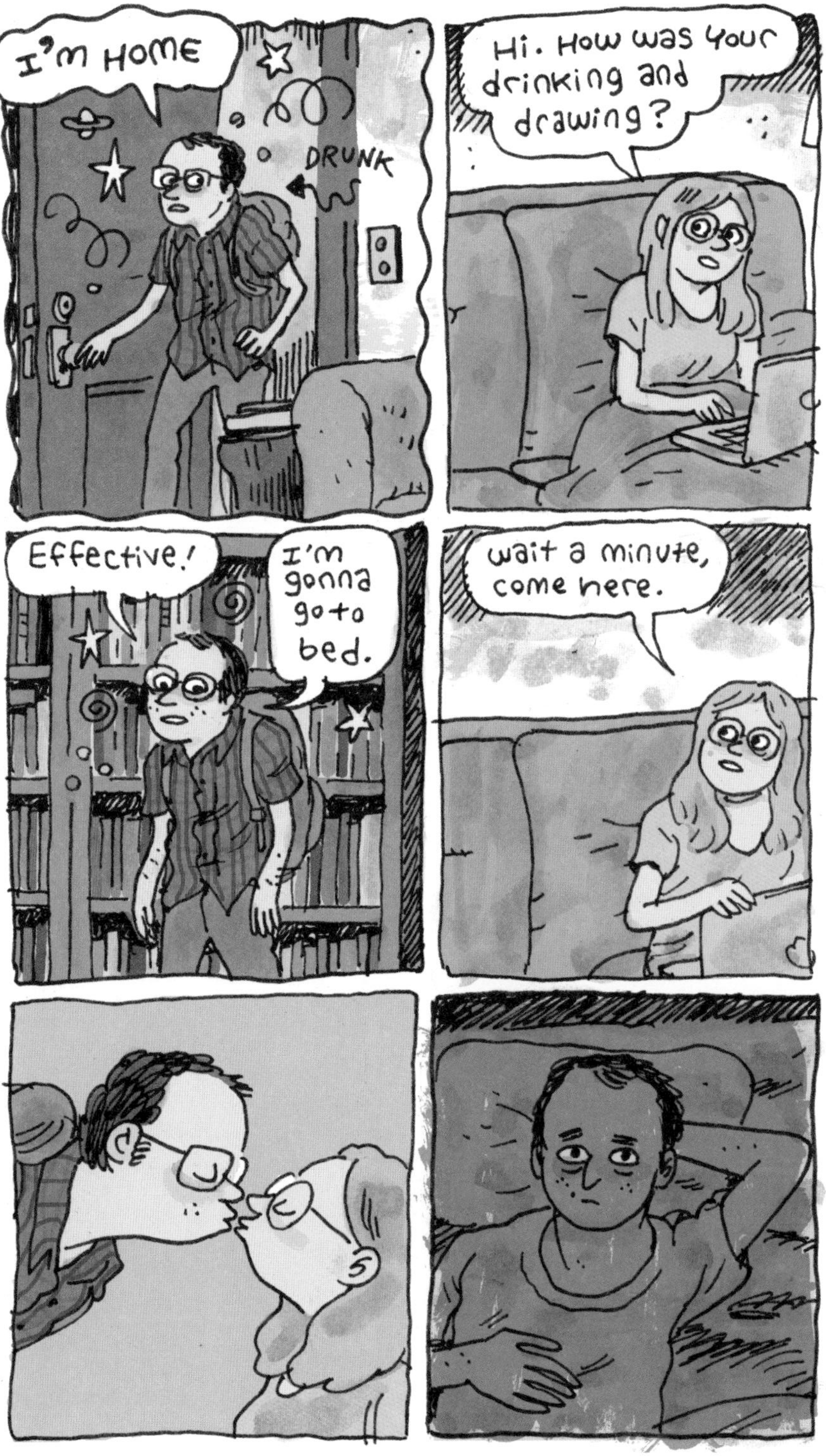
I'M HOME
DRUNK
Hi. How was your drinking and drawing?
Effective!
I'm gonna go to bed.
wait a minute, come here.

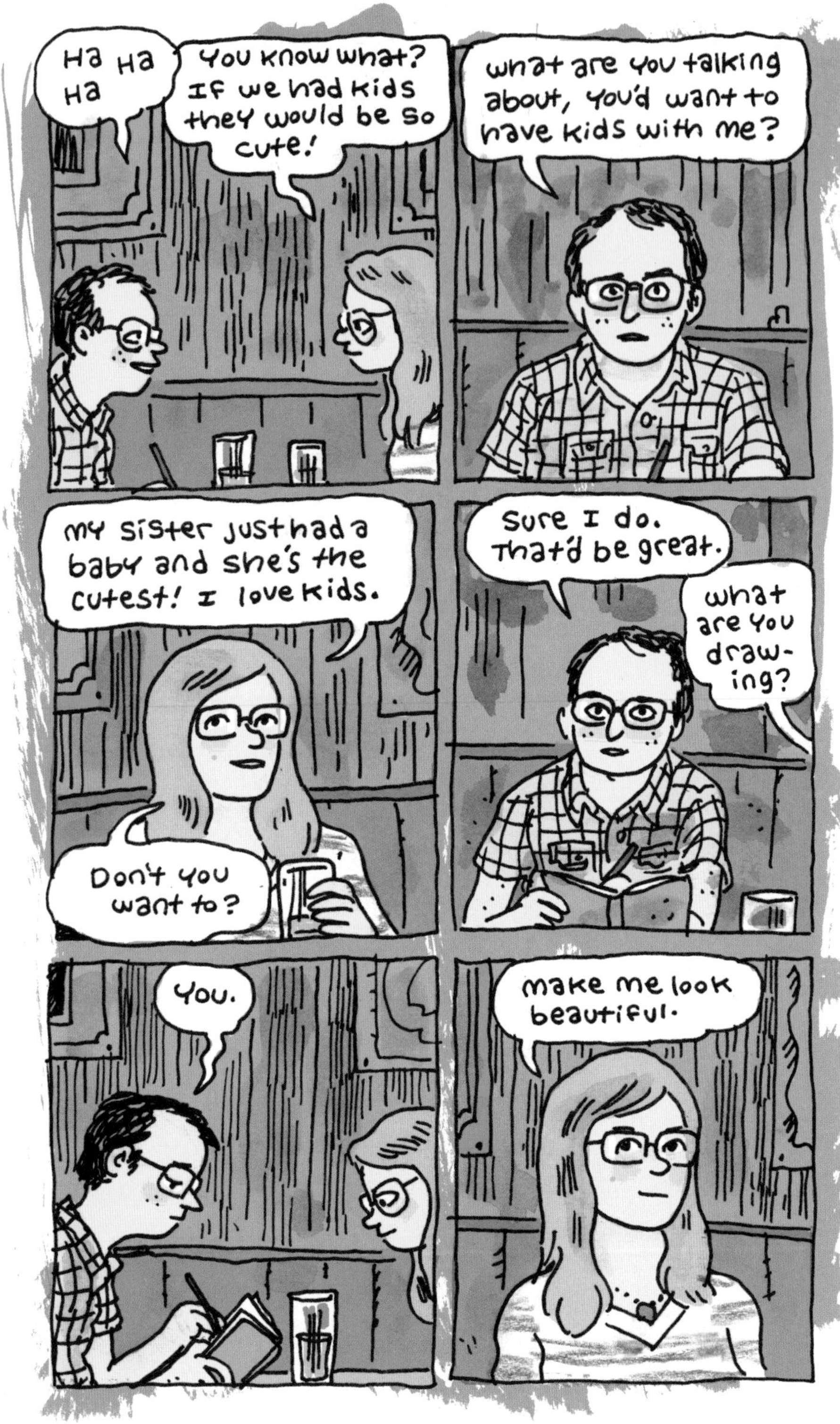
Ha Ha Ha
You know what? If we had kids they would be so cute!
what are you talking about, you'd want to have kids with me?
my sister just had a baby and she's the cutest! I love kids.
Don't you want to?
Sure I do. That'd be great.
what are you drawing?
You.
make me look beautiful.

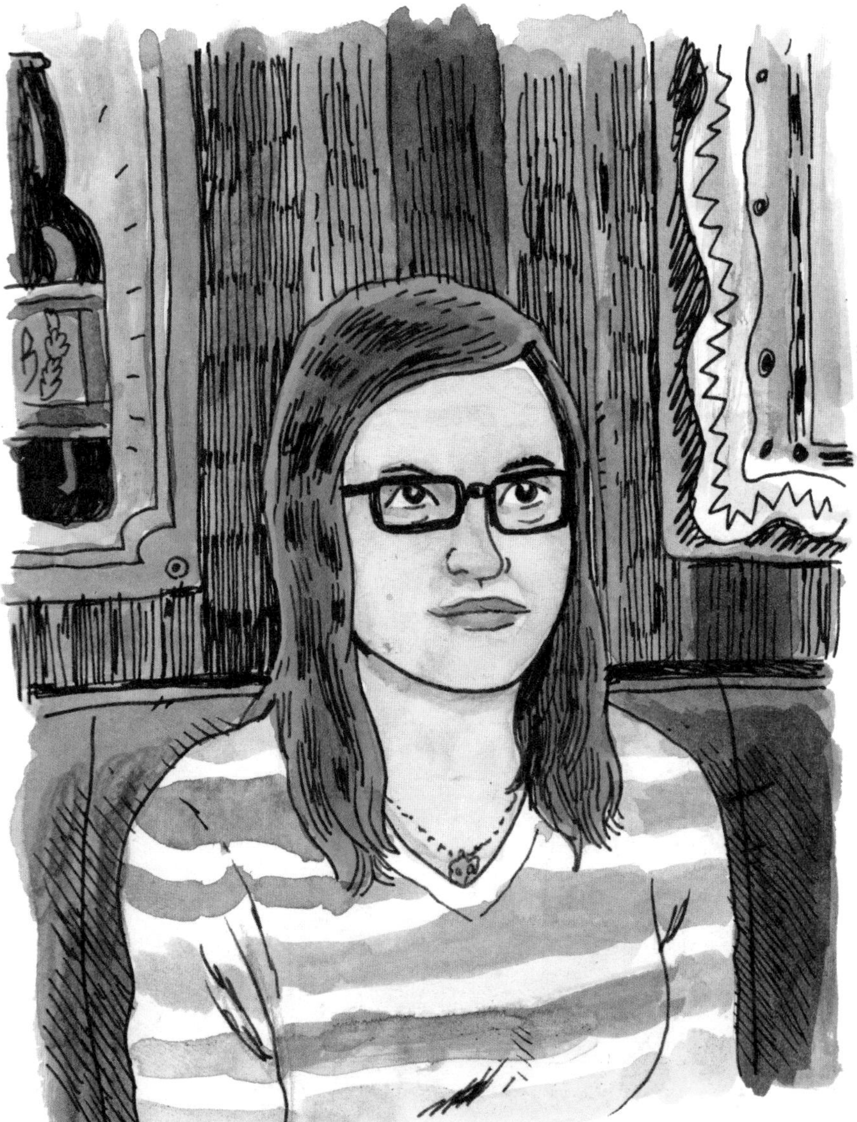

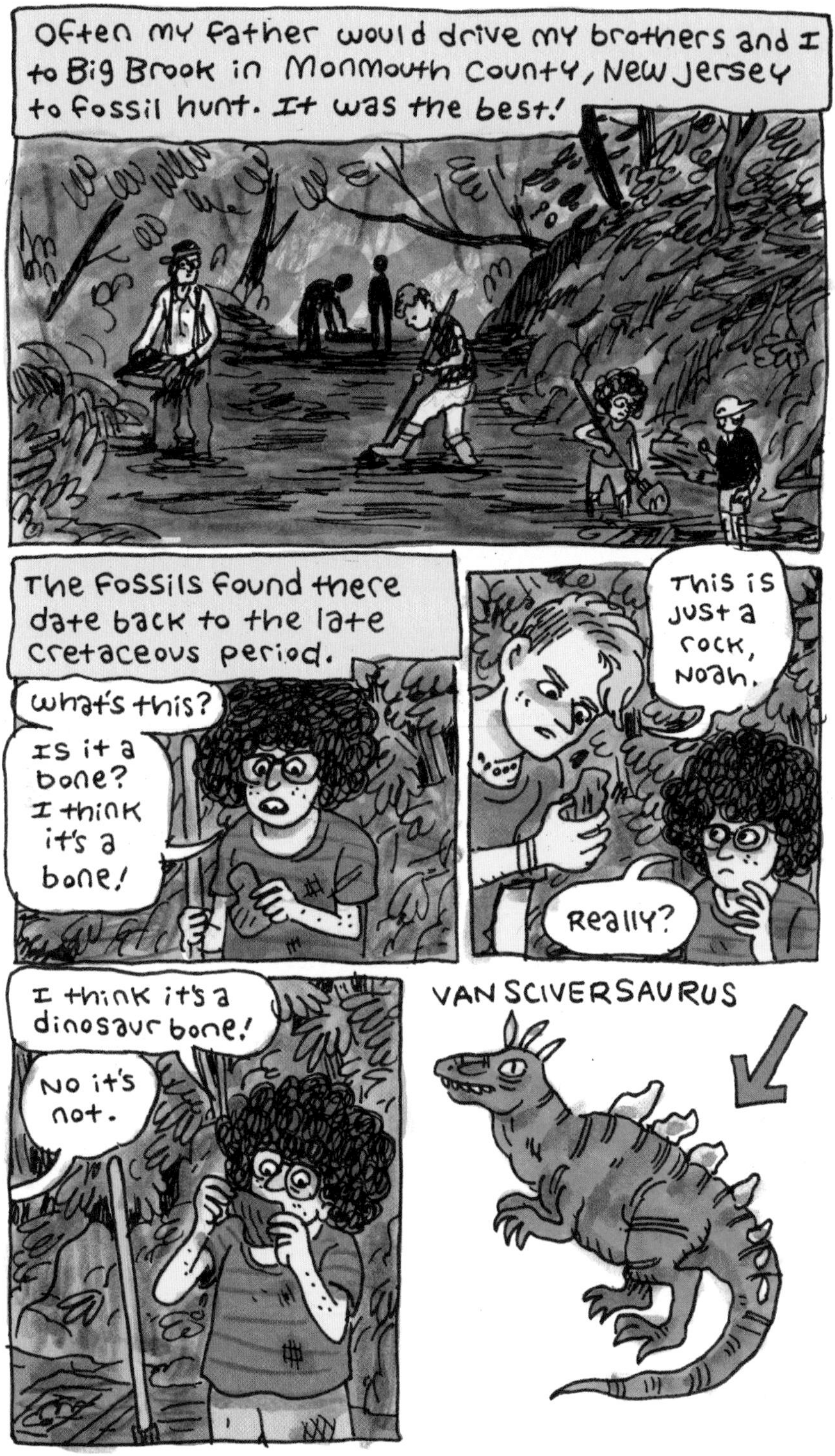
Often my father would drive my brothers and I to Big Brook in Monmouth County, New Jersey to fossil hunt. It was the best!
The fossils found there date back to the late cretaceous period.
what's this?
Is it a bone? I think it's a bone!
This is just a rock, Noah.
Really?
I think it's a dinosaur bone!
No it's not.
VAN SCIVERSAURUS

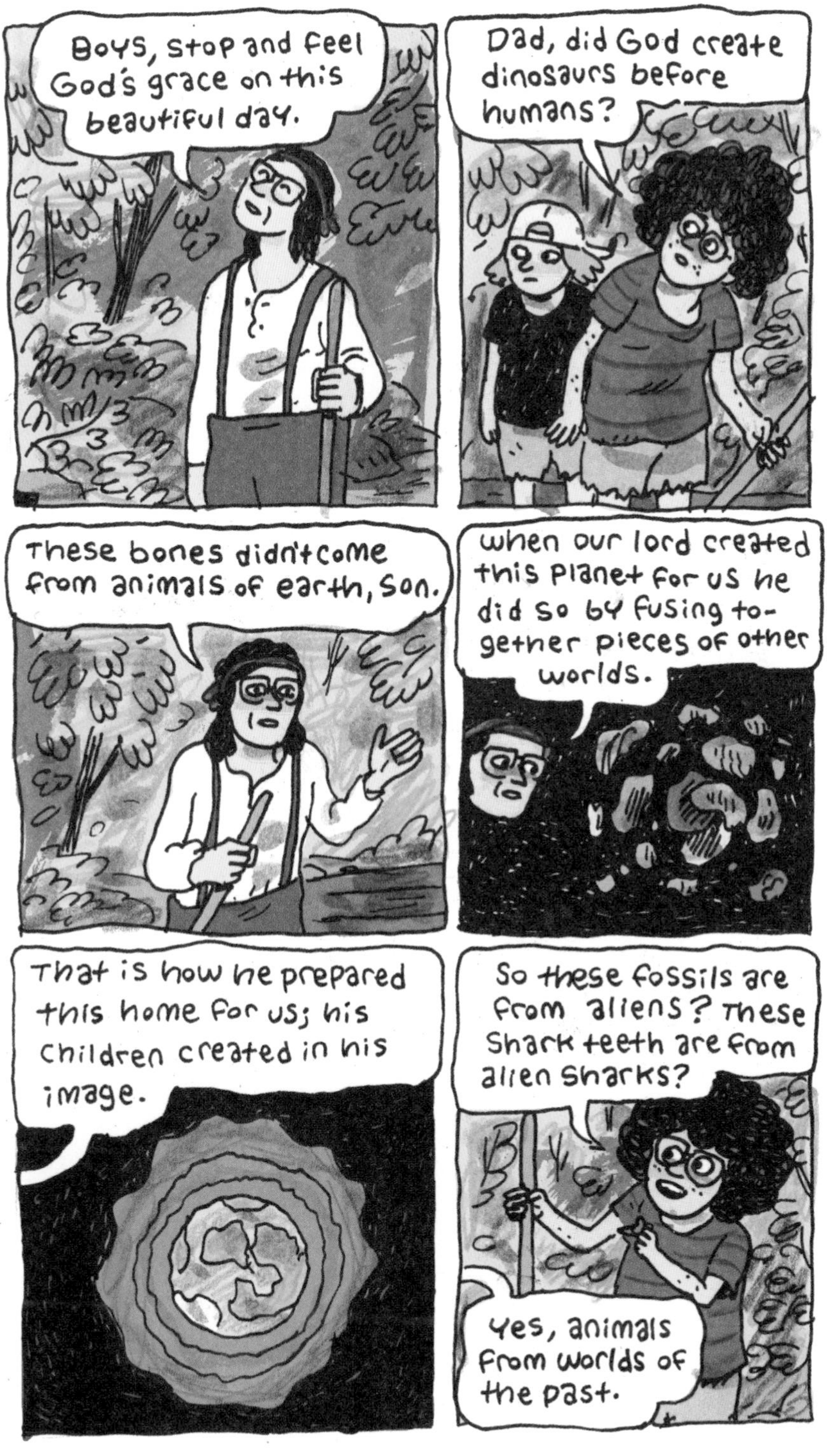
Boys, stop and feel God's grace on this beautiful day.
Dad, did God create dinosaurs before humans?
These bones didn't come from animals of earth, son.
When our lord created this planet for us he did so by fusing together pieces of other worlds.
That is how he prepared this home for us; his children created in his image.
So these fossils are from aliens? These shark teeth are from alien sharks?
Yes, animals from worlds of the past.

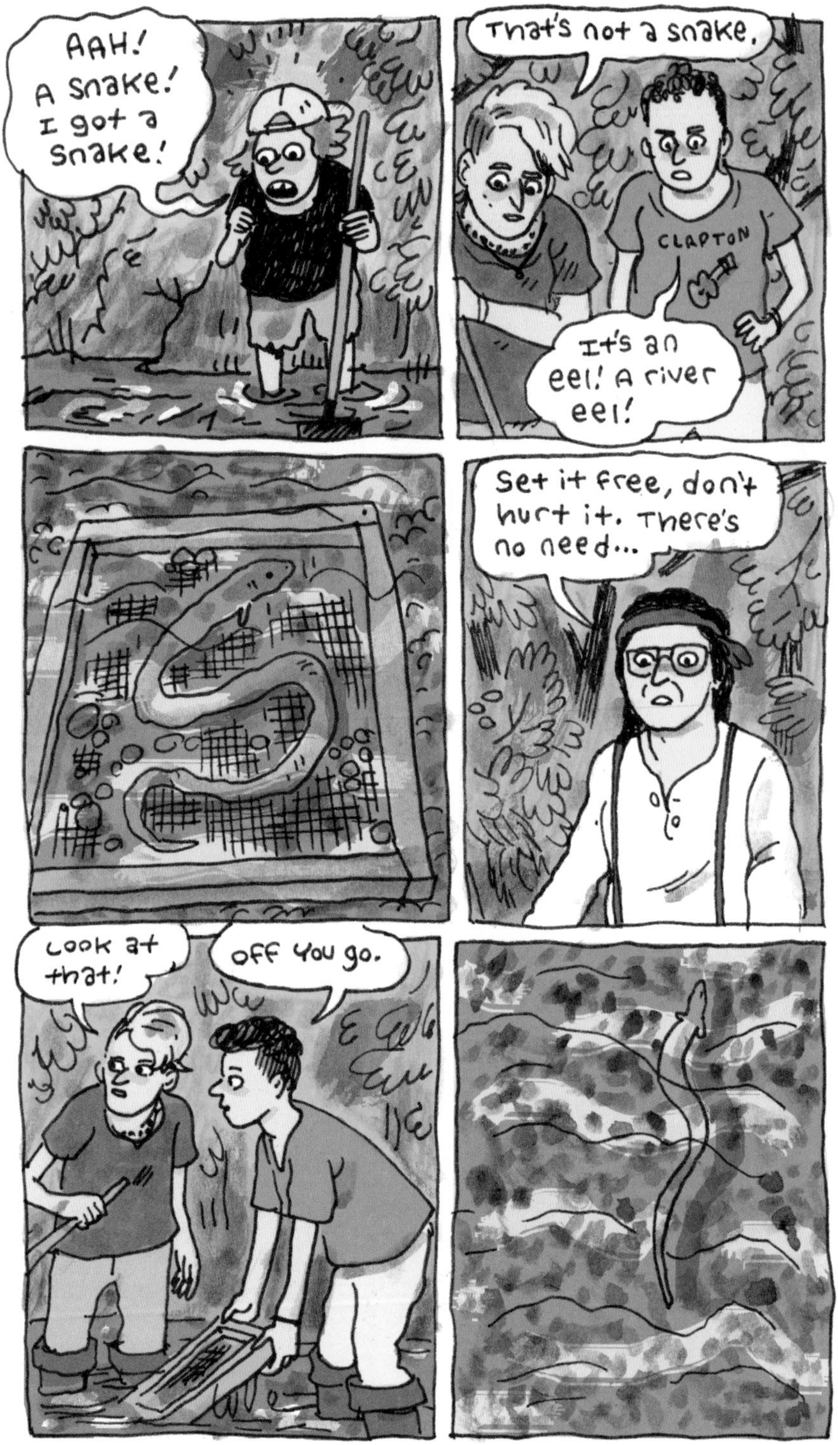

AAH! A snake! I got a snake!
That's not a snake.
It's an eel! A river eel!
Set it free, don't hurt it. There's no need...
Look at that!
Off you go.

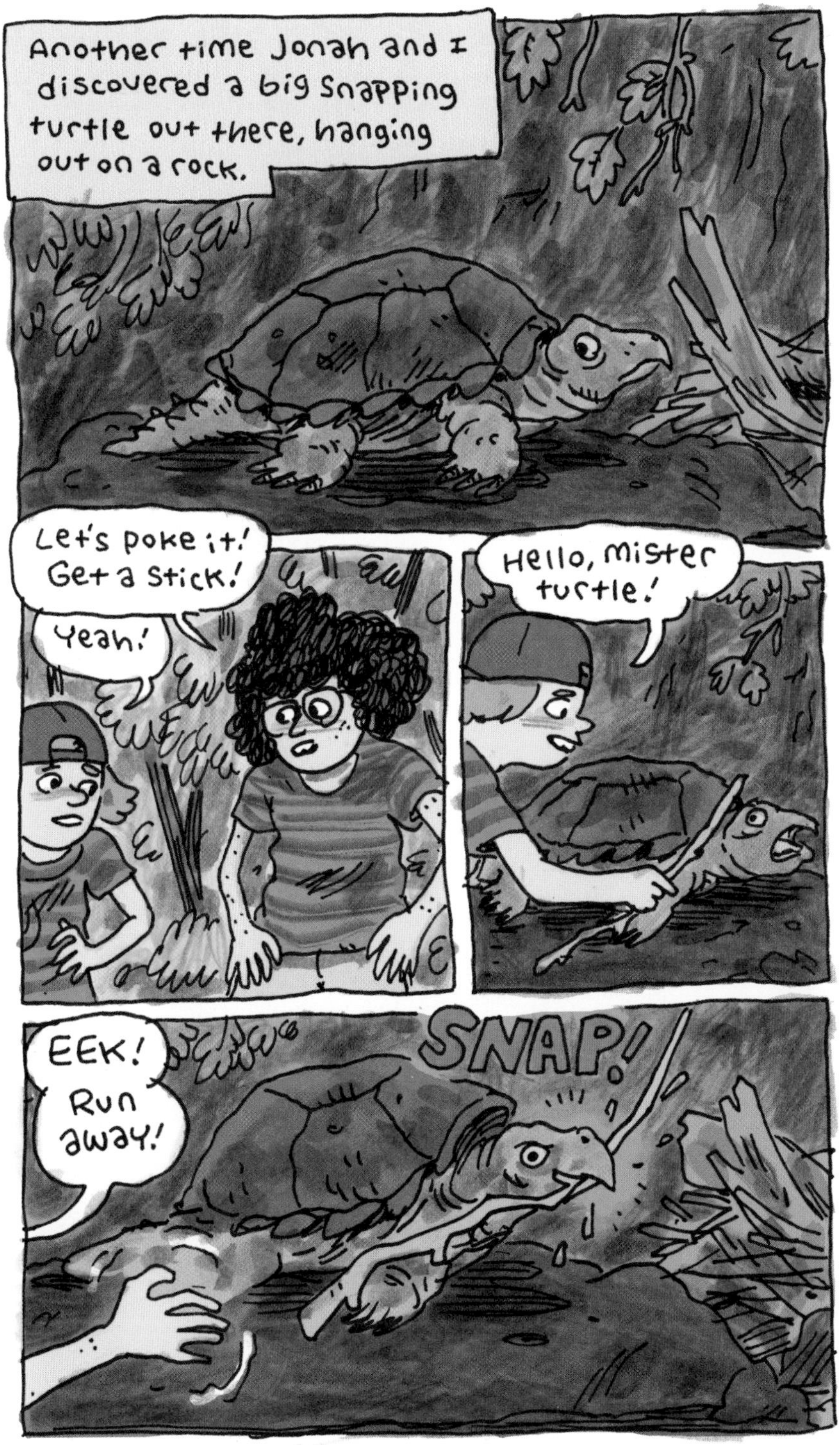
Another time Jonah and I discovered a big snapping turtle out there, hanging out on a rock.
Let's poke it! Get a stick!
Yeah!
Hello, mister turtle!
EEK! Run away!
SNAP!

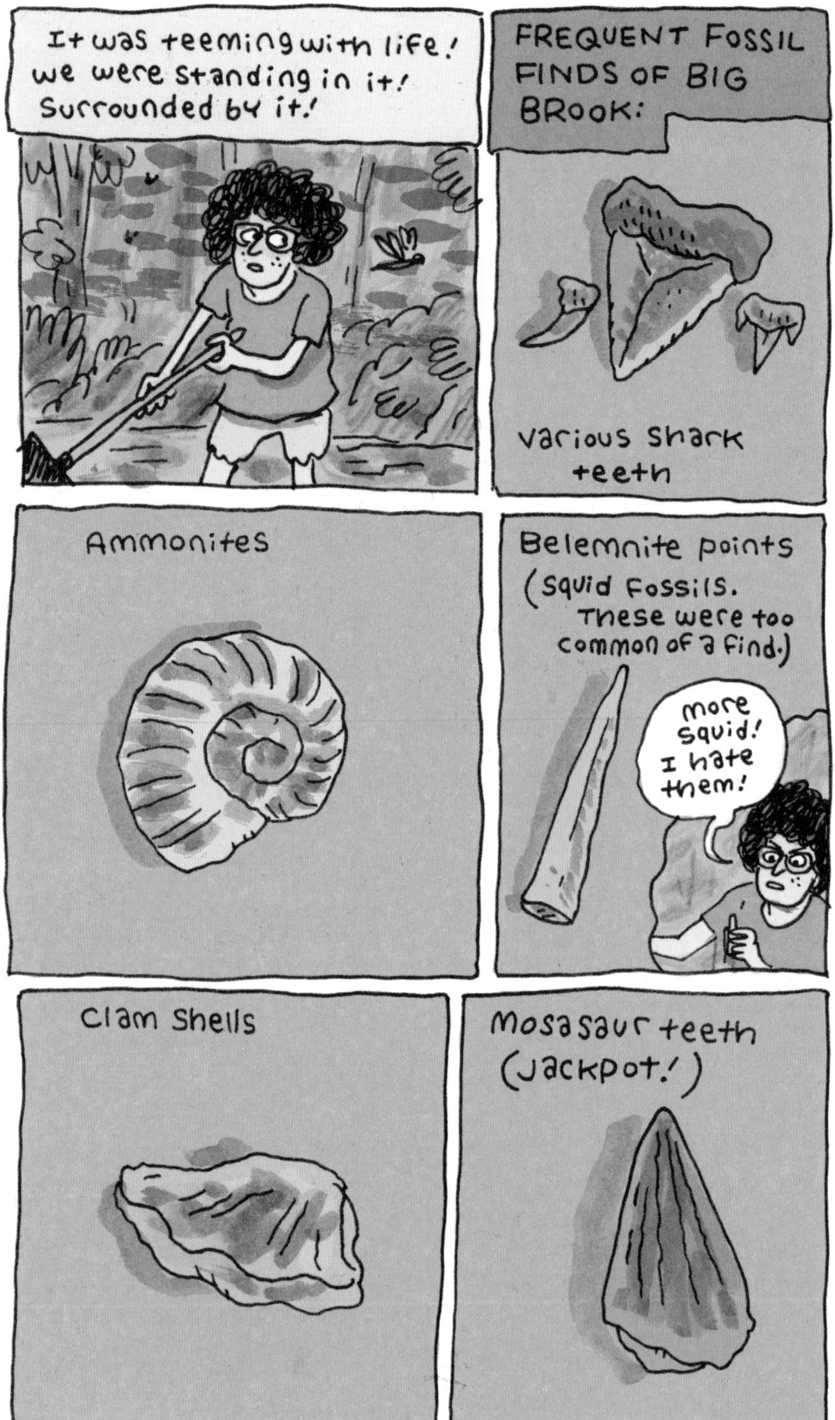
It was teeming with life! we were standing in it! Surrounded by it!
FREQUENT FOSSIL FINDS OF BIG BROOK:
Various shark teeth
Ammonites
Belemnite points (squid fossils. These were too common of a find.)
more squid! I hate them!
Clam shells
Mosasaur teeth (Jackpot!)

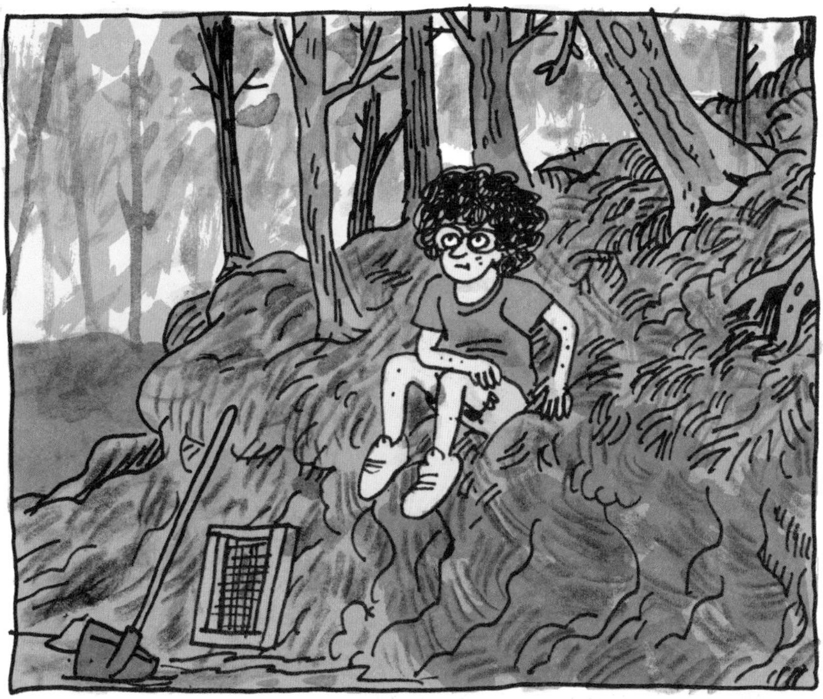

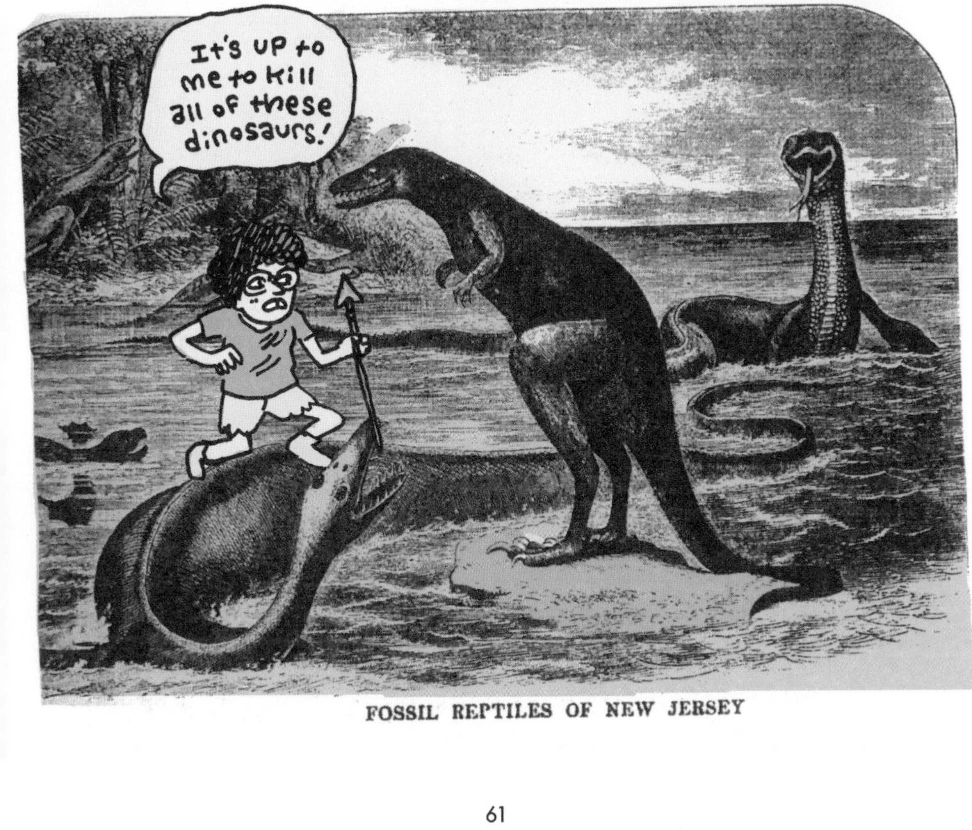
It's up to me to kill all of these dinosaurs!

FOSSIL REPTILES OF NEW JERSEY

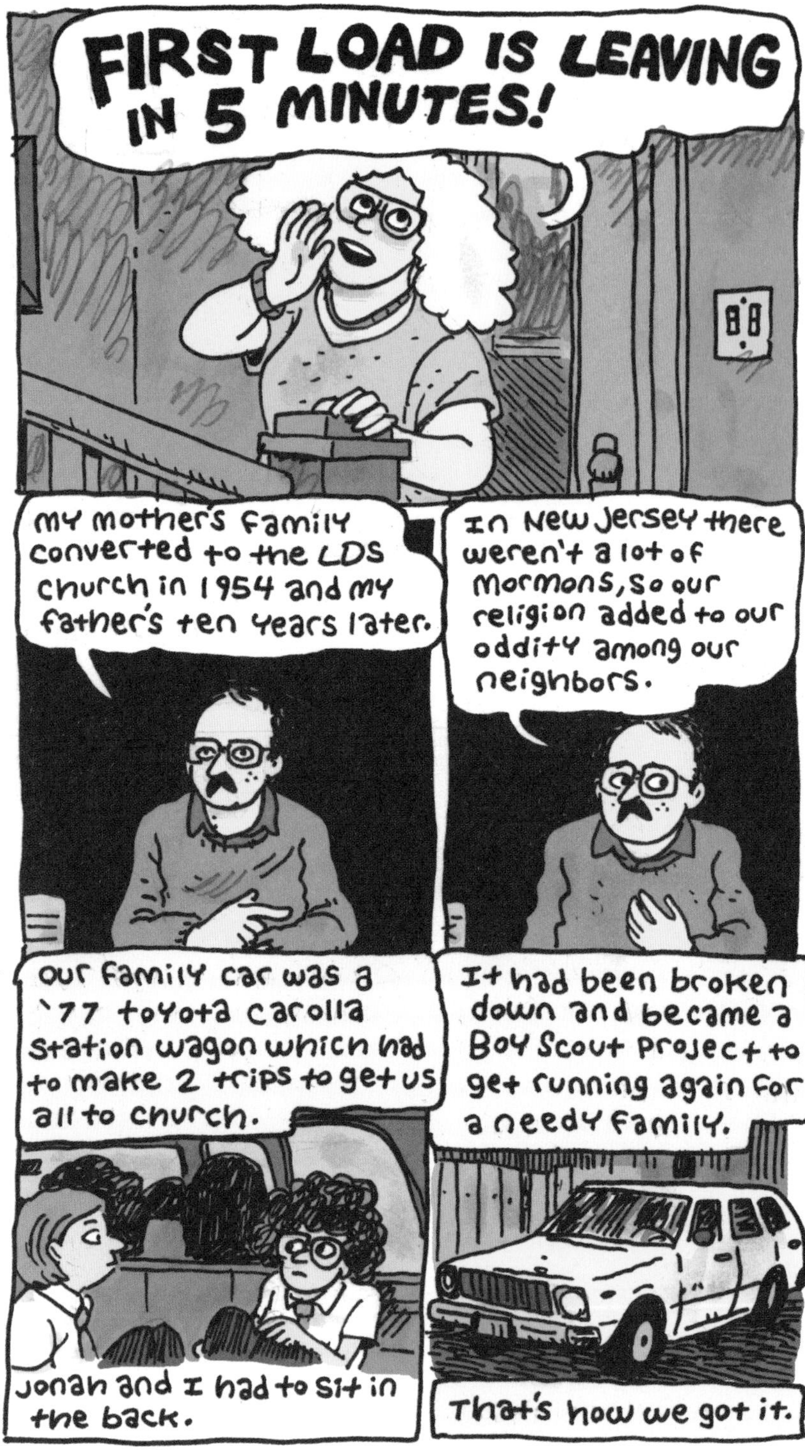
FIRST LOAD IS LEAVING IN 5 MINUTES!
my mother's family converted to the LDS church in 1954 and my father's ten years later.
In New Jersey there weren't a lot of Mormons, so our religion added to our oddity among our neighbors.
Our family car was a '77 toyota carolla station wagon which had to make 2 trips to get us all to church.
Jonah and I had to sit in the back.
It had been broken down and became a Boy Scout project to get running again for a needy family.
That's how we got it.

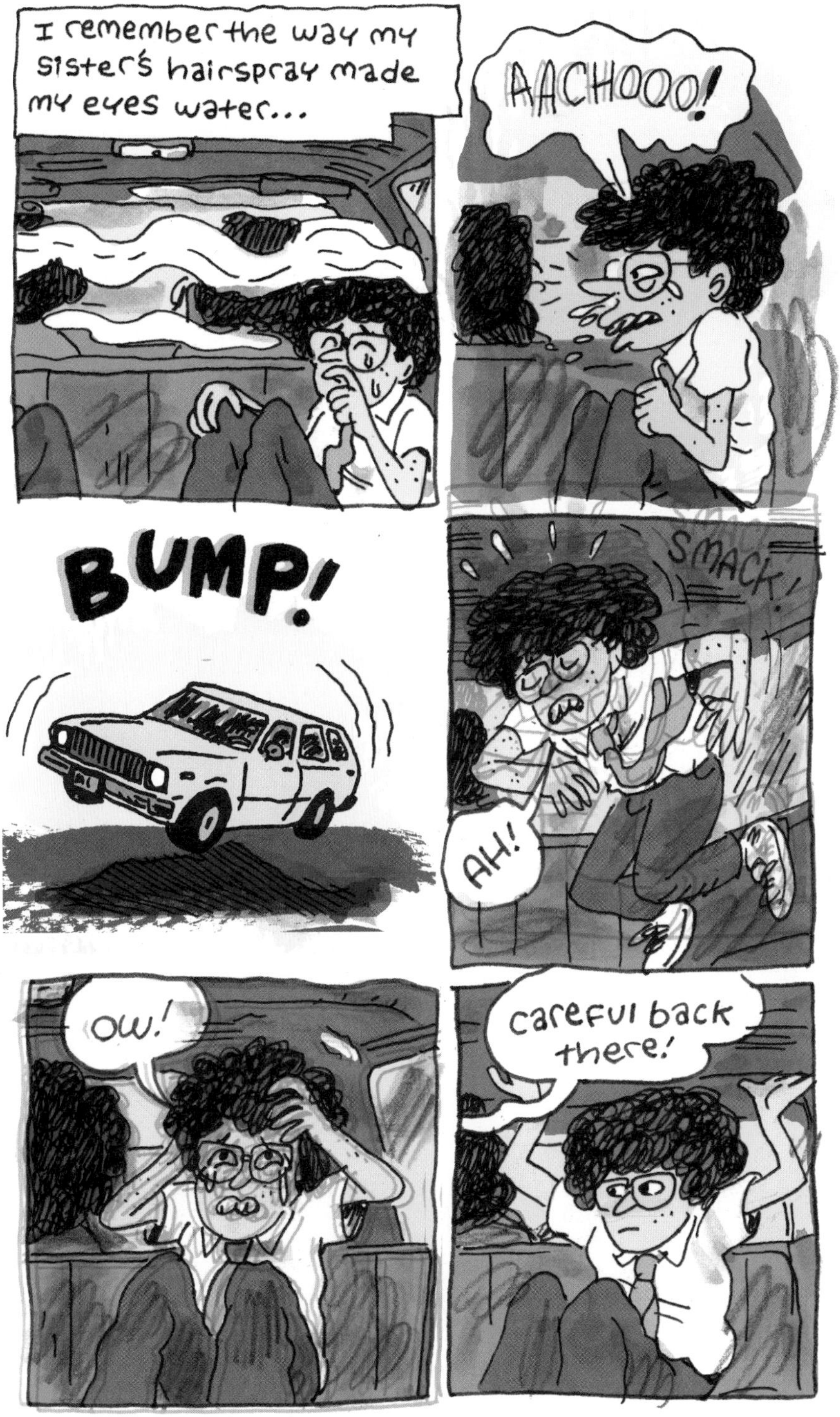
I remember the way my sister's hairspray made my eyes water...
AACHOOO!
BUMP!
SMACK!
AH!
OW!
careful back there!

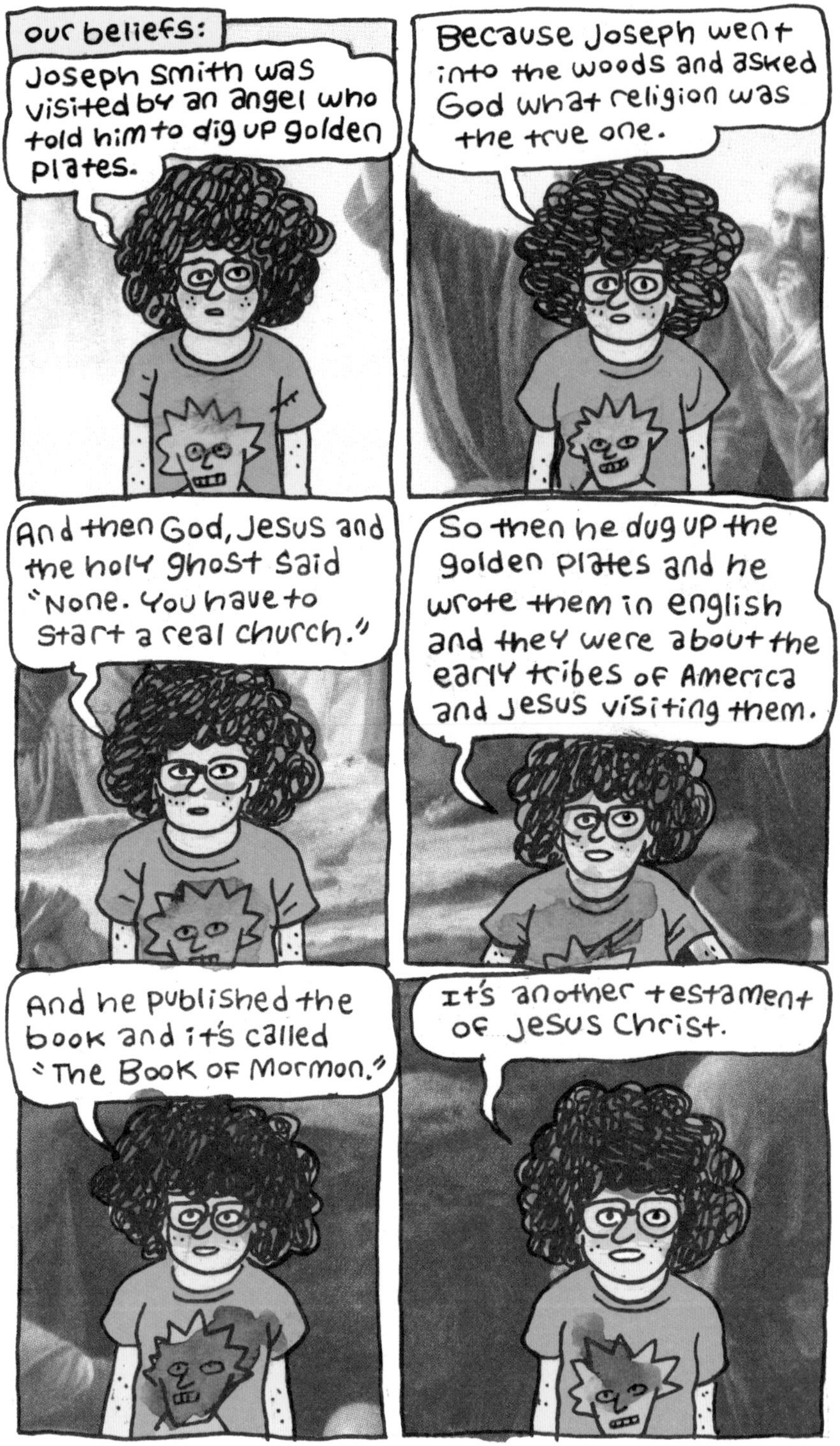
our beliefs:
Joseph Smith was visited by an angel who told him to dig up golden plates.
Because Joseph went into the woods and asked God what religion was the true one.
And then God, Jesus and the holy ghost said "None. You have to start a real church."
So then he dug up the golden plates and he wrote them in english and they were about the early tribes of America and Jesus visiting them.
And he published the book and it's called "The Book of Mormon."
It's another testament of Jesus Christ.

Moorestown, New Jersey...

Come, come, ye Saints, no toil nor labor fear;

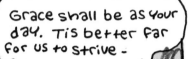

But with joy wend your way. Though hard to you this journey may appear -

Grace shall be as your day. 'Tis better far for us to strive -

Our useless cares from us to drive; Do this, and joy your hearts will swell - All is well! All is well!

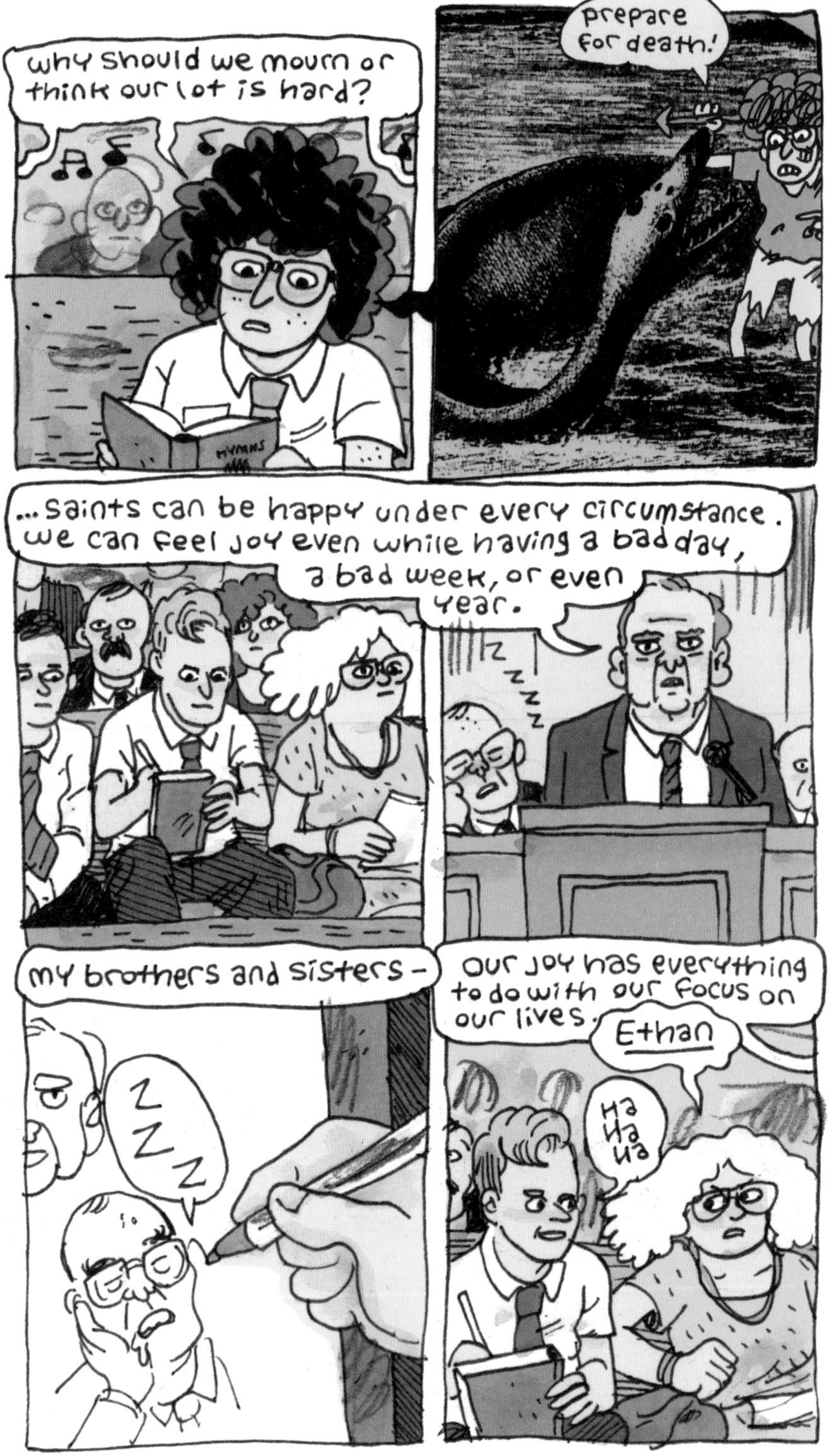
why should we mourn or think our lot is hard?
prepare for death!
...saints can be happy under every circumstance. we can feel joy even while having a bad day, a bad week, or even year.
my brothers and sisters -
our joy has everything to do with our focus on our lives.
Ethan
Ha Ha Ha

O God, the Eternal Father, we ask thee in the name of thy Son, Jesus Christ—

To bless and sanctify this bread to the souls of all those who partake of it—

That they may eat in remembrance of the body of thy Son, and witness unto thee, O God—

Heh heh

(shut up, Jonah)

Trying to make each other laugh during prayers was a daily game...

Torn up wonder bread in tray = Jesus's body

Doesn't taste like meat...

Eventually, all of our food would come from the church's food warehouse "Deseret."

TOASTY O's

TOASTY-O's cereal for breakfast, lunch and dinner!

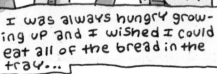

I was always hungry growing up and I wished I could eat all of the bread in the tray...

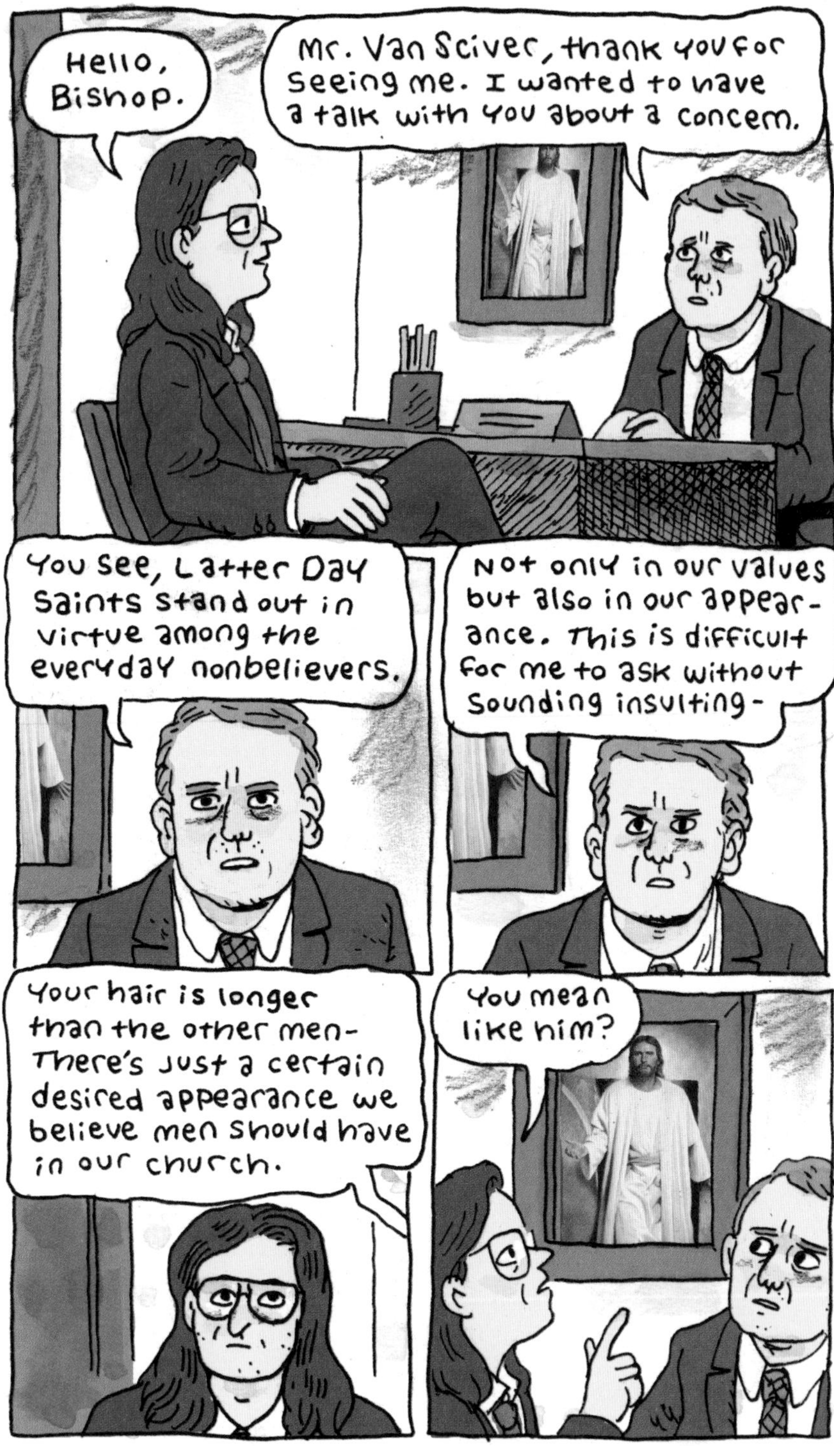
Hello, Bishop.
Mr. Van Sciver, thank you for seeing me. I wanted to have a talk with you about a concern.
You see, Latter Day Saints stand out in virtue among the everyday nonbelievers.
Not only in our values but also in our appearance. This is difficult for me to ask without sounding insulting-
Your hair is longer than the other men- There's just a certain desired appearance we believe men should have in our church.
You mean like him?

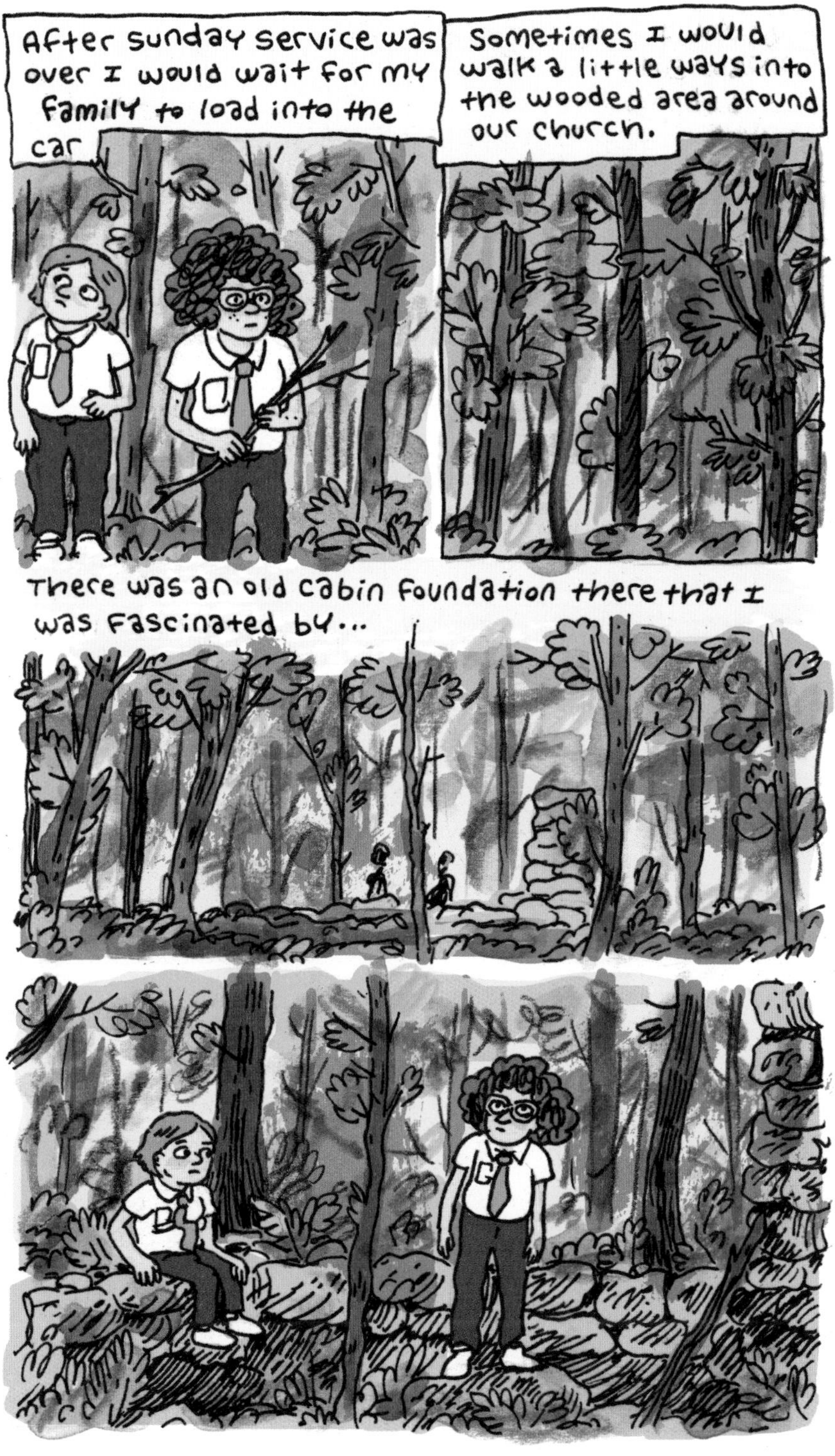
After sunday service was over I would wait for my family to load into the car
Sometimes I would walk a little ways into the wooded area around our church.
There was an old cabin foundation there that I was fascinated by...

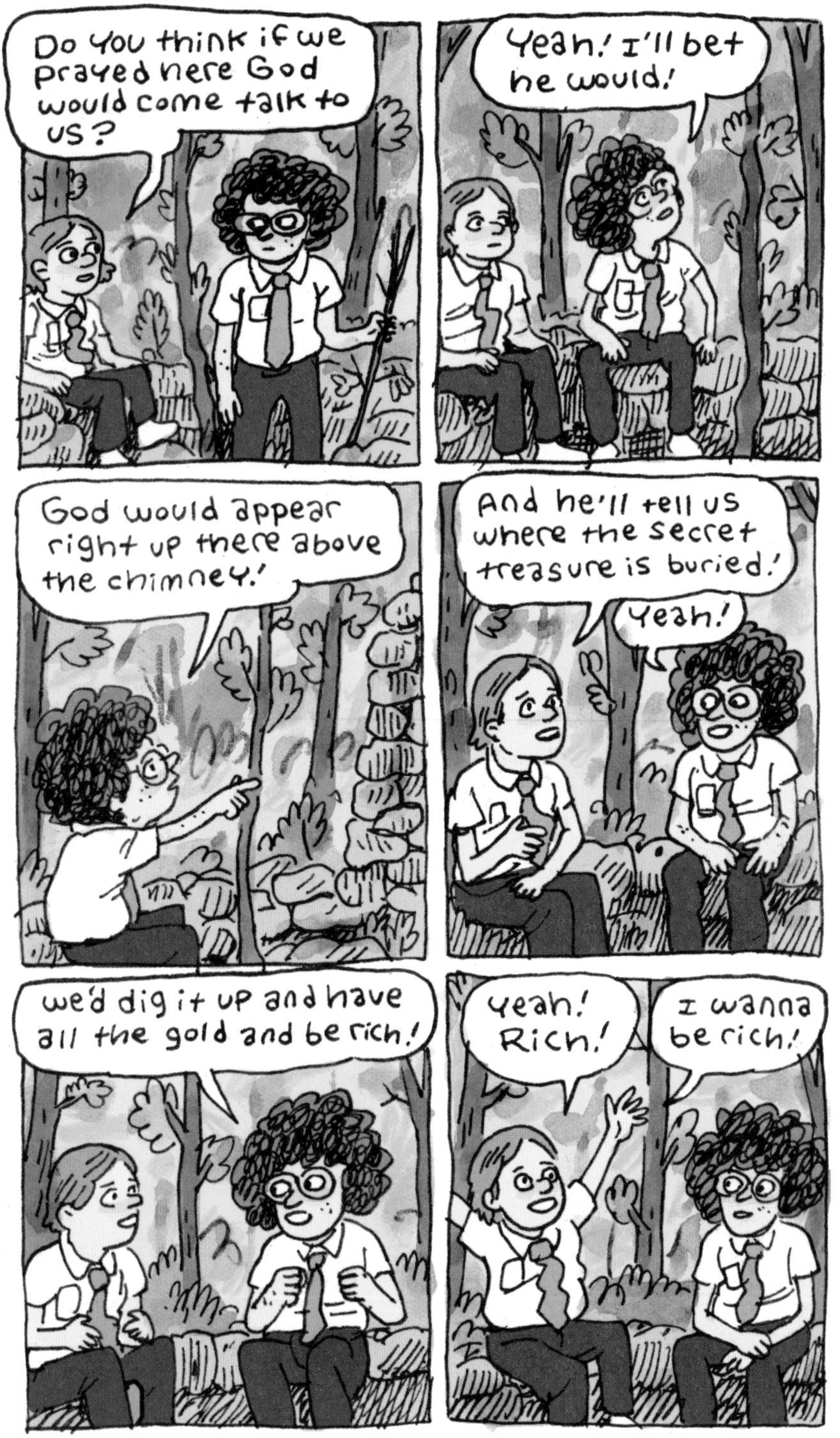
Do you think if we prayed here God would come talk to us?
Yeah! I'll bet he would!
God would appear right up there above the chimney!
And he'll tell us where the secret treasure is buried!
Yeah!
We'd dig it up and have all the gold and be rich!
Yeah! Rich!
I wanna be rich!

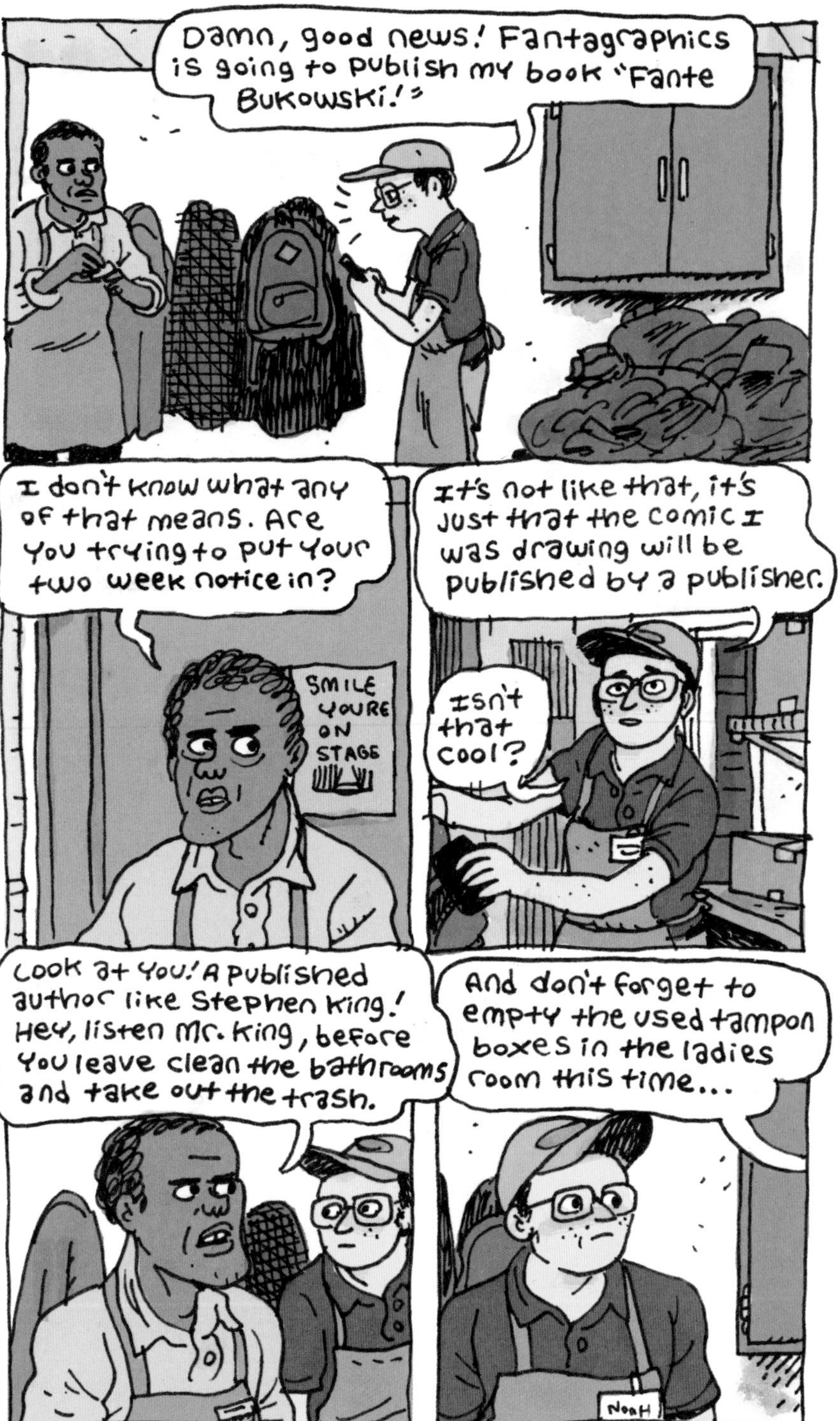
Damn, good news! Fantagraphics is going to publish my book "Fante Bukowski!"
I don't know what any of that means. Are you trying to put your two week notice in?
SMILE YOU'RE ON STAGE
It's not like that, it's just that the comic I was drawing will be published by a publisher.
Isn't that cool?
Look at you! A published author like Stephen King! Hey, listen Mr. King, before you leave clean the bathrooms and take out the trash.
And don't forget to empty the used tampon boxes in the ladies room this time...
NOAH

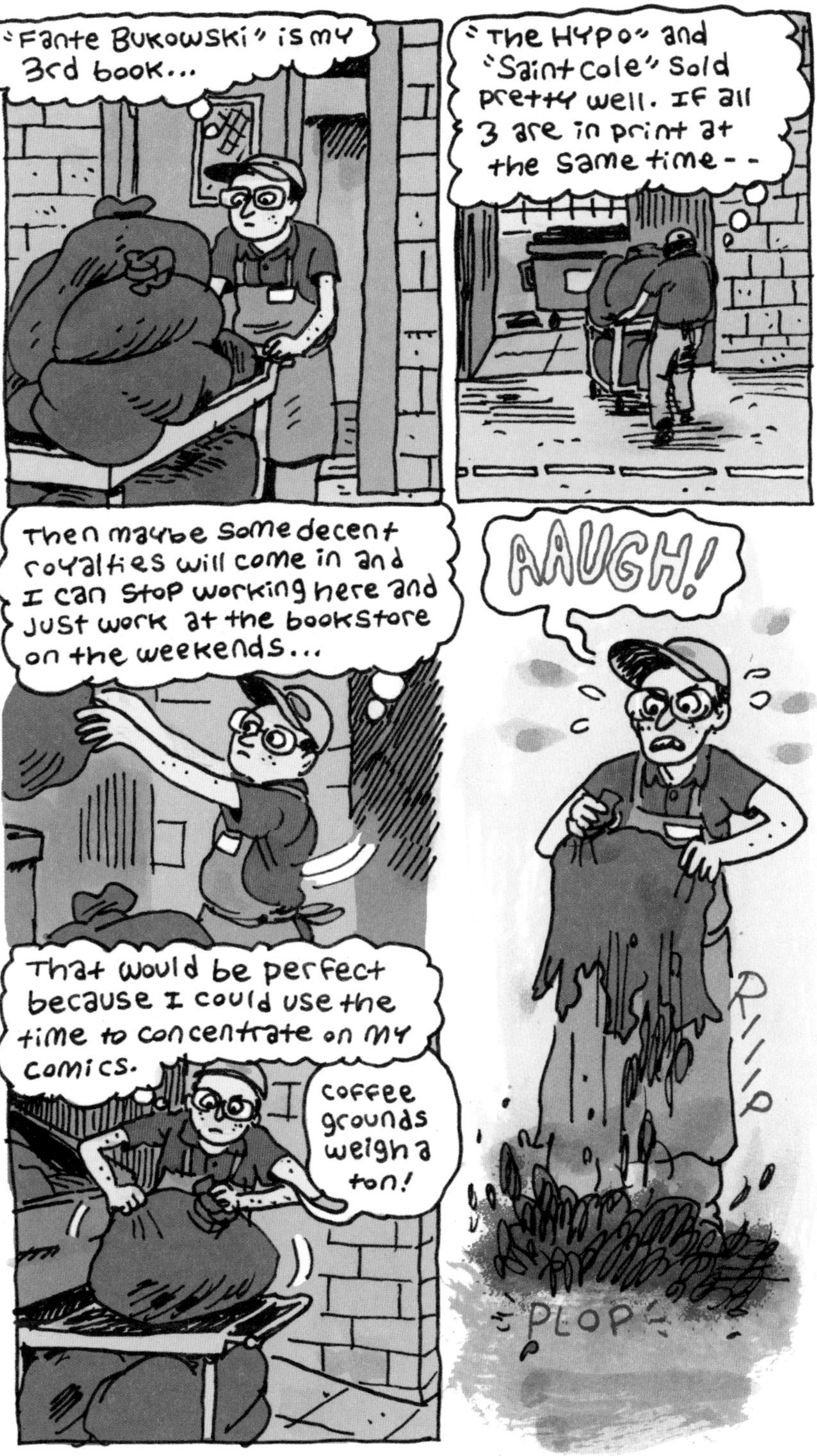
"Fante Bukowski" is my 3rd book...
"The Hypo" and "Saint Cole" sold pretty well. If all 3 are in print at the same time--
Then maybe some decent royalties will come in and I can stop working here and just work at the bookstore on the weekends...
That would be perfect because I could use the time to concentrate on my comics.
Coffee grounds weigh a ton!
AAUGH!
RIIIP
PLOP

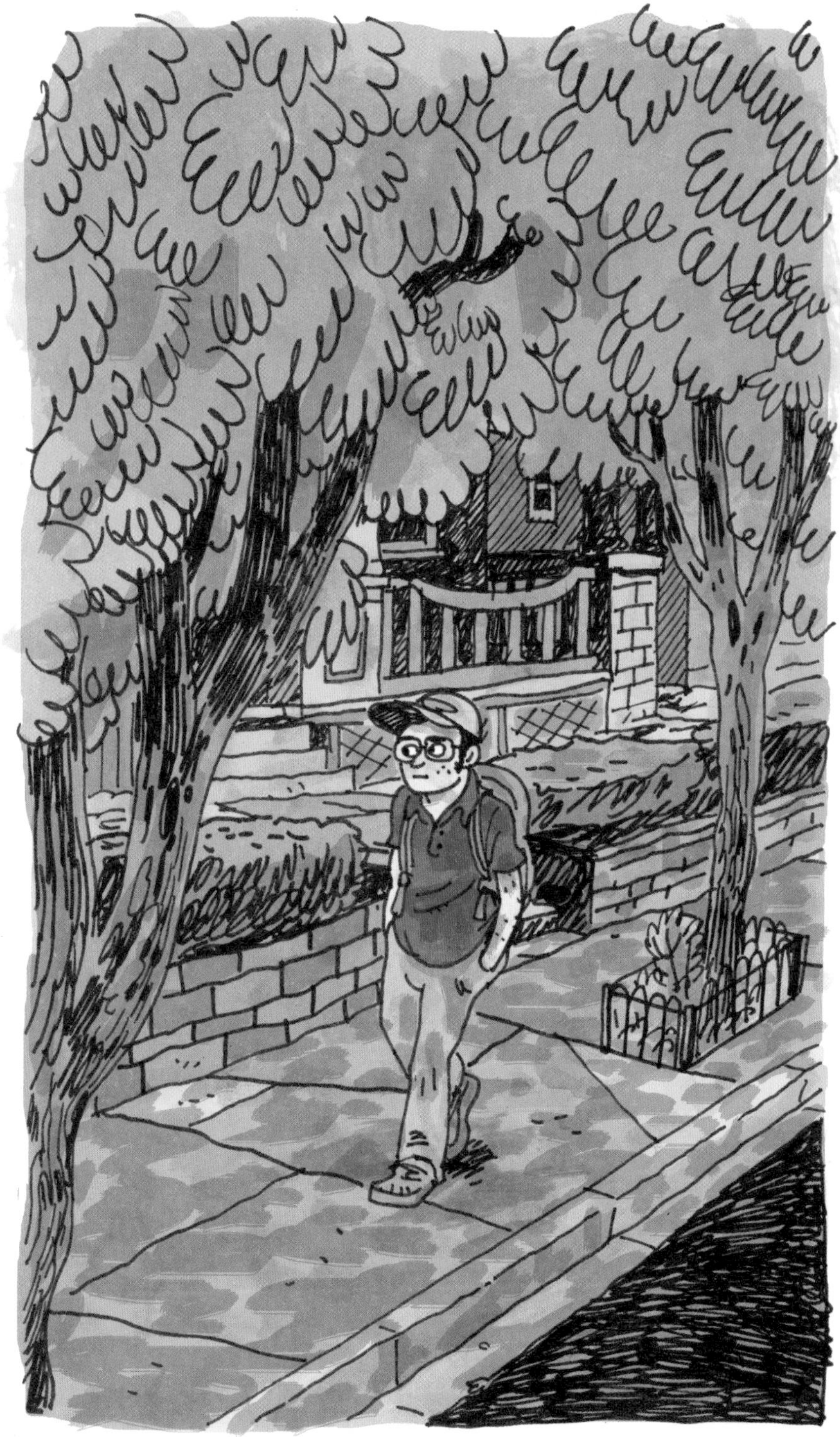

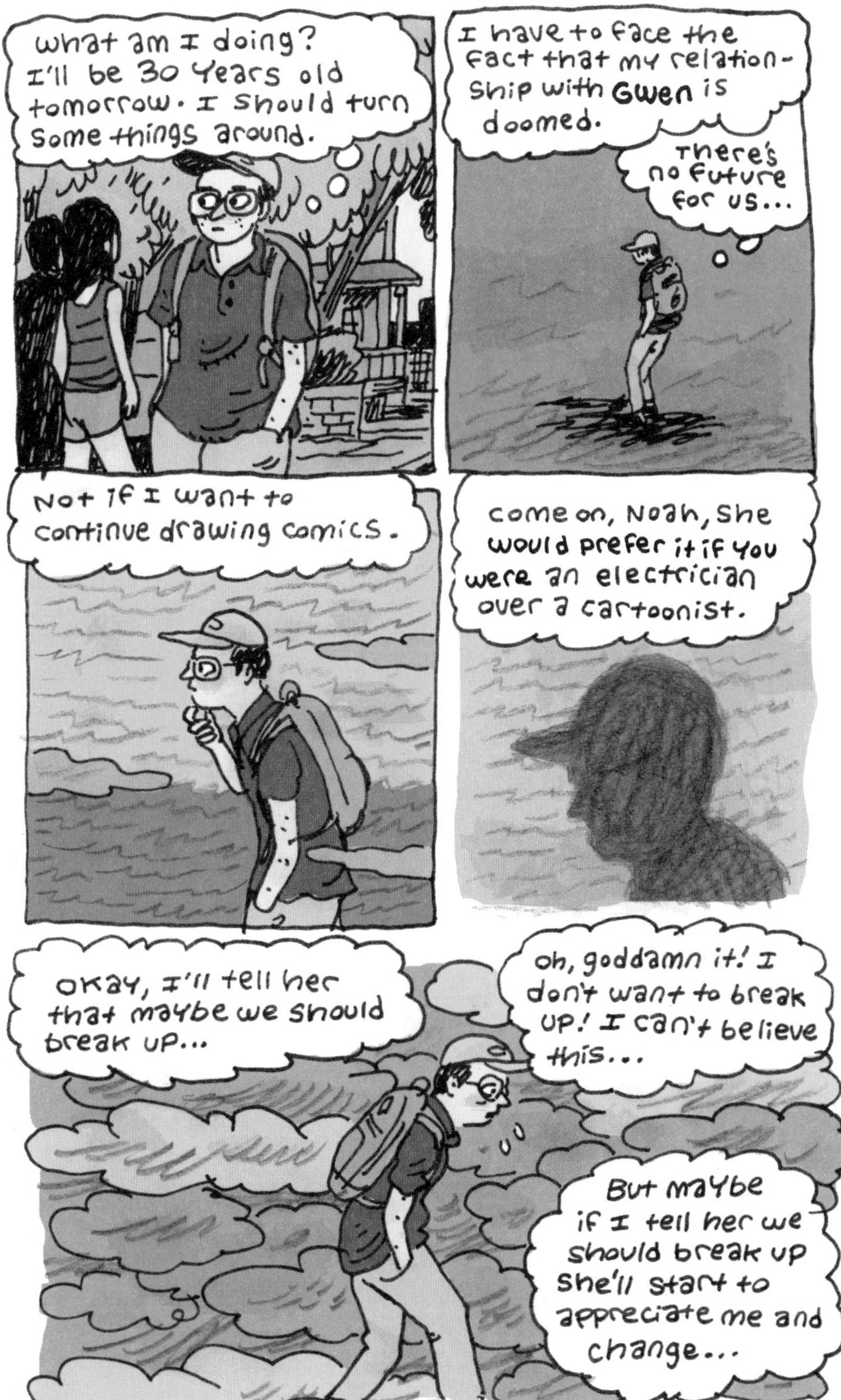
What am I doing? I'll be 30 years old tomorrow. I should turn some things around.
I have to face the fact that my relationship with Gwen is doomed.
There's no future for us...
Not if I want to continue drawing comics.
Come on, Noah, she would prefer it if you were an electrician over a cartoonist.
Okay, I'll tell her that maybe we should break up...
Oh, goddamn it! I don't want to break up! I can't believe this...
But maybe if I tell her we should break up she'll start to appreciate me and change...

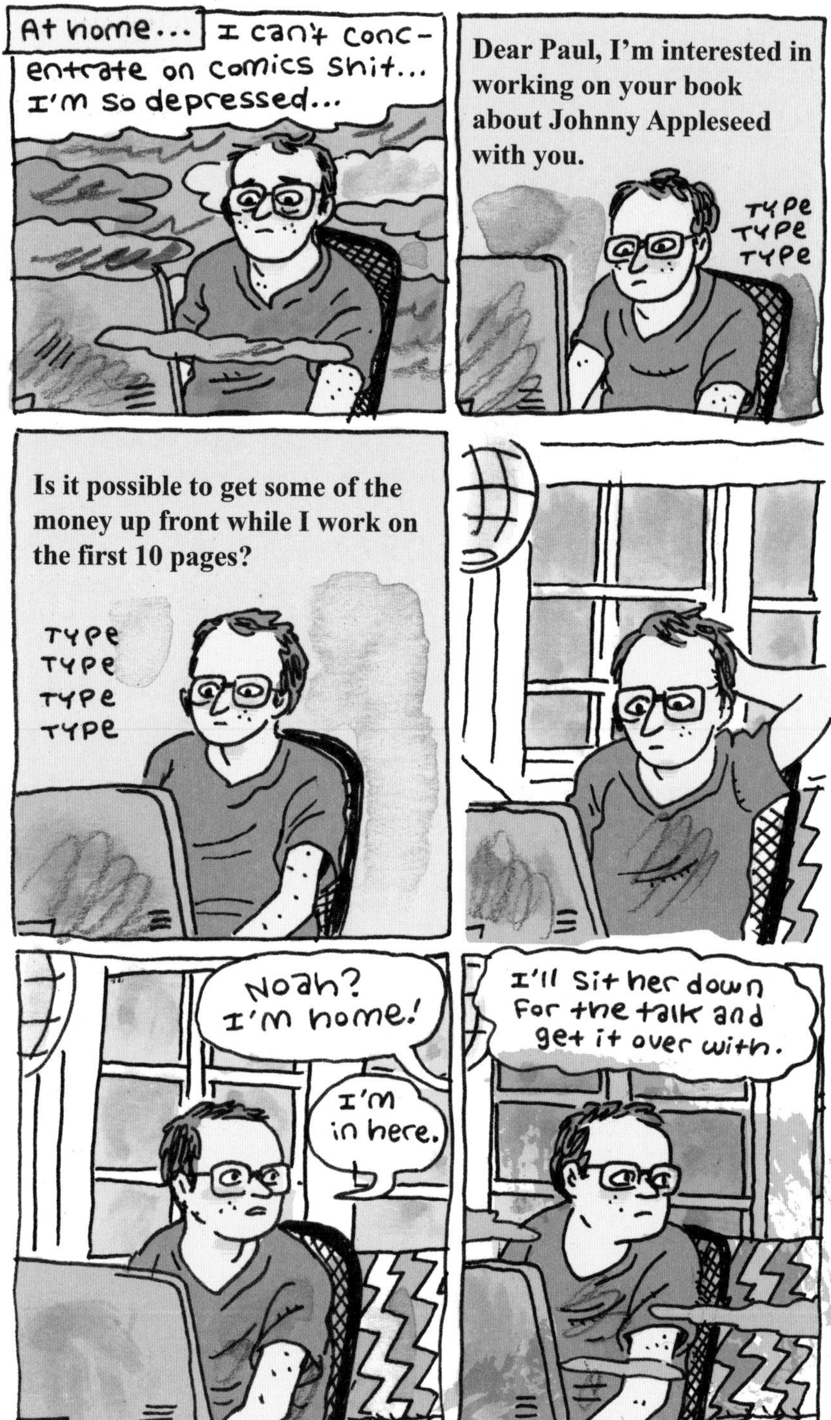
At home...
I can't concentrate on comics shit... I'm so depressed...
Dear Paul, I'm interested in working on your book about Johnny Appleseed with you.
TYPE TYPE TYPE
Is it possible to get some of the money up front while I work on the first 10 pages?
TYPE TYPE TYPE TYPE
Noah? I'm home!
I'm in here.
I'll sit her down for the talk and get it over with.

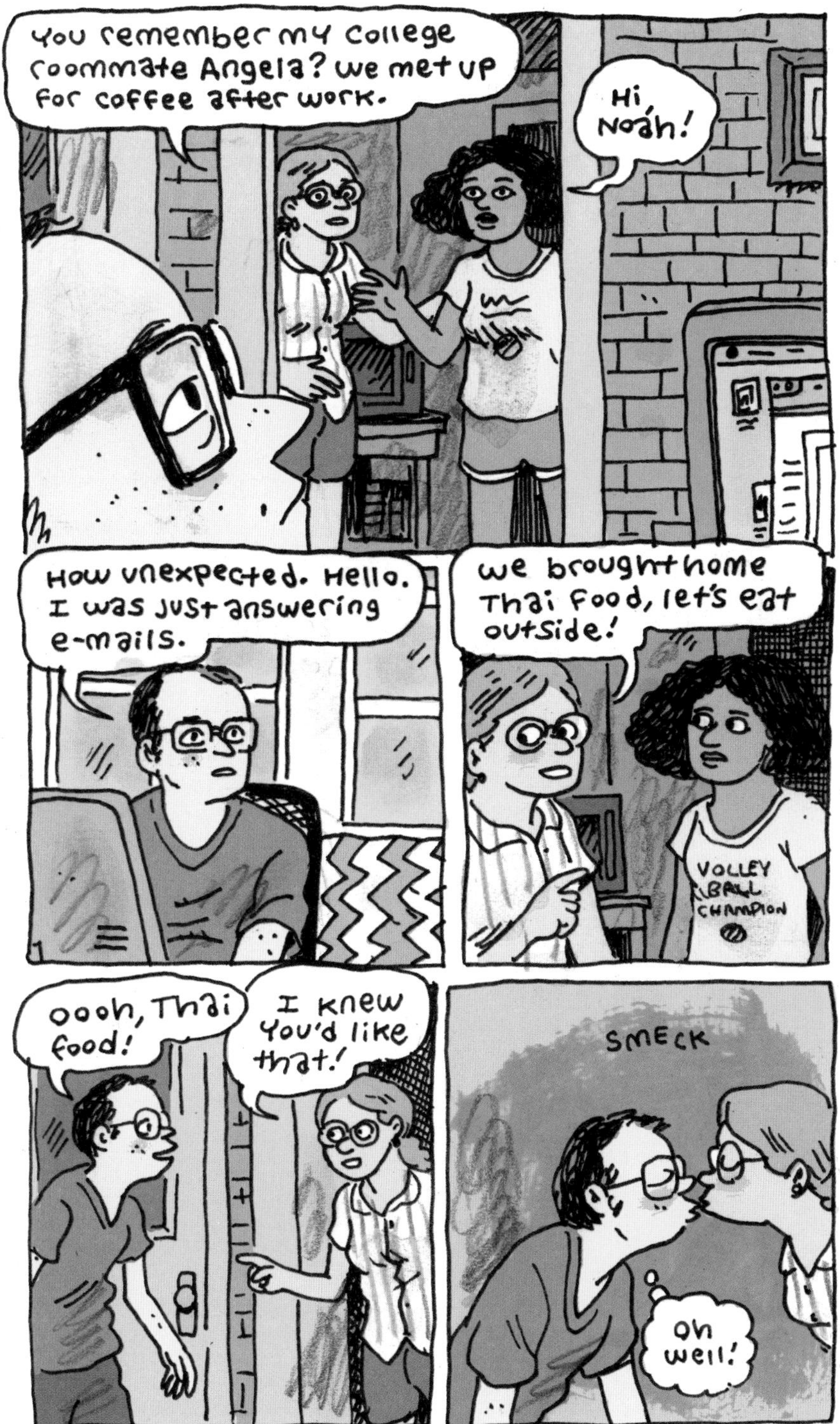
You remember my college roommate Angela? We met up for coffee after work.
Hi, Noah!
How unexpected. Hello. I was just answering e-mails.
We brought home Thai food, let's eat outside!
VOLLEY BALL CHAMPION
Oooh, Thai food!
I knew you'd like that!
SMECK
Oh well!

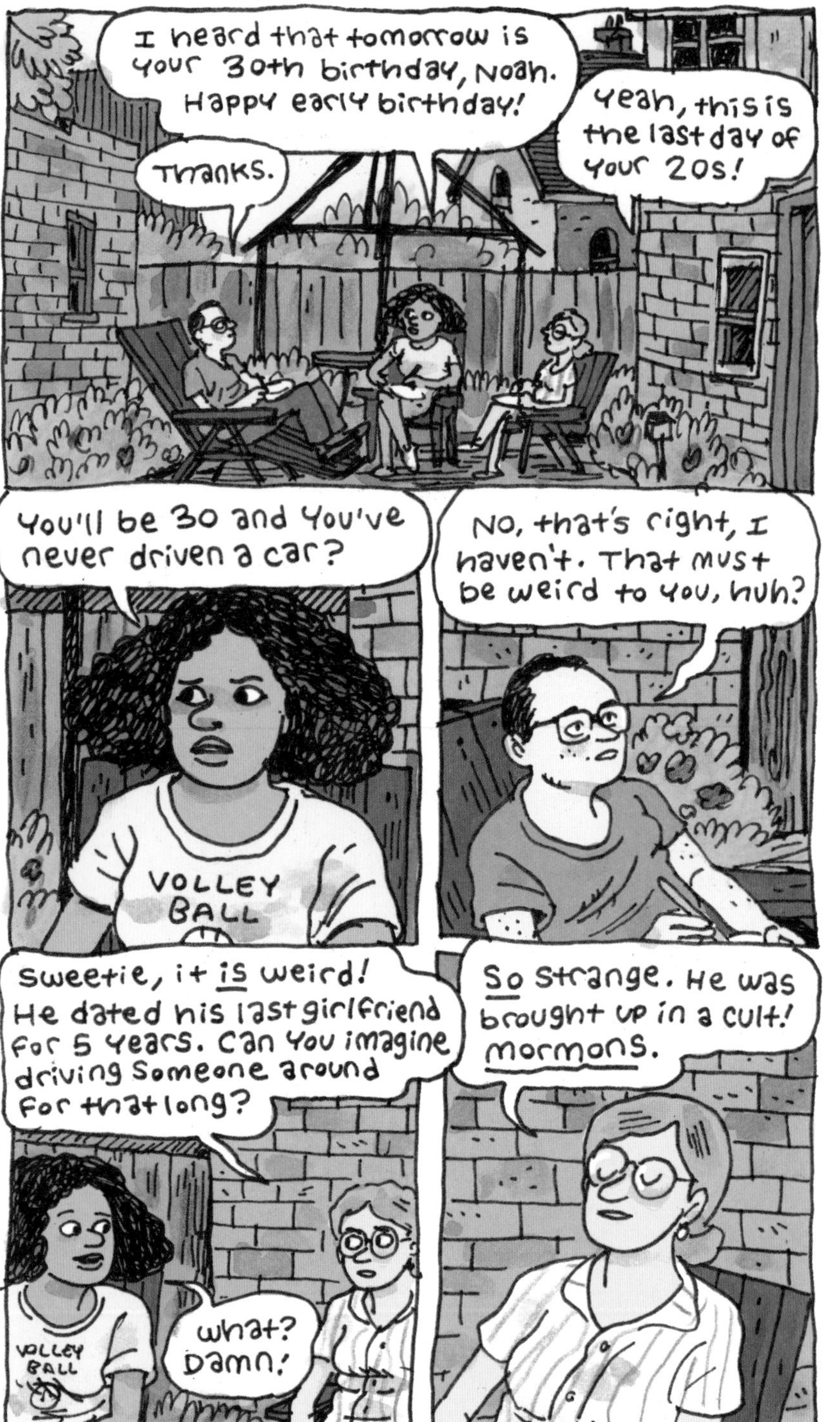
I heard that tomorrow is your 30th birthday, Noah. Happy early birthday!
Thanks.
Yeah, this is the last day of your 20s!
You'll be 30 and you've never driven a car?
No, that's right, I haven't. That must be weird to you, huh?
Sweetie, it is weird! He dated his last girlfriend for 5 years. Can you imagine driving someone around for that long?
VOLLEY BALL
What? Damn!
So strange. He was brought up in a cult! Mormons.

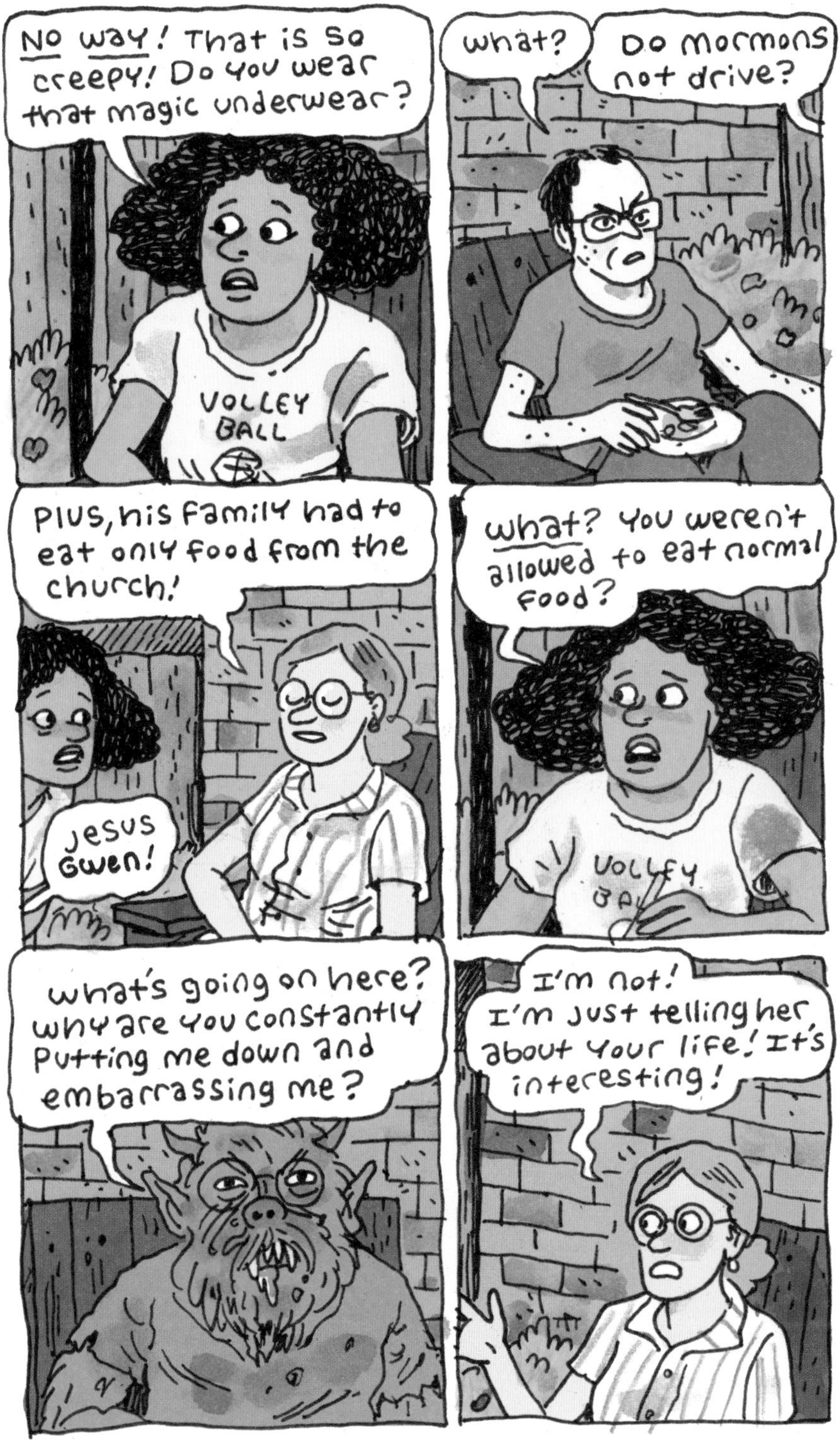
No way! That is so creepy! Do you wear that magic underwear?
VOLLEY BALL
What?
Do mormons not drive?
Plus, his family had to eat only food from the church!
Jesus Gwen!
What? You weren't allowed to eat normal food?
What's going on here? Why are you constantly putting me down and embarrassing me?
I'm not! I'm just telling her about your life! It's interesting!

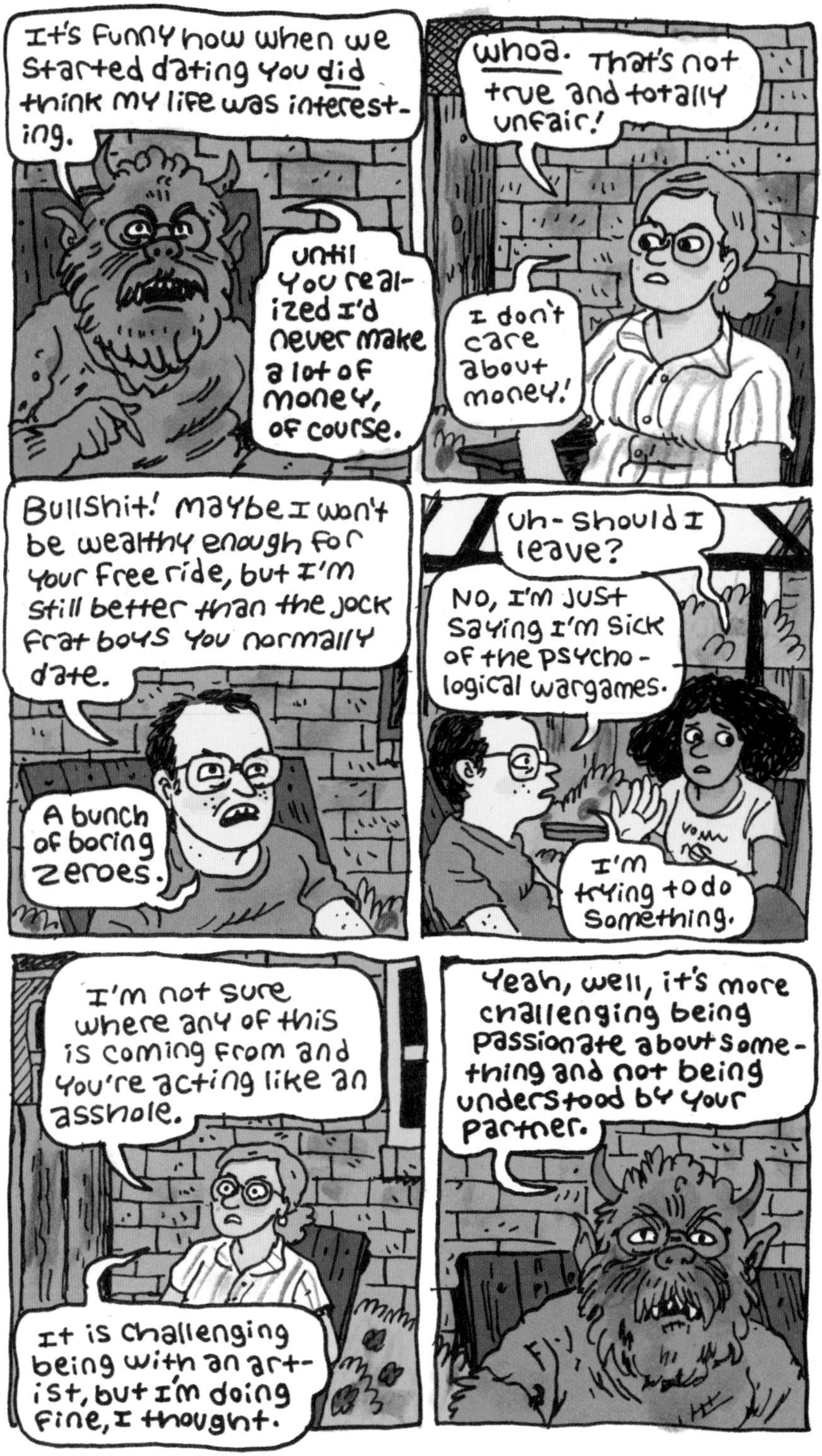

It's funny how when we started dating you did think my life was interesting.
Until you realized I'd never make a lot of money, of course.
Whoa. That's not true and totally unfair!
I don't care about money!
Bullshit! Maybe I won't be wealthy enough for your free ride, but I'm still better than the jock frat boys you normally date.
A bunch of boring zeroes.
Uh- should I leave?
No, I'm just saying I'm sick of the psychological wargames.
I'm trying to do something.
I'm not sure where any of this is coming from and you're acting like an asshole.
It is challenging being with an artist, but I'm doing fine, I thought.
Yeah, well, it's more challenging being passionate about something and not being understood by your partner.

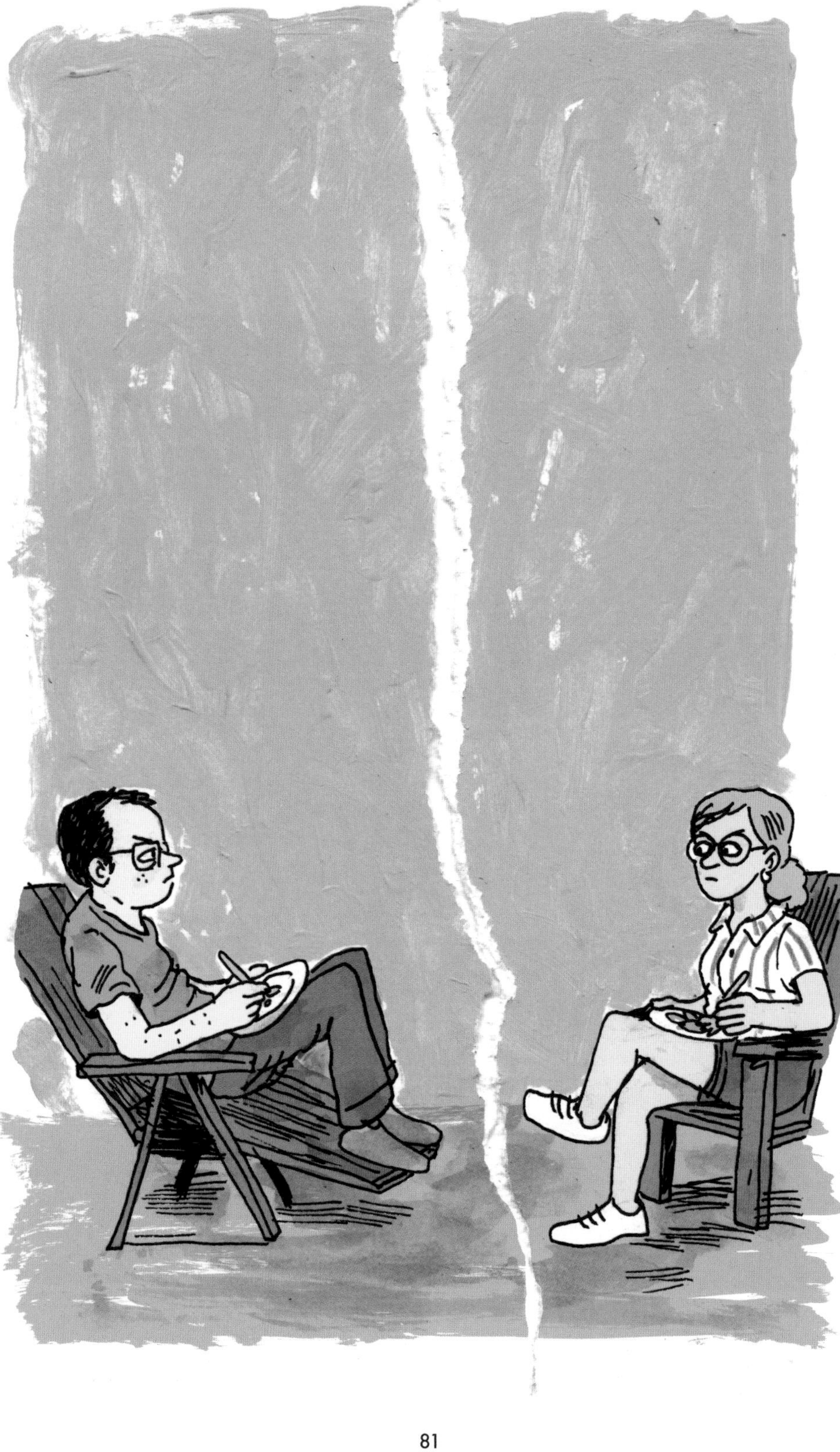

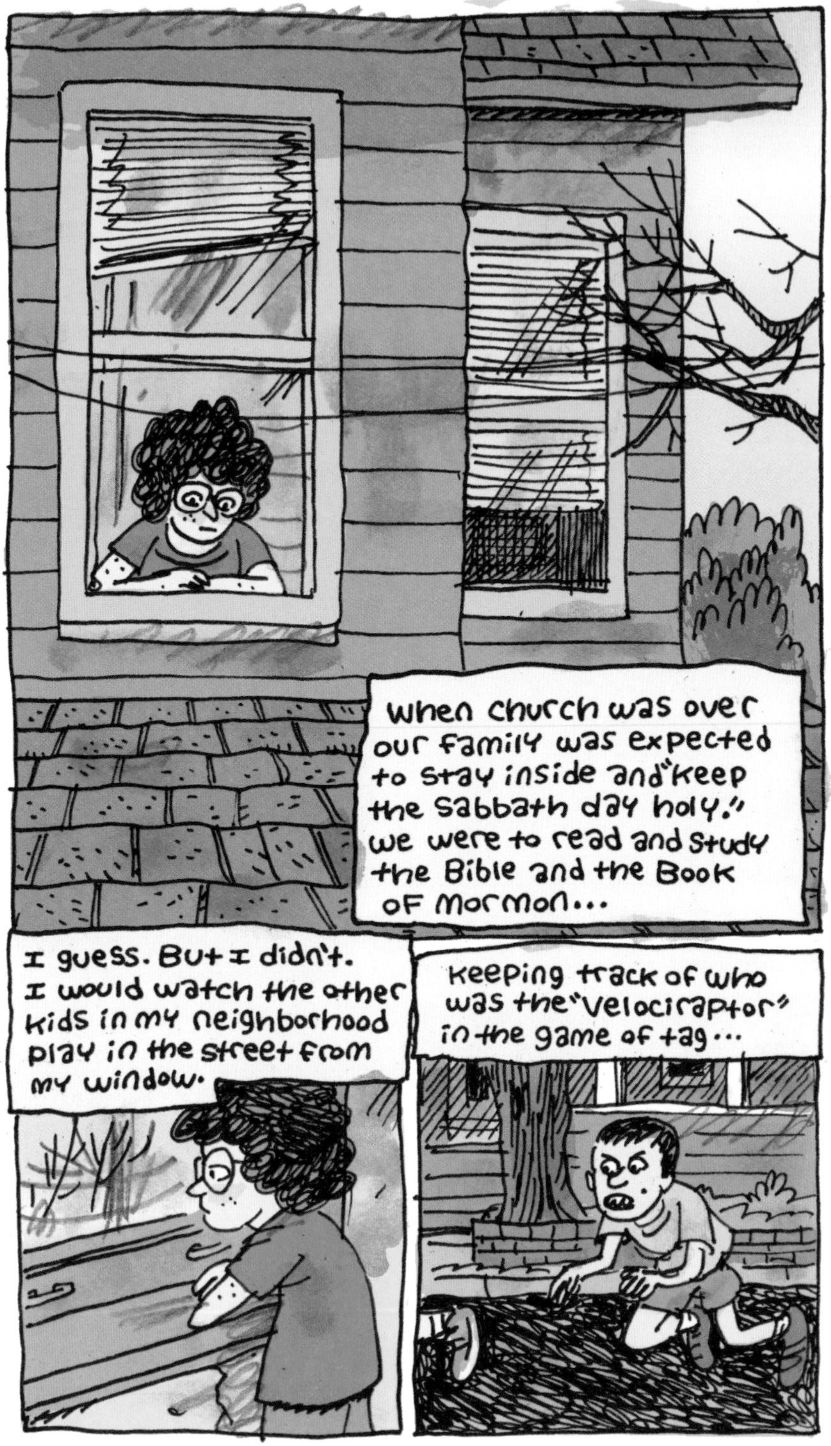
When church was over our family was expected to stay inside and "keep the Sabbath day holy." We were to read and study the Bible and the Book of Mormon...
I guess. But I didn't. I would watch the other kids in my neighborhood play in the street from my window.
Keeping track of who was the "Velociraptor" in the game of tag...

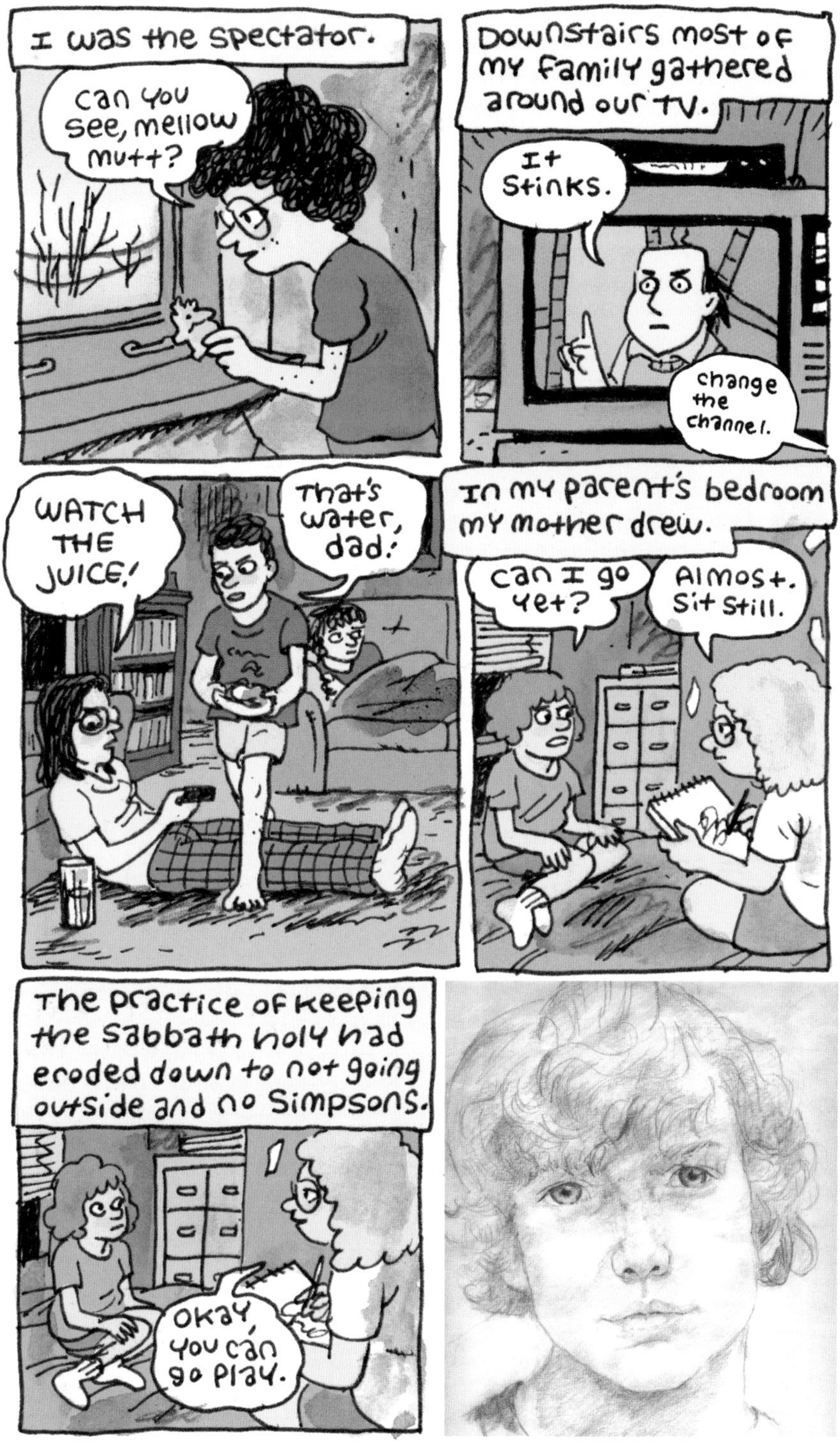
I was the spectator.
Can you see, mellow mutt?
Downstairs most of my family gathered around our TV.
It stinks.
change the channel.
WATCH THE JUICE!
That's water, dad.
In my parent's bedroom my mother drew.
Can I go yet?
Almost. Sit still.
The practice of keeping the sabbath holy had eroded down to not going outside and no Simpsons.
Okay, you can go play.

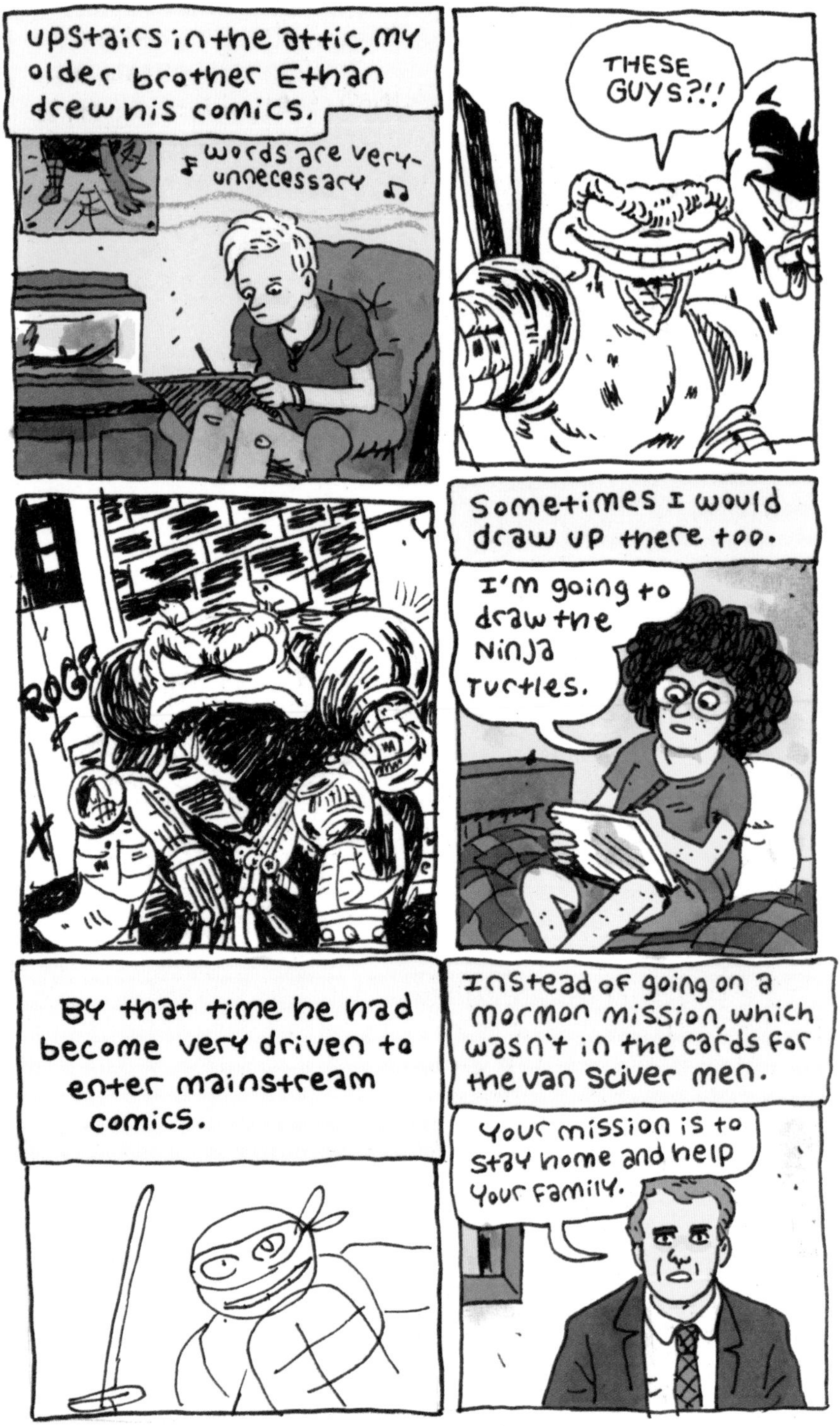
upstairs in the attic, my older brother Ethan drew his comics.
words are very-unnecessary
THESE GUYS?!!
Sometimes I would draw up there too.
I'm going to draw the Ninja Turtles.
By that time he had become very driven to enter mainstream comics.
Instead of going on a mormon mission, which wasn't in the cards for the van Sciver men.
Your mission is to stay home and help your family.

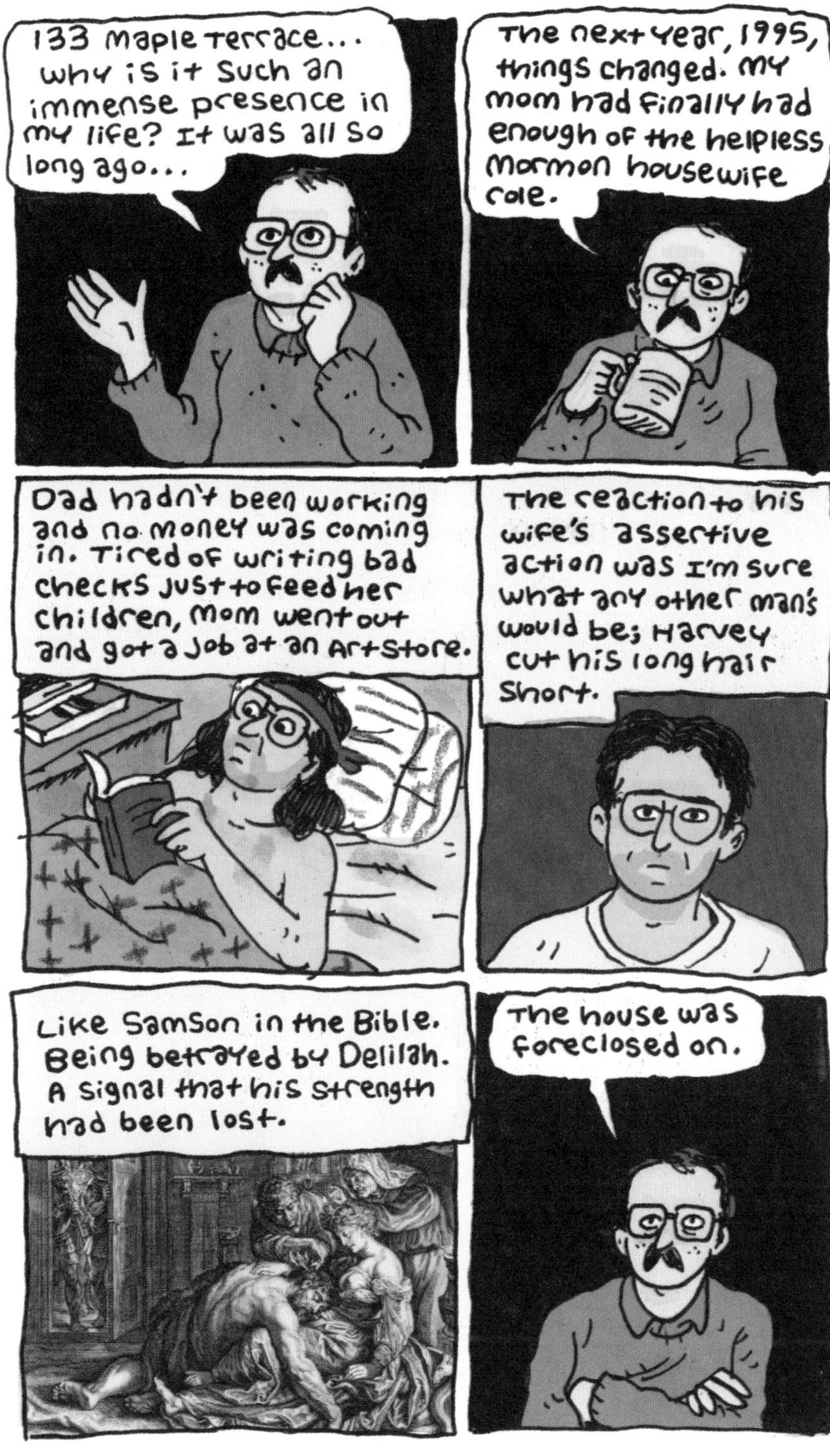
133 Maple Terrace... why is it such an immense presence in my life? It was all so long ago...
The next year, 1995, things changed. My mom had finally had enough of the helpless Mormon housewife role.
Dad hadn't been working and no money was coming in. Tired of writing bad checks just to feed her children, Mom went out and got a job at an Art Store.
The reaction to his wife's assertive action was I'm sure what any other man's would be; Harvey cut his long hair short.
Like Samson in the Bible. Being betrayed by Delilah. A signal that his strength had been lost.
The house was foreclosed on.

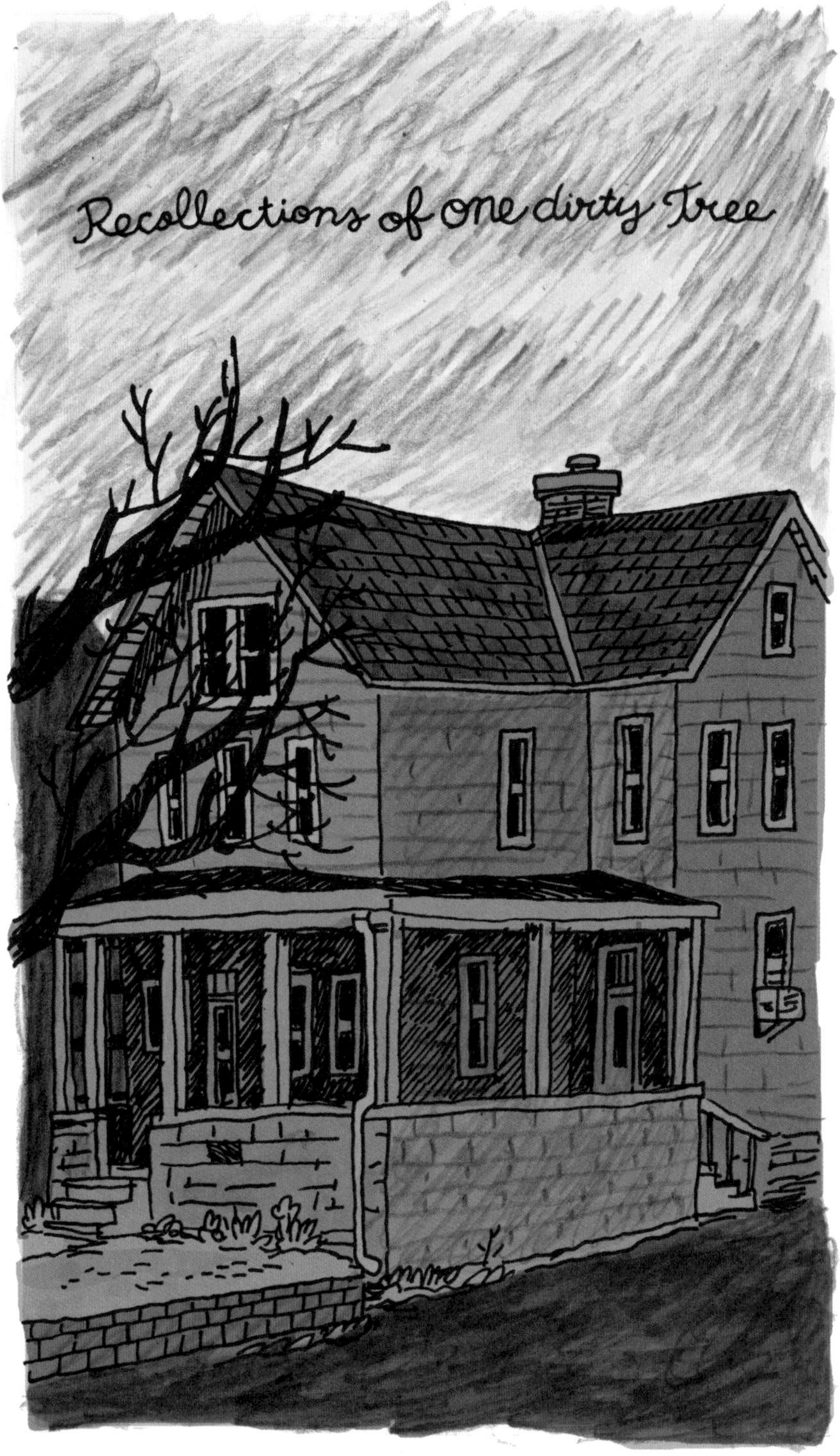
Recollections of one dirty tree

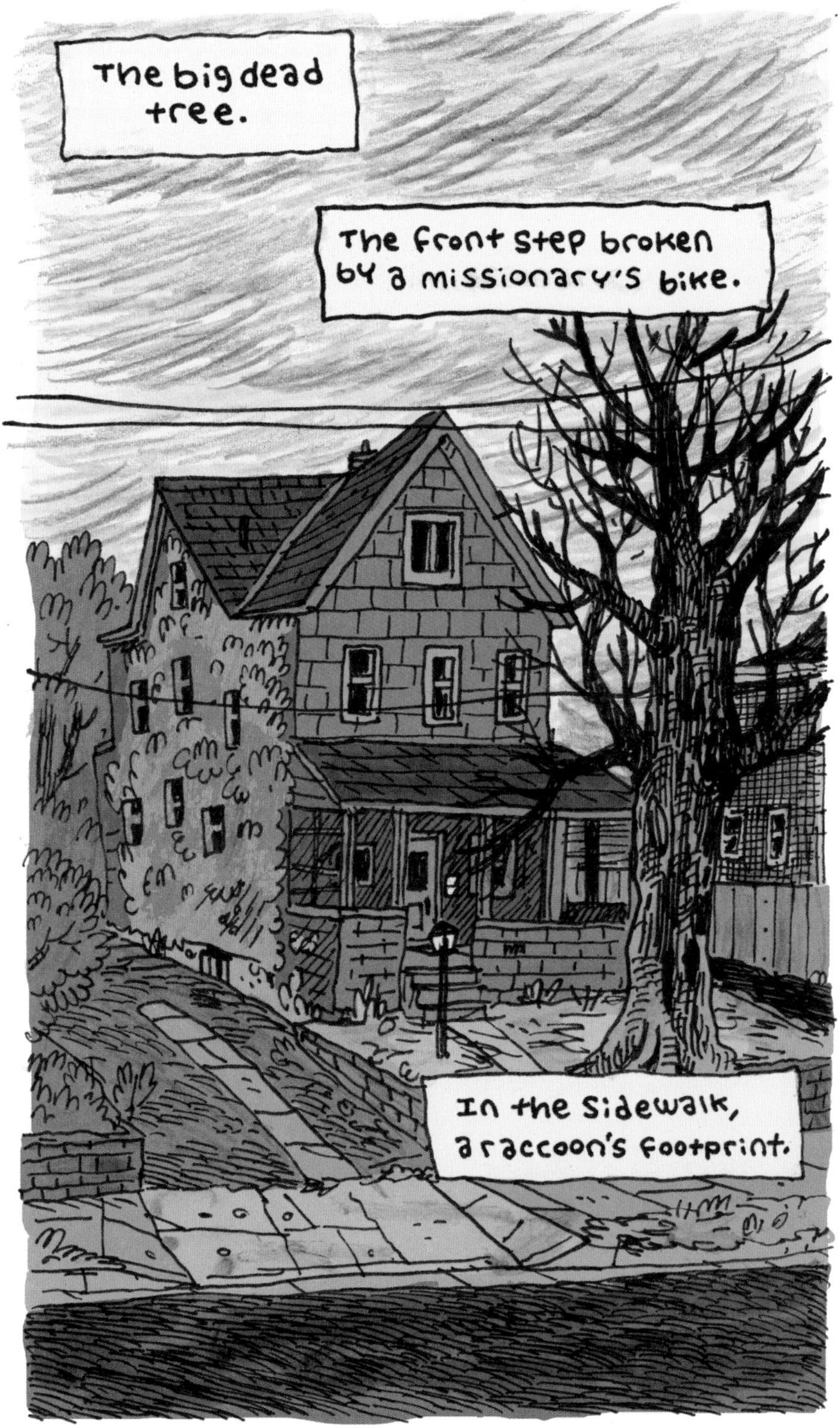
The big dead tree.
The front step broken by a missionary's bike.
In the sidewalk, a raccoon's footprint.

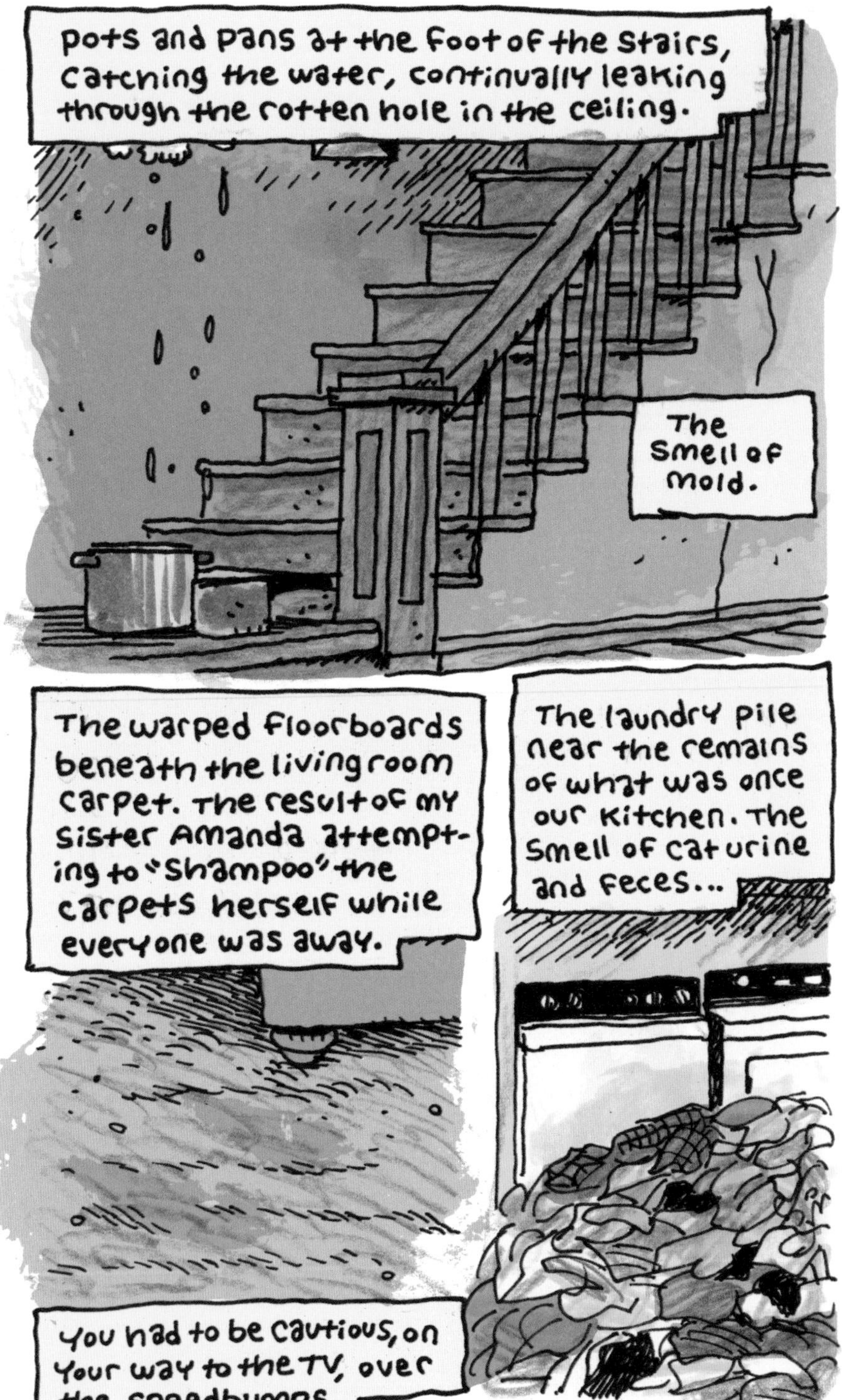
pots and pans at the foot of the stairs, catching the water, continually leaking through the rotten hole in the ceiling.
The smell of mold.
The warped floorboards beneath the living room carpet. The result of my sister Amanda attempting to "shampoo" the carpets herself while everyone was away.
You had to be cautious, on your way to the TV, over the speedbumps.
The laundry pile near the remains of what was once our kitchen. The smell of cat urine and feces...

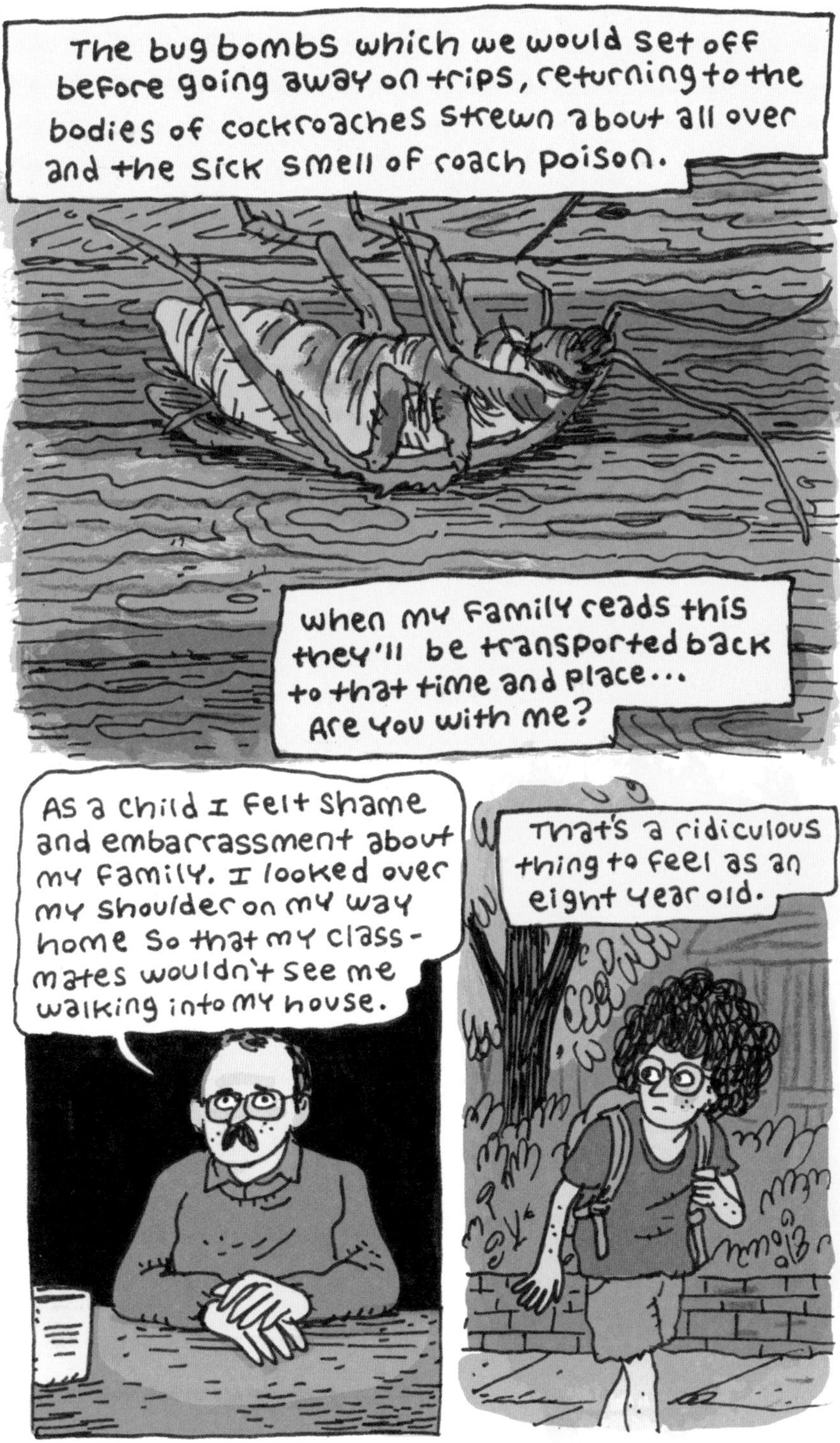
The bug bombs which we would set off before going away on trips, returning to the bodies of cockroaches strewn about all over and the sick smell of roach poison.
When my family reads this they'll be transported back to that time and place... Are you with me?
As a child I felt shame and embarrassment about my family. I looked over my shoulder on my way home so that my class-mates wouldn't see me walking into my house.
That's a ridiculous thing to feel as an eight year old.

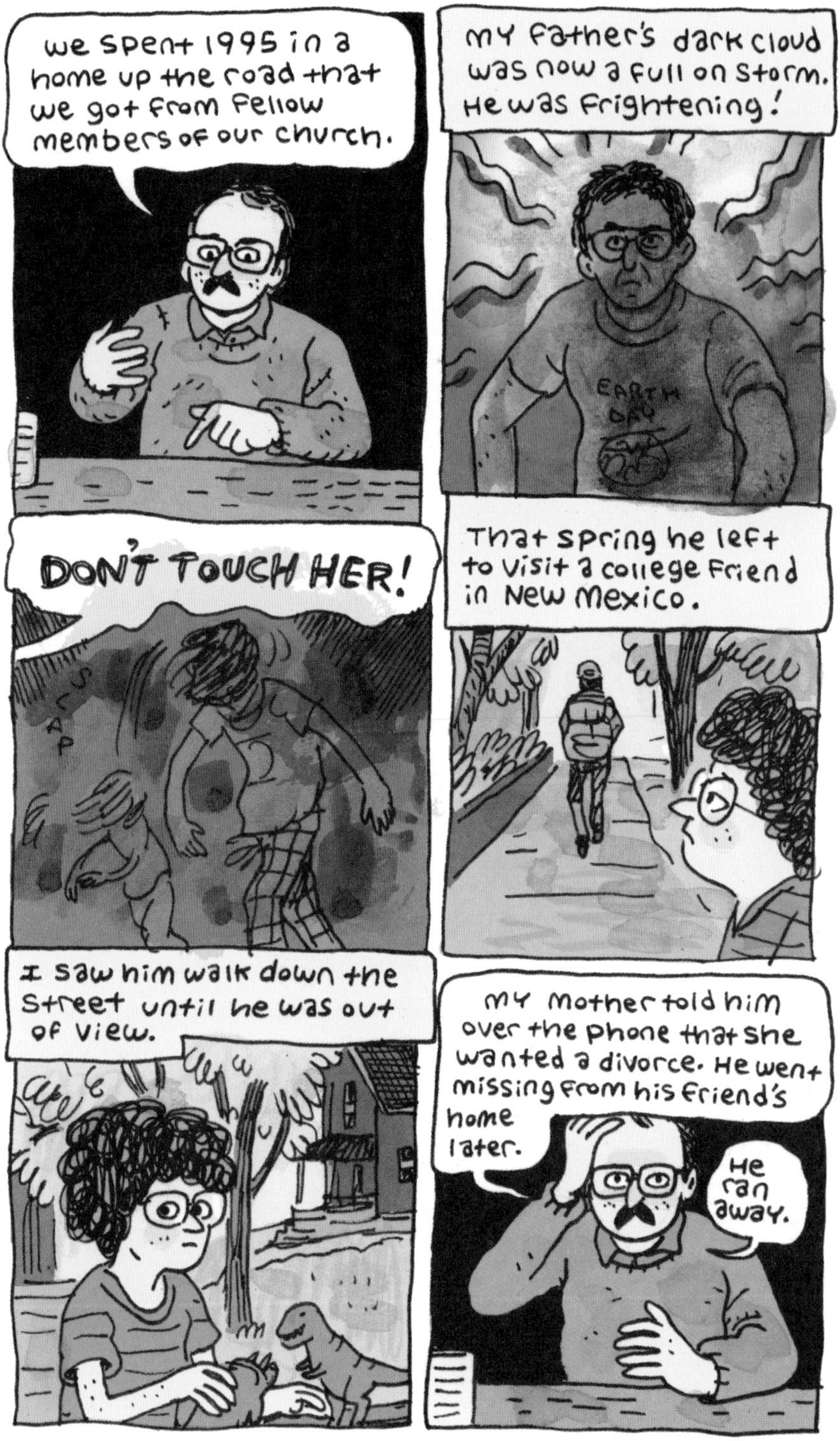
we spent 1995 in a home up the road that we got from fellow members of our church.
My father's dark cloud was now a full on storm. He was frightening!
EARTH DAY
DON'T TOUCH HER!
SLAP
That spring he left to visit a college friend in New Mexico.
I saw him walk down the street until he was out of view.
My mother told him over the phone that she wanted a divorce. He went missing from his friend's home later.
He ran away.

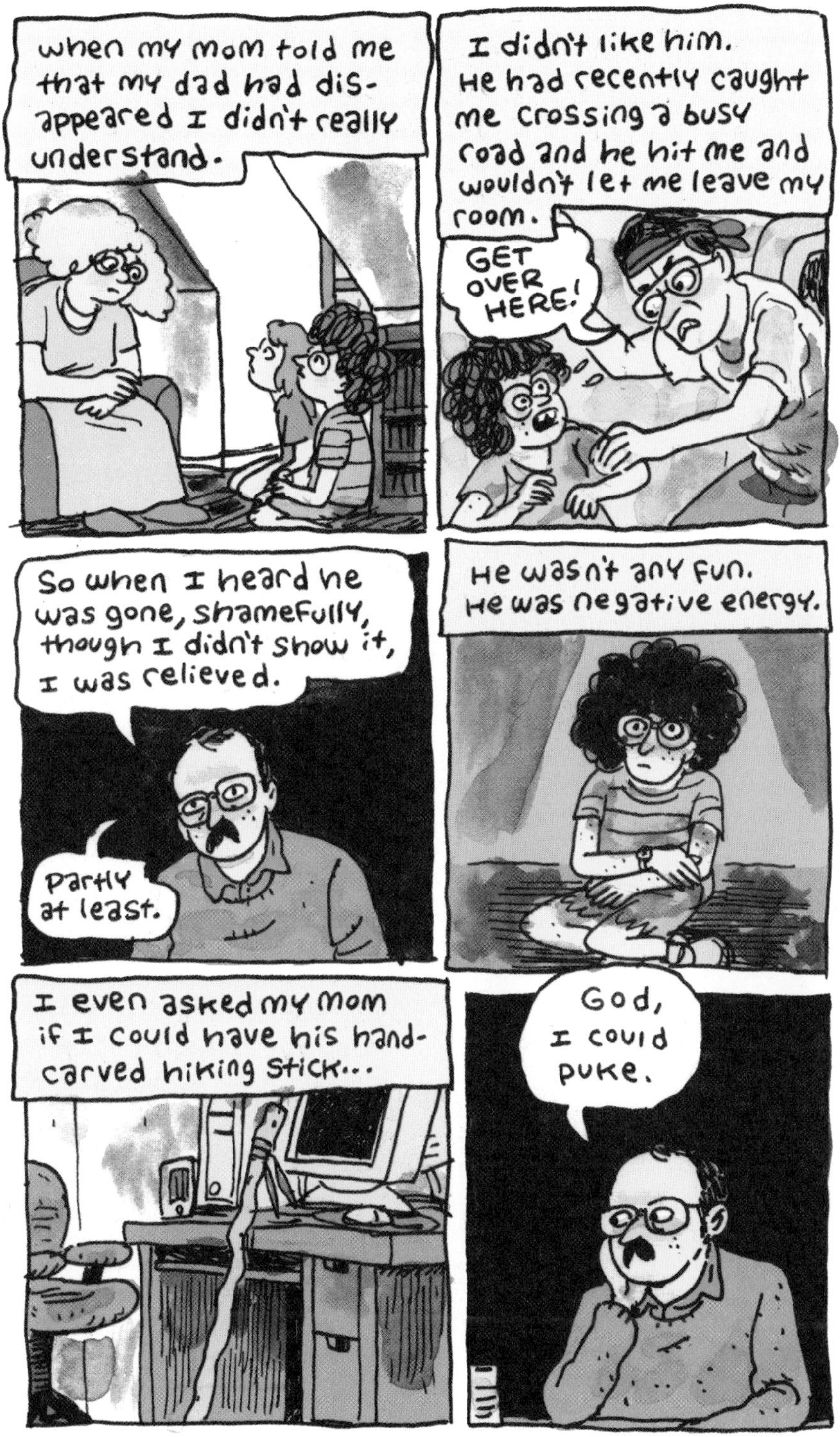
when my mom told me that my dad had disappeared I didn't really understand.
I didn't like him. He had recently caught me crossing a busy road and he hit me and wouldn't let me leave my room.
GET OVER HERE!
So when I heard he was gone, shamefully, though I didn't show it, I was relieved.
Partly at least.
He wasn't any fun. He was negative energy.
I even asked my mom if I could have his hand-carved hiking stick...
God, I could puke.

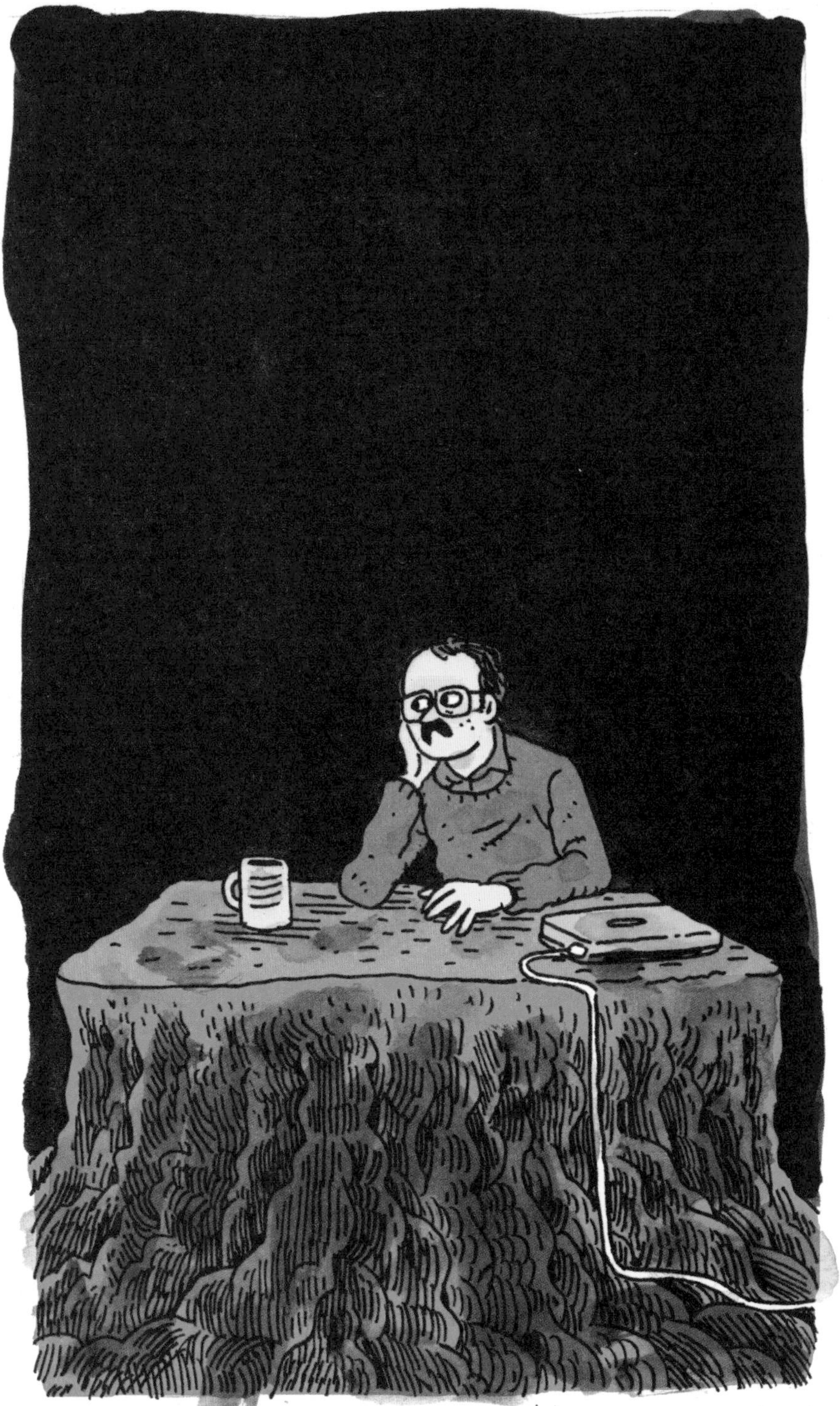

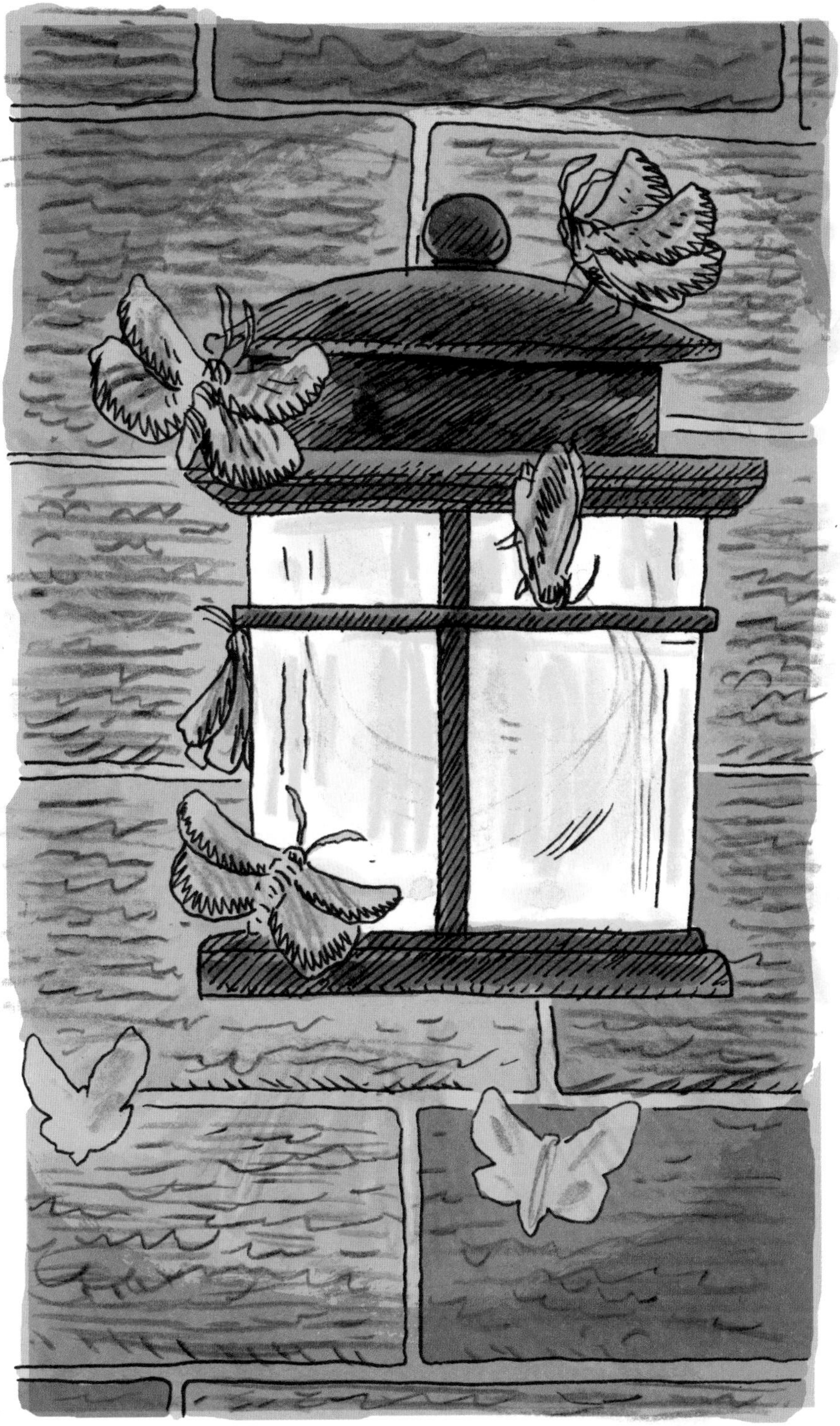

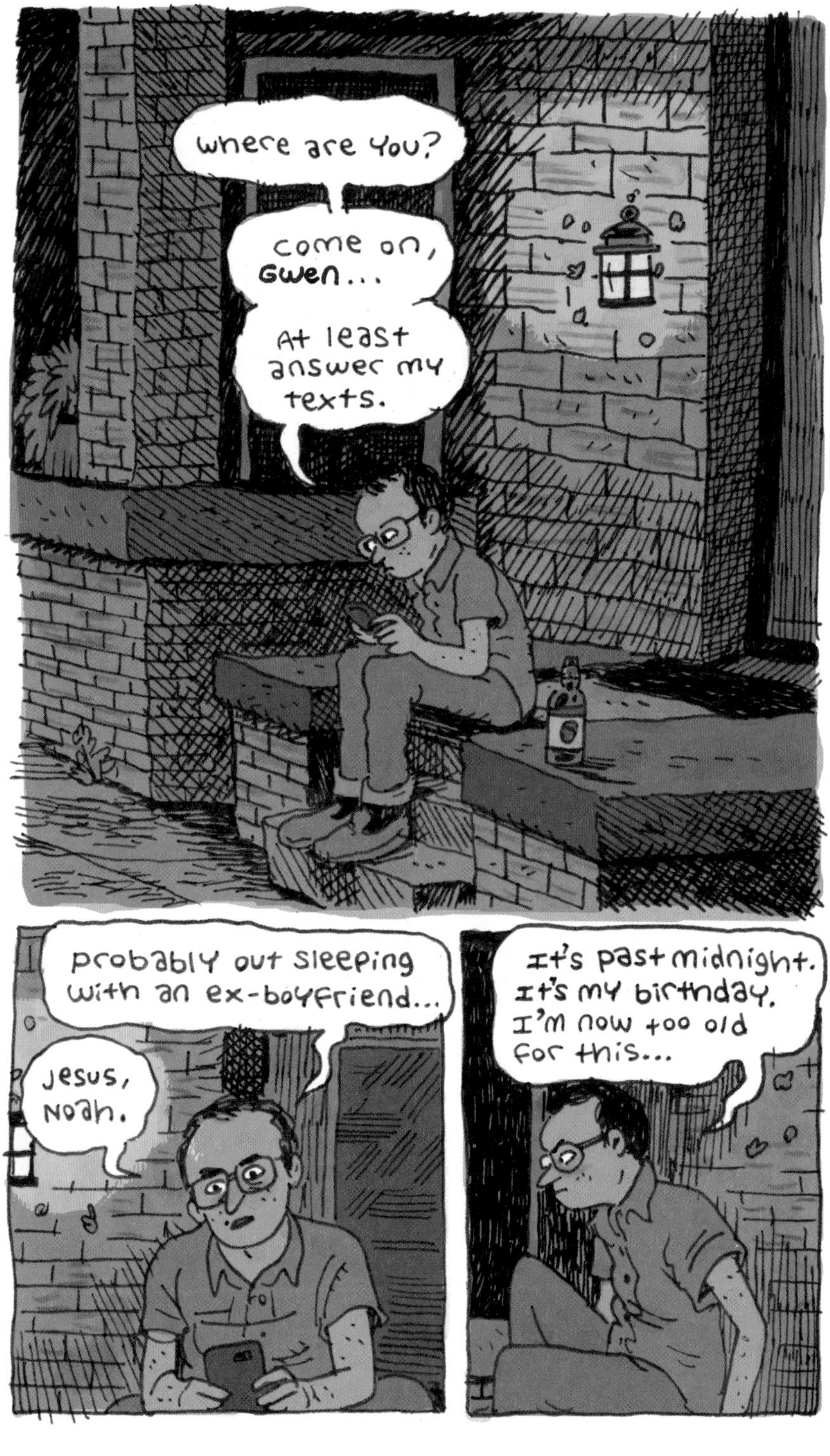
where are you?
come on, Gwen...
At least answer my texts.
probably out sleeping with an ex-boyfriend...
Jesus, Noah.
It's past midnight. It's my birthday. I'm now too old for this...

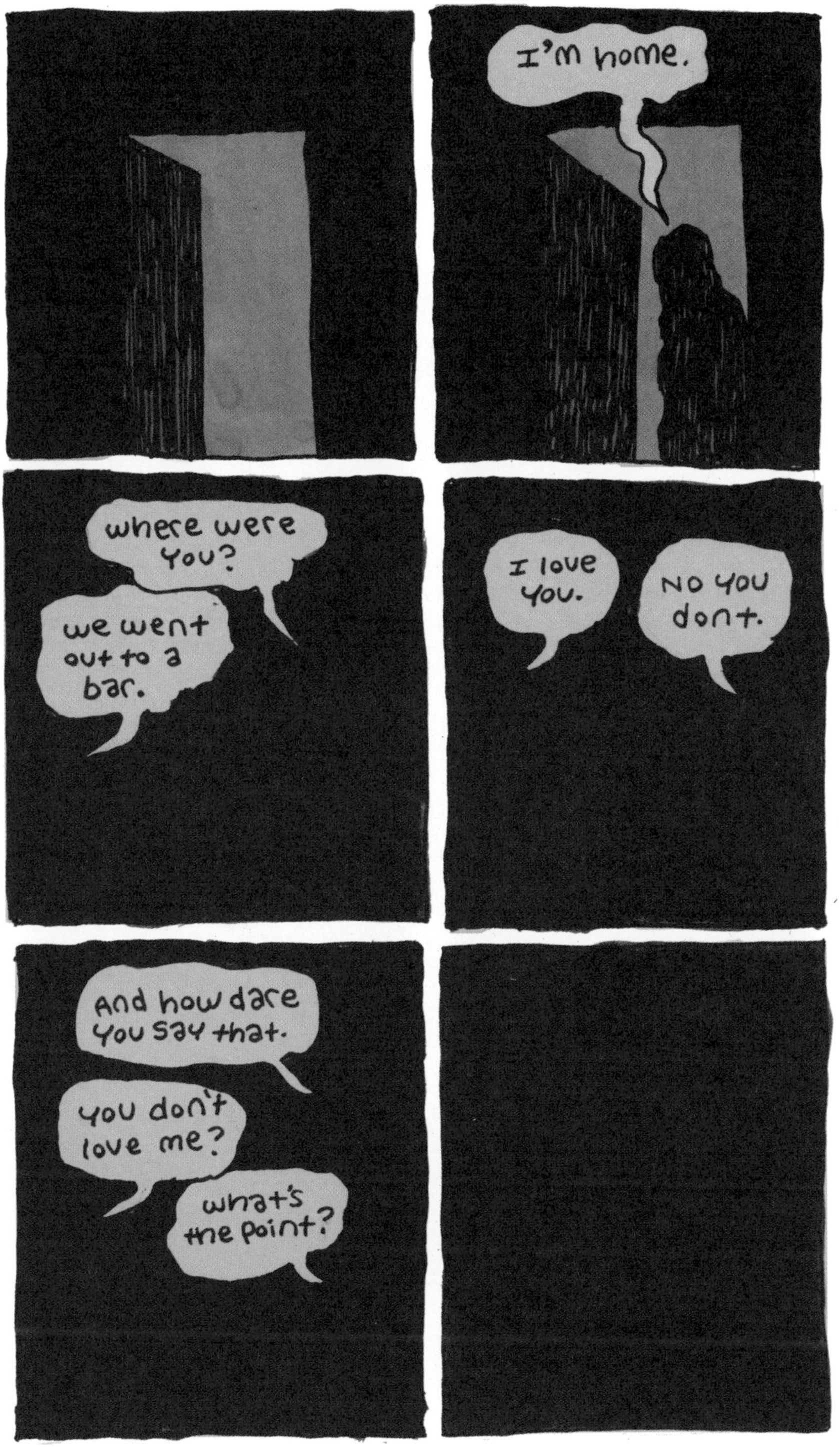
I'm home.
where were you?
we went out to a bar.
I love you.
No you dont.
And how dare you say that.
you don't love me?
what's the point?

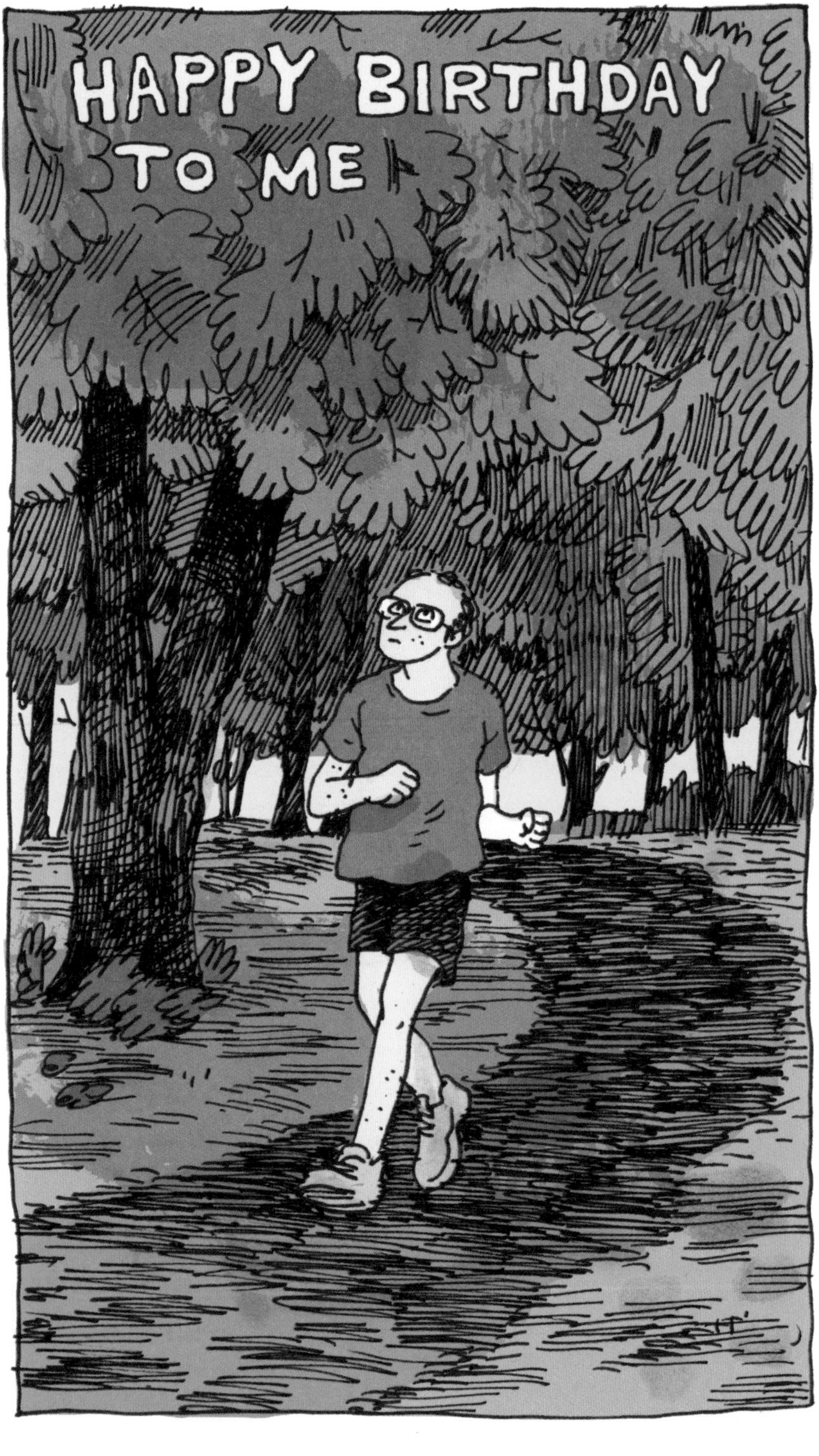
HAPPY BIRTHDAY TO ME

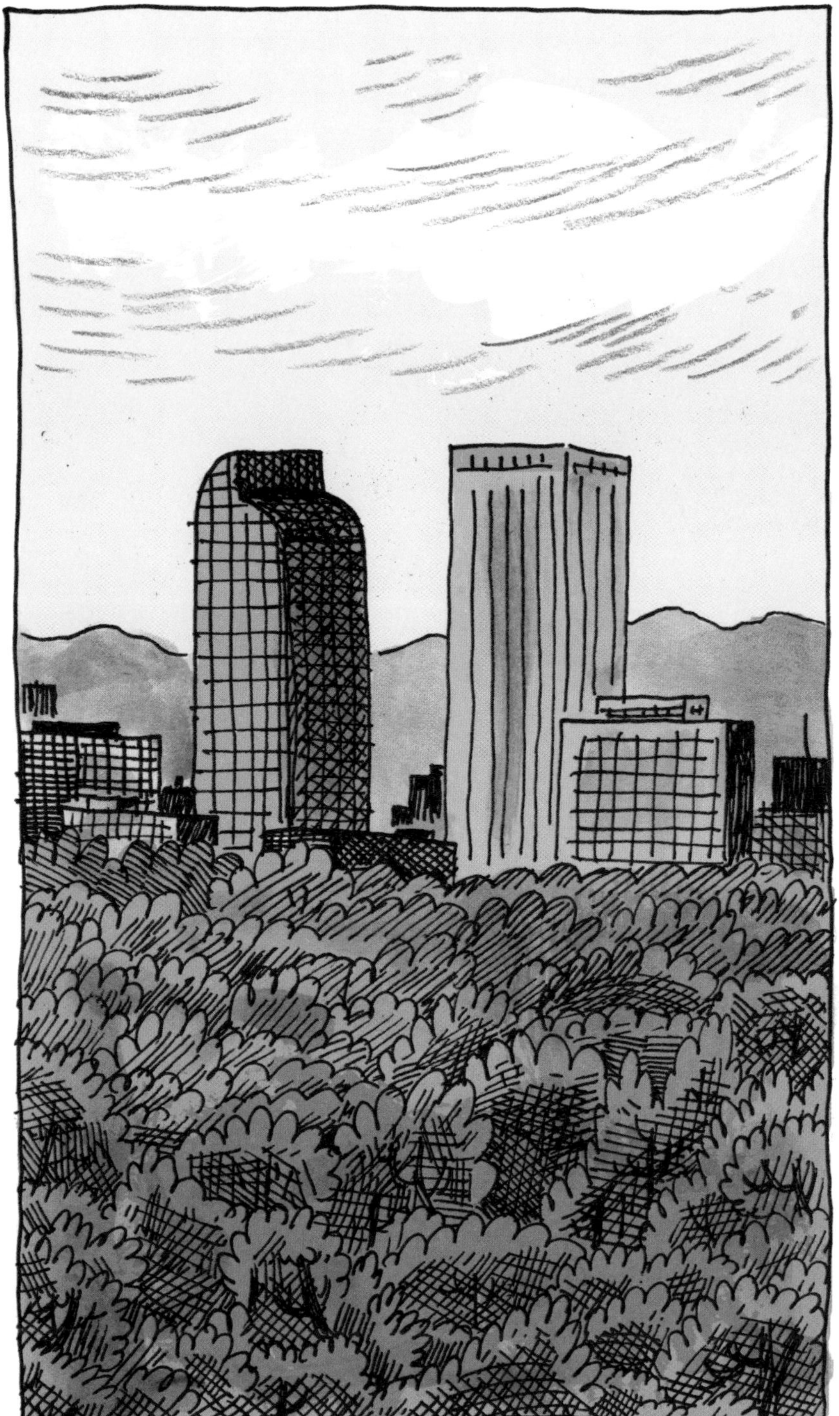

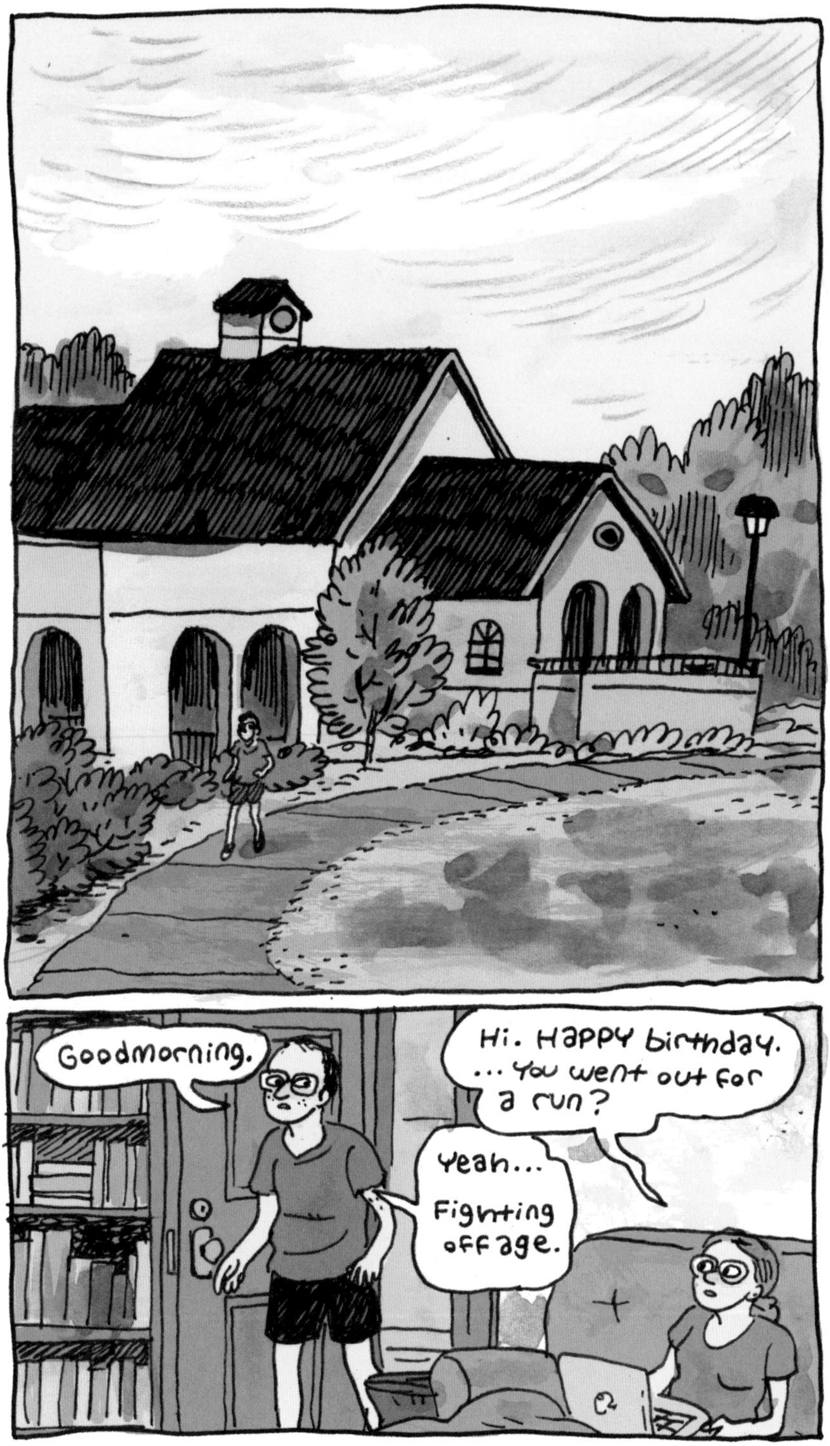
Goodmorning.
Hi. Happy birthday. ... You went out for a run?
Yeah... Fighting off age.

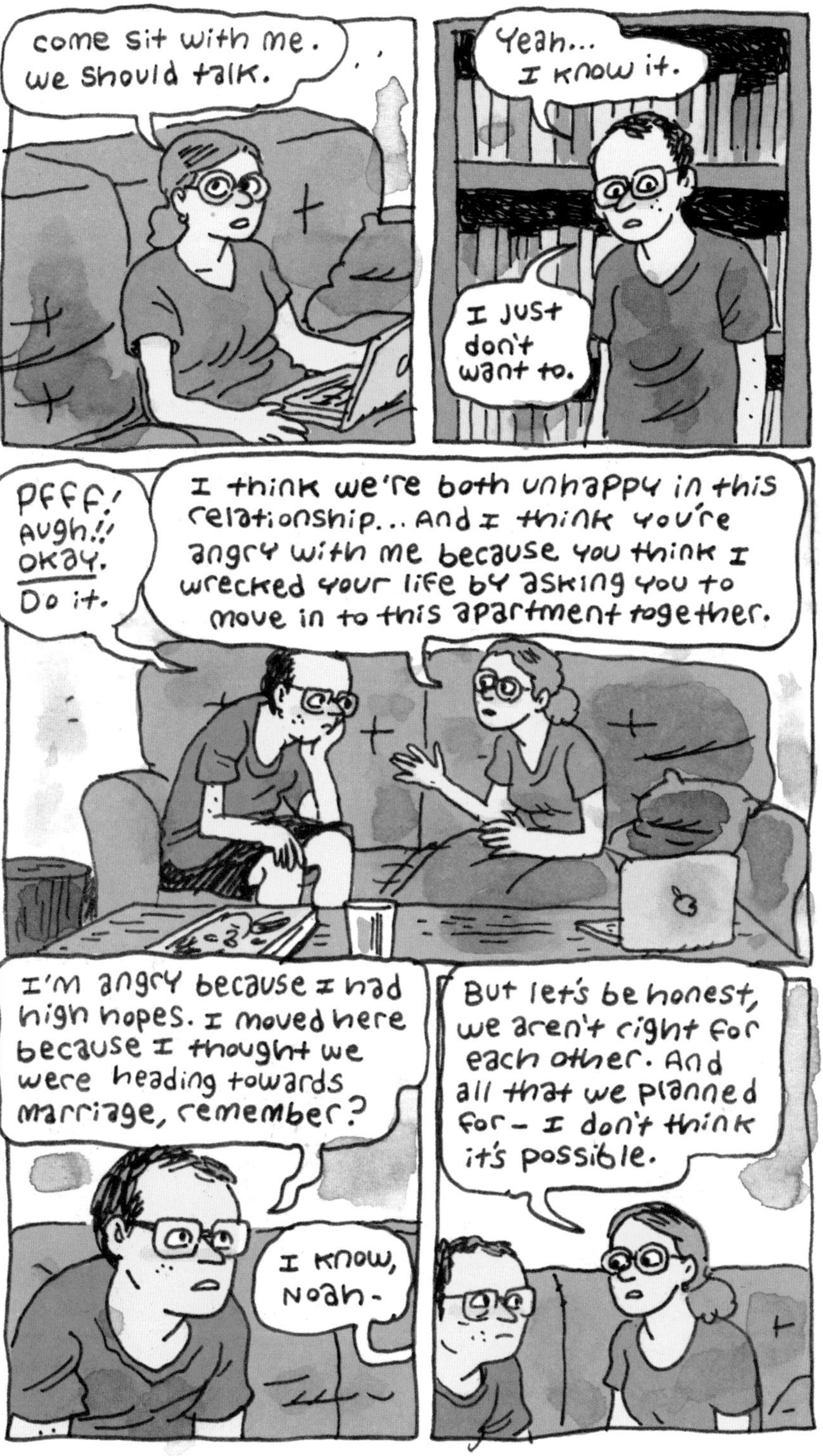
come sit with me. we should talk.
Yeah... I know it.
I just don't want to.
PFFF! Augh!! OKAY. Do it.
I think we're both unhappy in this relationship... And I think you're angry with me because you think I wrecked your life by asking you to move in to this apartment together.
I'm angry because I had high hopes. I moved here because I thought we were heading towards marriage, remember?
I know, Noah-
But let's be honest, we aren't right for each other. And all that we planned for - I don't think it's possible.

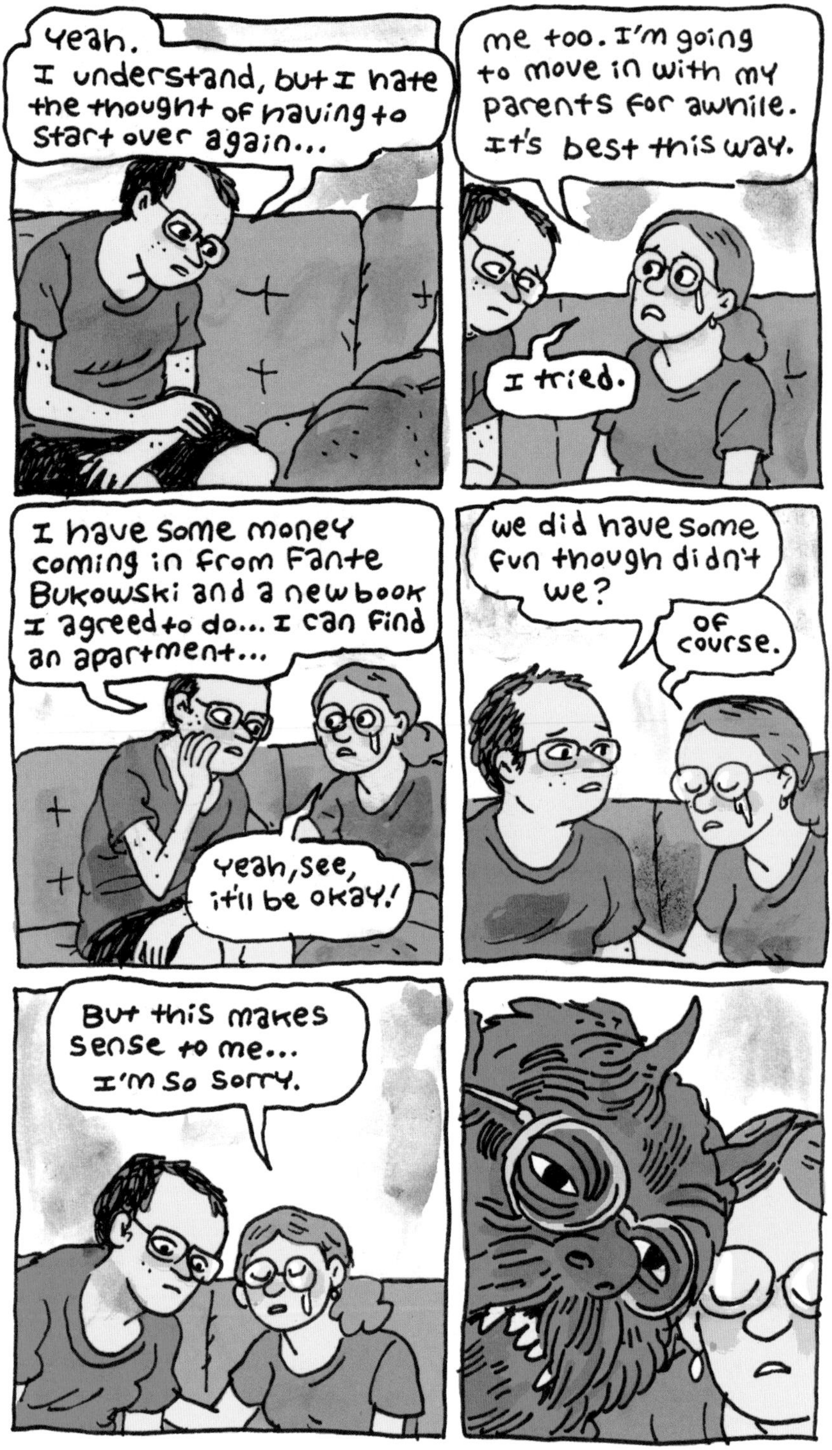
Yeah.
I understand, but I hate the thought of having to start over again...
me too. I'm going to move in with my parents for awhile. It's best this way.
I tried.
I have some money coming in from Fante Bukowski and a new book I agreed to do... I can find an apartment...
yeah, see, it'll be okay!
we did have some fun though didn't we?
of course.
But this makes sense to me... I'm so sorry.

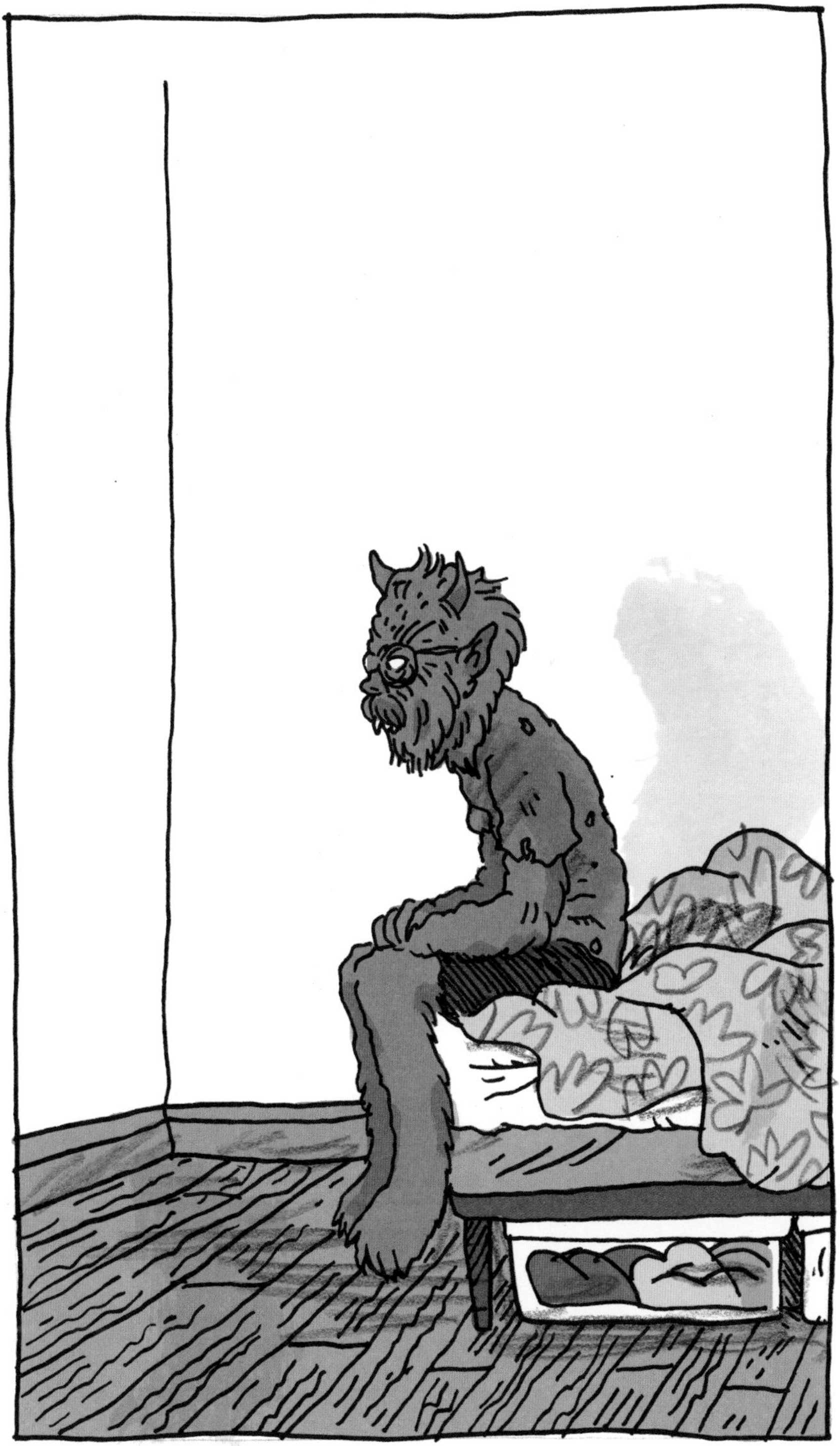

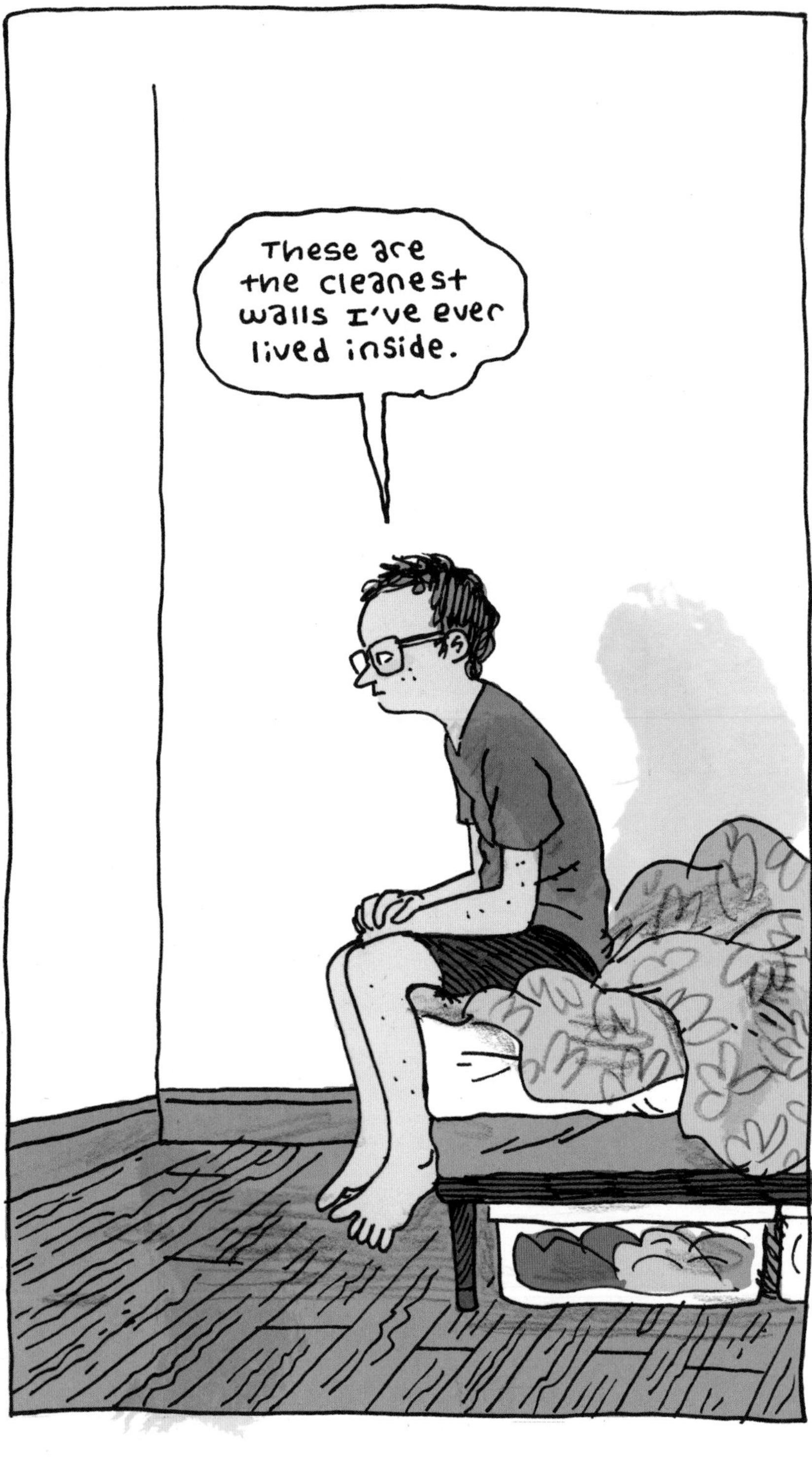
These are the cleanest walls I've ever lived inside.

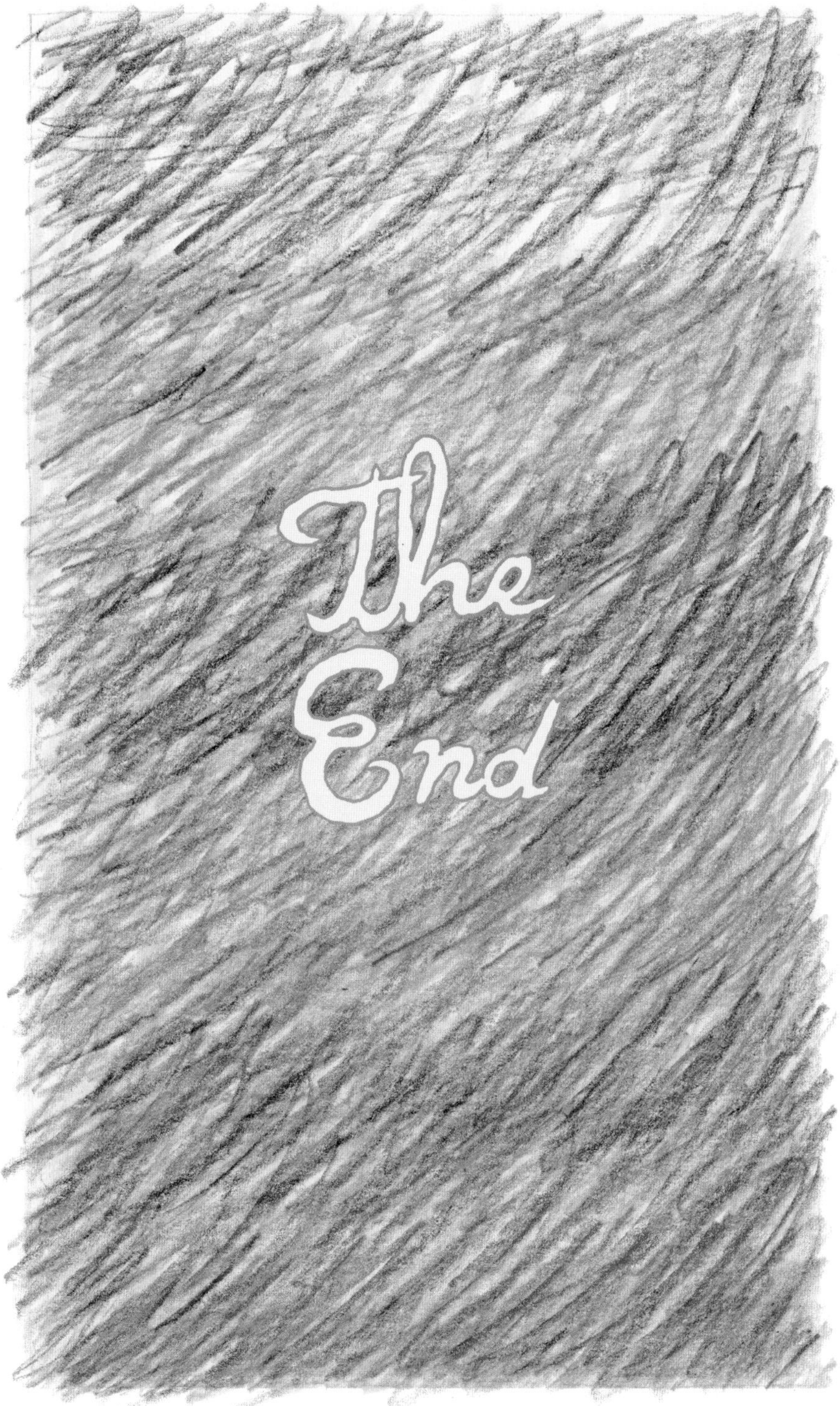
The End

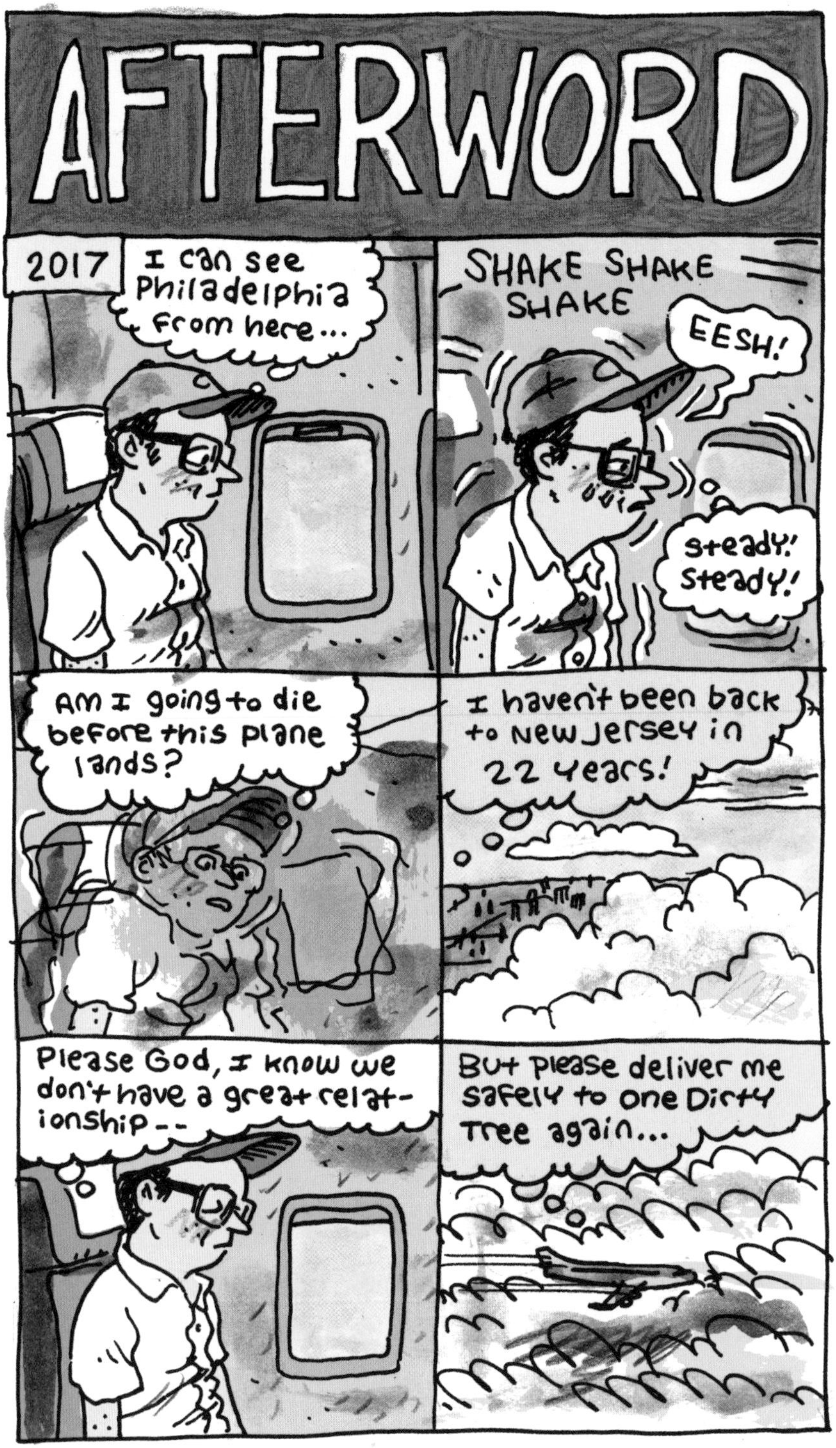
AFTERWORD
2017
I can see Philadelphia from here...
SHAKE SHAKE SHAKE
EESH!
steady! steady!
Am I going to die before this plane lands?
I haven't been back to New Jersey in 22 years!
Please God, I know we don't have a great relationship--
But please deliver me safely to One Dirty Tree again...

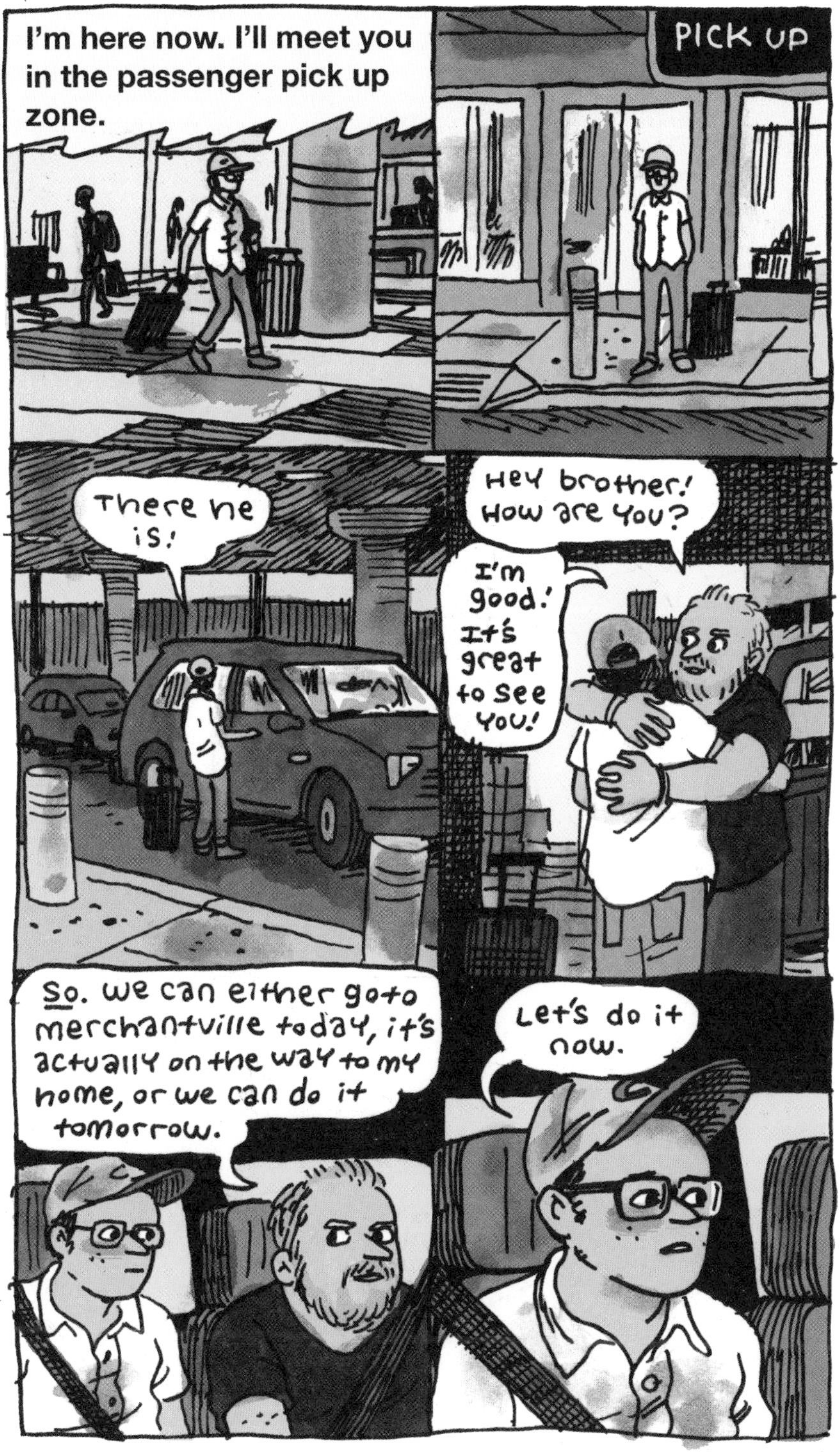
I'm here now. I'll meet you in the passenger pick up zone.
PICK UP
There he is!
Hey brother! How are you?
I'm good! It's great to see you!
So. We can either go to merchantville today, it's actually on the way to my home, or we can do it tomorrow.
Let's do it now.

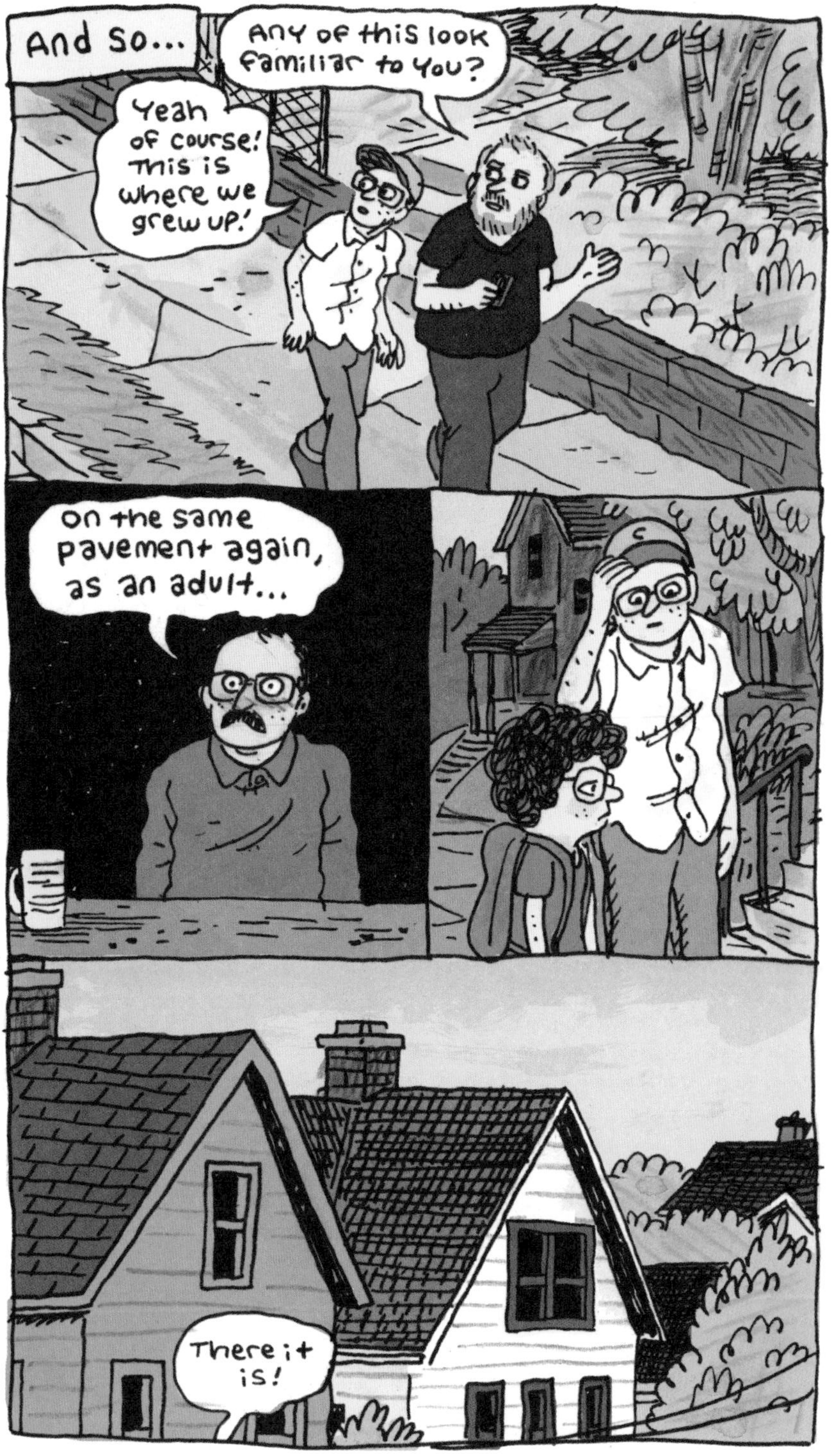
And so...
Any of this look familiar to you?
Yeah of course! This is where we grew up!
On the same pavement again, as an adult...
There it is!

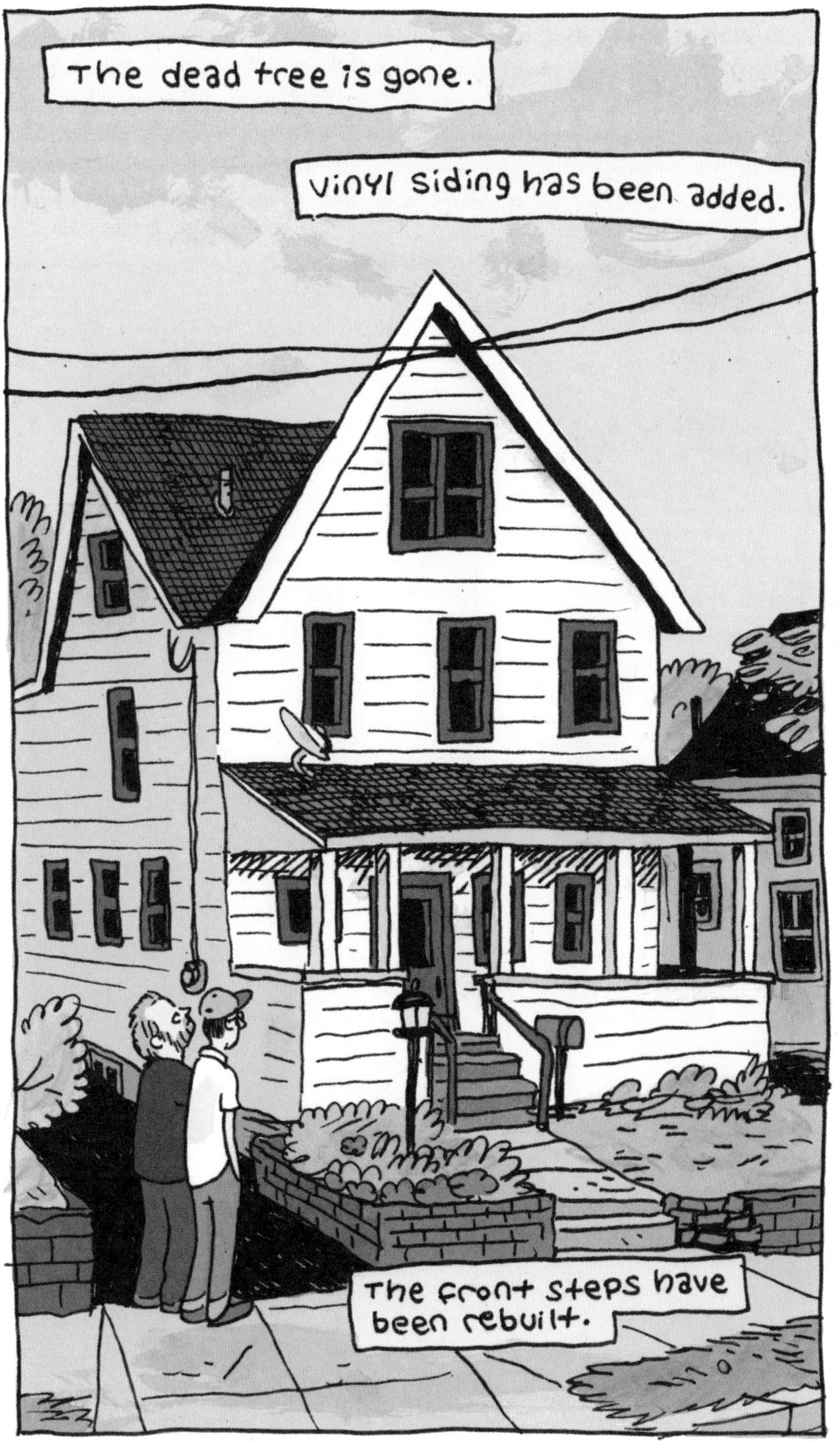
The dead tree is gone.
Vinyl siding has been added.
The front steps have been rebuilt.

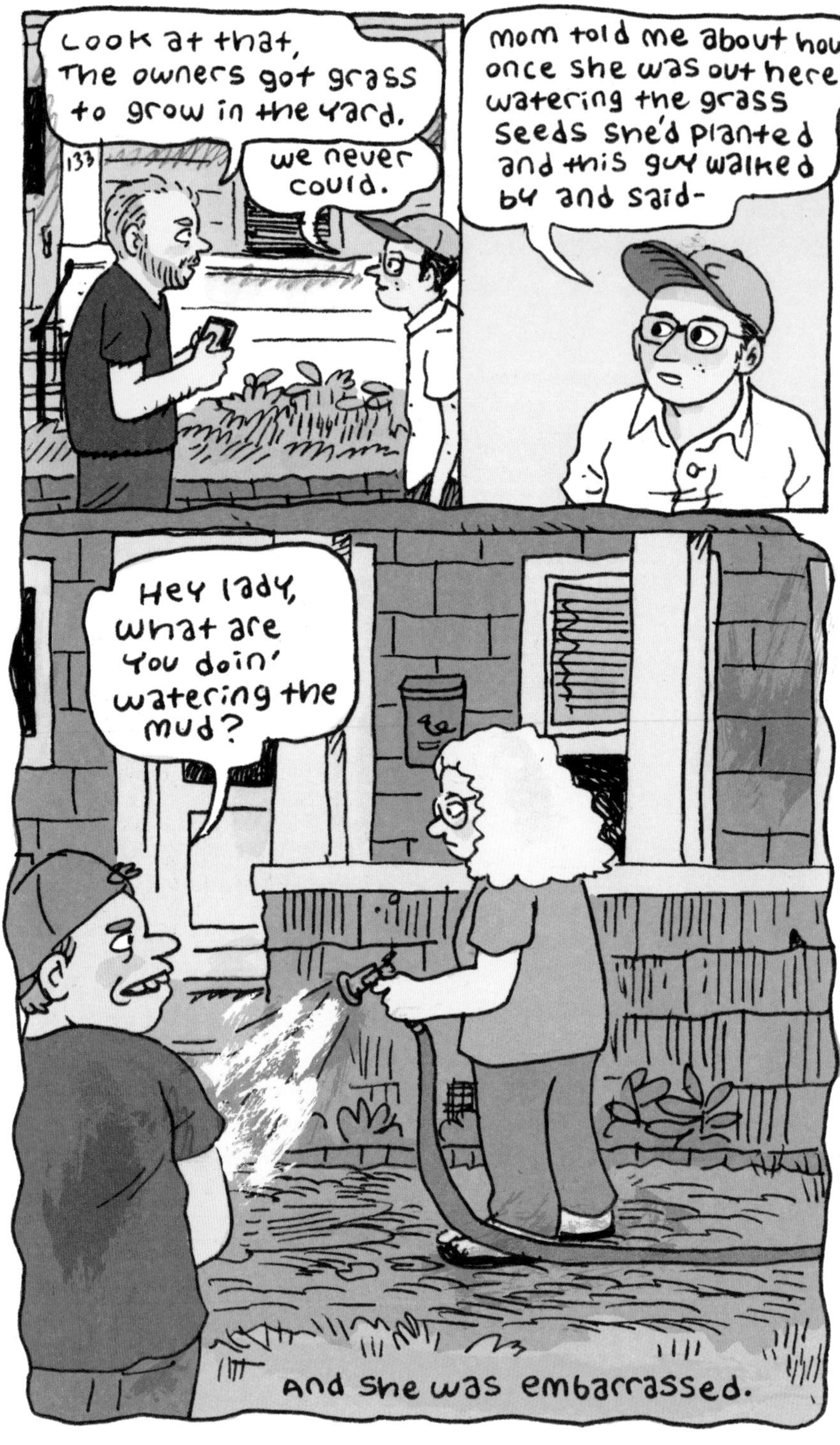
Look at that, The owners got grass to grow in the yard.
133
We never could.
Mom told me about how once she was out here watering the grass seeds she'd planted and this guy walked by and said-
Hey lady, what are you doin' watering the mud?
And she was embarrassed.

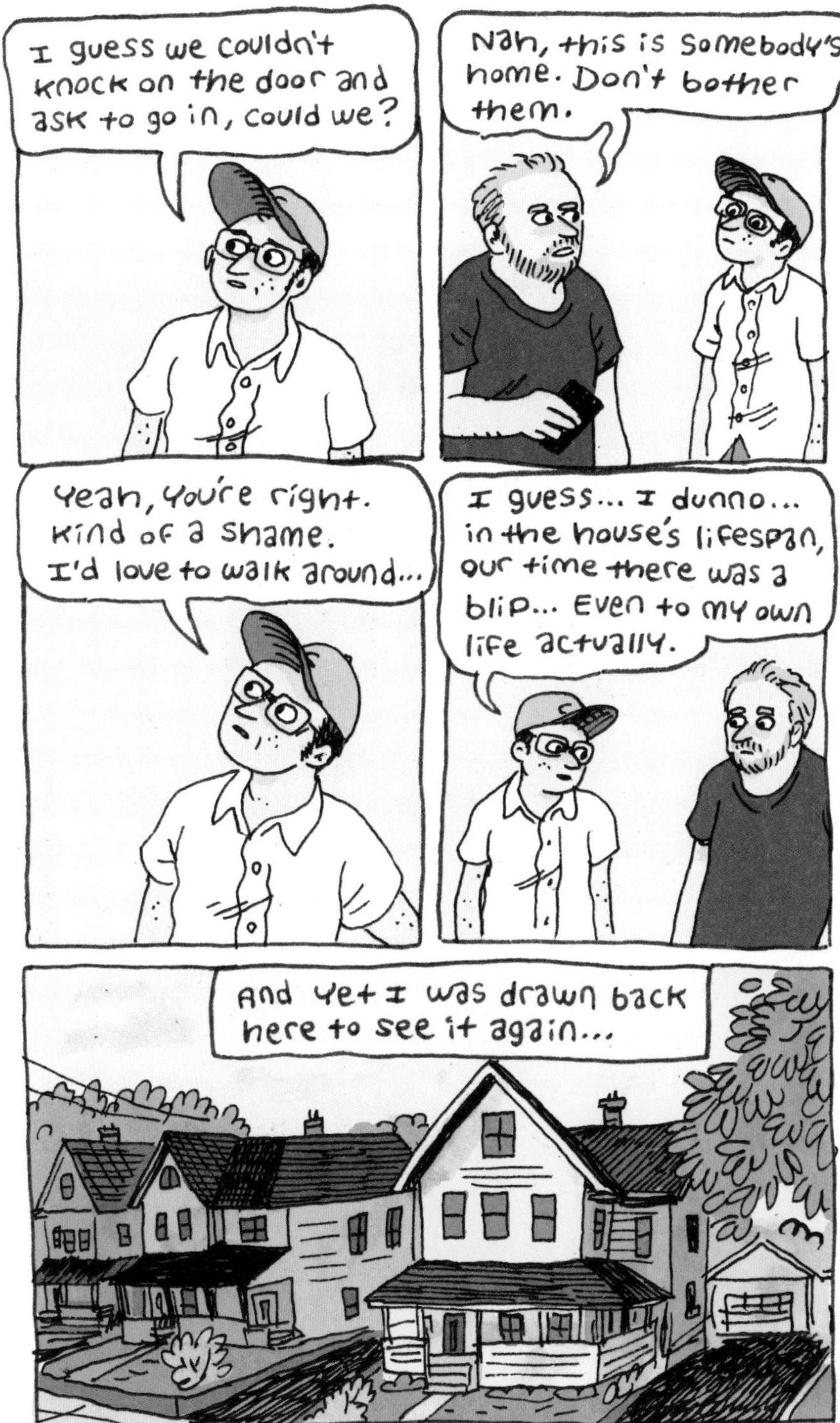
I guess we couldn't knock on the door and ask to go in, could we?
Nah, this is somebody's home. Don't bother them.
Yeah, you're right. Kind of a shame. I'd love to walk around...
I guess... I dunno... in the house's lifespan, our time there was a blip... Even to my own life actually.
And yet I was drawn back here to see it again...

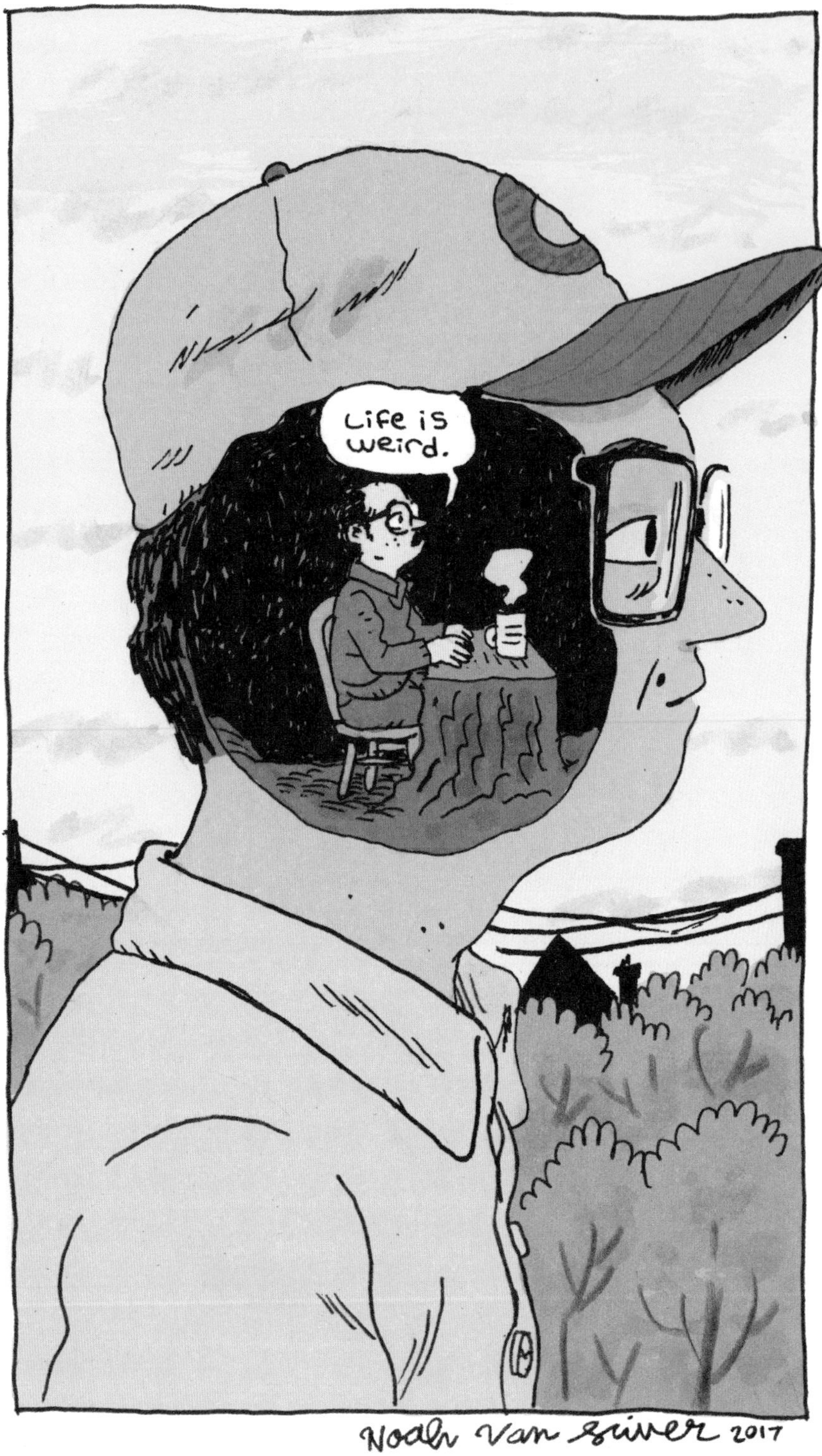
Life is weird.
Noah Van Sciver 2017

Special Thanks to:

First and most importantly,
my family for allowing me to
draw so much of us, though I
know they probably won't read
these words. With the exception
of Ethan who championed me along
the whole way. To Bruce Simon,
John Porcellino and Leslie Stein
(who read the first draft and hated
it). Dan Stafford (who gave me
great advice on fixing the problems
of that first draft). Thank you
everyone who supported and kept
up with this story on patreon.'
Thank you Igort, and Tom Kaczynski,
Jordan Shiveley, Eric Reynolds and
Amy Chalmers ♡

Noah Van Sciver is an Ignatz award-winning cartoonist currently living in Columbus, Ohio.

He is the author of several acclaimed graphic novels and the ongoing Eisner-nominated comic book series "Blammo."